Amplifying That Still, Small Voice

To John,

Thanks for all your assistance with administering the General Chair.

Frank

by
Frank Brennan SJ

The Scholar's Collection

1. *Opening the Bible*, 2014, Antony Campbell SJ,

Amplifying That Still, Small Voice

A Collection of Essays

by
Frank Brennan SJ

ATF Theology
Adelaide

2015

National Library of Australia Cataloguing-in-Publication entry
Creator: Brennan, Frank, 1954- author.
Title: Amplifying that still, small voice : a collection of essays /
 Frank Tenison Brennan.
ISBN: 9781925232097 (paperback)
ISBN: 9781925232080 (hardback)
ISBN: 9781925232110 (ebook : Kindle, Kobo, Amazon)
ISBN: 9781925232103 (ebook : pdf)
Notes: Includes index.
Subjects: Catholic Church--Australia.
        Church and social problems--Catholic Church.
        Church and state--Australia.
        Aboriginal Australians--Land tenure.
        Sex crimes--Religious aspects--Catholic Church.
        Same-sex marriage--Religious aspects--Catholic Church.

Dewey Number: 282.94

Cover original artwork:
Photographs
Cover design by Astrid Sengkey
Layout/Artwork by

Text Minion Pro Size 11 & 12

Published by:

An imprint of the ATF Ltd.
PO Box 504
Hindmarsh, SA 5007
ABN 90 116 359 963
www.atfpress.com

Dedicated
to

Gerard and Patricia

who made a home for conscience

CONTENTS

Introduction   1

I

Amplifying that still, small voice
…in the Church

1. Celebrating a New Pope   5
2. Scrutinising a Non-Transparent Hierarchy   23
3. Handing on the Faith   37
4. Making Room for Aborigines in the Church   59
5. Dealing with Child Sexual Abuse   81
6. Bringing the Church to the World   109

II

At Bridges and Frontiers in the Church and the World   133

III

Amplifying that still, small voice
…in the World

7. Pursuing Human Rights   145
8. Insisting on the Separation of Powers   165
9. Respecting Religious Freedom and Freedom of Conscience   181
10. Recognising Aboriginal Rights   207
11. Dealing with Asylum Claims   247
12. Respecting Autonomy and Protecting the Vulnerability
of the Dying   291
13. Espousing marriage and respecting the dignity
of same sex couples   323

Conclusion   359
Index   363

INTRODUCTION

This year I am thirty years a priest and forty years a Jesuit. I have spent much of my time as a Catholic priest in the public square in Australia agitating for human rights both in society, and in the Catholic Church. For Human Rights Day in 1985, the year I was ordained a priest, Seamus Heaney wrote his poem *From the Republic of Conscience* for Amnesty International. Constantly getting on and off planes, speaking and meeting people all over the country, I have long been inspired by the closing stanzas of that poem:

> I came back from that frugal republic
> with my two arms the one length, the customs woman
> having insisted my allowance was myself.
>
> The old man rose and gazed into my face
> and said that was official recognition
> that I was now a dual citizen.
>
> He therefore desired me when I got home
> to consider myself a representative
> and to speak on their behalf in my own tongue.
>
> Their embassies, he said, were everywhere
> but operated independently
> and no ambassador would ever be relieved.

As priest and lawyer, I have always regarded myself as an ambassador for conscience. Often it means speaking or standing alone. I believe every authentic human being needs to form and inform their conscience, and to that conscience be true. It is parody to suggest to the religious person that this is simply a recipe for doing one's own thing, or to suggest to the citizen that it is the road to lawlessness, or to intimate to either that it is the path to arrogant egoism.

I am one of those many Catholics who has found a new spring in my step and a new confidence in our religious tradition and

1

sacramental celebrations since the election of Pope Francis. He wrote in his first apostolic exhortation: 'The great danger in today's world, pervaded as it is by consumerism, is the desolation and anguish born of a complacent yet covetous heart, the feverish pursuit of frivolous pleasures, and a blunted conscience.'[1] The great reformers and contributors I know inside and outside the Church, and inside and outside the corridors of political power, are those untouched by materialism, those with open passionate hearts, and those with finely honed consciences blunted neither by self-interest nor by unquestioning acceptance of authority.

Marking the sixtieth anniversary of the *UN Declaration of Human Rights* in 2008, Seamus Heaney wrote:

> Since it was framed, the Declaration has succeeded in creating an international moral consensus. It is always there as a means of highlighting abuse if not always as a remedy: it exists instead in the moral imagination as an equivalent of the gold standard in the monetary system. The articulation of its tenets has made them into world currency of a negotiable sort. Even if its Articles are ignored or flouted—in many cases by governments who have signed up to them—it provides a worldwide amplification system for the 'still, small voice'.[2]

In the Old Testament, the prophet Elijah finds that the Lord is not in the wind, fire or earthquake, but in the still, small voice.[3] In the world of human rights violations, justice is often not found in the law, the politics, or the media frenzy, but in the still, small voice of conscience. I am grateful to Boston College for giving me the time to write as Gasson Professor and to Hilary Regan at ATF Press for giving me the opportunity to bring together between one set of covers some of my reworked written and spoken attempts to be attentive to that voice in myself and others, and to provide the occasional slight amplification. I hope you the reader enjoy your dual citizenship as much as I do.

---

1. Pope Francis, *Evangelii Gaudium*, 2013, #2
2. Seamus Heaney, 'Human Rights, Poetic Redress', *The Irish Times*, Weekend Review, 15 March 2008: 1
3. 1 Kings 19:11–13

PART ONE
Amplifying That Still, Small, Voice
... in the Church

1

Celebrating a New Pope

Jorge Mario Bergoglio, the Jesuit cardinal archbishop of Buenos Aires was elected pope on evening of 13 March 2013. There was great excitement and curiosity about this first Jesuit pope, this first pope from South America. The media was fascinated by him. Parishioners were delighted. In Canberra, I help out on weekends in the Parish of the Transfiguration at Curtin. The long time parish priest, Tony Frey, is the 'go to' priest for so many people in Canberra in situations of pastoral need. When celebrating his fortieth anniversary as a priest, he invited me to speak at the annual parish dinner in September 2013 offering a parish reflection on Pope Francis.

At mass at Curtin on the Fifth Sunday of Lent in 2013, just after the election of our new pope, I recall greeting parishioners with these words: 'Good evening. My name is Frank and I am a Jesuit. I've had a good week. I hope you have too.' I have been overwhelmed by the positive response by all sorts of people to the election of the first Jesuit pope. I have happily received the congratulations without quite knowing what to do with them, nor what I did to deserve them! Francis has opened up a vast new panorama and not just for Catholics. He is theologically orthodox, politically conservative, comfortable in his own skin, infectiously pastoral, and truly committed to the poor. Of late, most thinking Catholics engaged in the world have wondered how you could possibly be theologically orthodox and infectiously pastoral at the one time, how you could be politically conservative and still have a commitment to the poor, how you could be comfortable in your own skin—at ease in Church and in the public square, equally comfortable and uncomfortable in

5

conversation with fawning devotees and hostile critics. Think only of Francis's remark during the press conference on the plane on the way back from World Youth Day: 'If a person is gay and seeks the Lord and has good will, who am I to judge him?' Gone are the days of rainbow sashes outside cathedrals and threats of communion bans.

As Francis says in the lengthy interview he did for the Jesuit journal *La Civilta Cattolica*: 'We need to proclaim the Gospel on every street corner, preaching the good news of the kingdom and healing, even with our preaching, every kind of disease and wound. In Buenos Aires I used to receive letters from homosexual persons who are "socially wounded" because they tell me that they feel like the church has always condemned them.' [1] In that interview reproduced in full in the Jesuit magazine *America*, he recalls:

> A person once asked me, in a provocative manner, if I approved of homosexuality. I replied with another question: 'Tell me: when God looks at a gay person, does he endorse the existence of this person with love, or reject and condemn this person?' We must always consider the person. Here we enter into the mystery of the human being. In life, God accompanies persons, and we must accompany them, starting from their situation. It is necessary to accompany them with mercy. When that happens, the Holy Spirit inspires the priest to say the right thing. [2]

Here is a pope who is not just about creating wiggle room or watering down the teachings of the Church. No, he wants to admit honestly to the world that we hold in tension definitive teachings and pastoral yearnings—held together coherently only by mercy and forgiveness. He explains:

---

1. Pope Francis, 'A Big Heart Open to the World', *America*, 30 September 2013: 15, 24
2. Pope Francis, 'A Big Heart Open to the World', 26

We cannot insist only on issues related to abortion, gay marriage and the use of contraceptive methods. This is not possible. I have not spoken much about these things, and I was reprimanded for that. But when we speak about these issues, we have to talk about them in a context. The teaching of the church, for that matter, is clear and I am a son of the church, but it is not necessary to talk about these issues all the time. The dogmatic and moral teachings of the church are not all equivalent. The church's pastoral ministry cannot be obsessed with the transmission of a disjointed multitude of doctrines to be imposed insistently. Proclamation in a missionary style focuses on the essentials, on the necessary things: this is also what fascinates and attracts more, what makes the heart burn, as it did for the disciples at Emmaus. We have to find a new balance; otherwise even the moral edifice of the church is likely to fall like a house of cards, losing the freshness and fragrance of the Gospel. The proposal of the Gospel must be more simple, profound, radiant. It is from this proposition that the moral consequences then flow. [3]

If we are honest with ourselves, many of us have wondered how we can maintain our Christian faith and our commitment to the Catholic Church in the wake of the sexual abuse crisis and the many judgmental utterances about sexuality and reproduction— the Church that has spoken longest and loudest about sex in all its modalities seems to be one of the social institutions most needing to get its own house in order in relation to trust, fidelity, love, respect and human dignity. Revelations out of Melbourne and Newcastle and the national royal commission hearings leave us with heavy hearts especially about some of our local church leadership before 1996. But we do have a spring in our step that this new Pope, together with rigorous, independent legal processes (even in the face of much media pre-judgment) and local church commitments to transparency and solicitous care of victims, including the establishment of the 'Truth

---

3. Pope Francis, 'A Big Heart Open to the World', 26

Justice and Healing Council', provide us with the structures and leadership necessary for 'cooperation, openness, full disclosure and justice for victims and survivors'. The chief Christian paradox is that we are lowly sinners who dare to profess the highest ideals, and that sometimes we cannot do it on our own—we need the help of our critics and the state. Our greatest possibilities are born of the promise of forgiveness and redemption, the hope of new life emerging from suffering and even death. Out of our past failings and our present shame can come future promise and hope.

Something crystallised for me at an appearance in March this year at the Opera House with the British philosopher AC Grayling, author of *The God Argument*, and Sean Faircloth, a US director of one of the Dawkins Institutes passionately committed to atheism. We were there to discuss their certainty about the absurdity of religious faith. Mr Faircloth raised what has already become a hoary old chestnut, the failure of Pope Francis when provincial of the Jesuits in Argentina during the Dirty Wars to adequately defend his fellow Jesuits who were detained and tortured by unscrupulous soldiers. Being a Jesuit, I thought I was peculiarly well situated to respond. I confess to having got a little carried away. I exclaimed: Yes, how much better it would have been if there had been just one secular, humanist, atheist philosopher who had stood up in the city square in Buenos Aires and shouted, 'Stop it!' The military junta would have collectively come to their senses, stopped it, and Argentinians would have lived happily ever after. The luxury for such philosophers is that they never have to get their hands dirty and they think that religious people who do are hypocrites unless of course they take the course of martyrdom. It is only as church that I think we can hold together ideals and reality, commitment and forgiveness.

Before we canonise Francis too quickly, let us concede that he was a divisive figure in his home province of Argentina when he was made Jesuit Provincial at the age of only thirty-six. The London *Tablet* has carried extracts from Paul Vallely's book *Pope Francis: Untying the Knots* which includes the explosive email sent by one of the serving Jesuit provincials in another Latin American country when Bergoglio's election was announced in St Peter's Square. This Jesuit provincial wrote:

> Yes I know Bergoglio. He's a person who's caused a lot of problems in the Society and is highly controversial in his own country. In addition to being accused of having allowed the arrest of two Jesuits during the time of the Argentinian dictatorship, as provincial he generated divided loyalties: some groups almost worshipped him, while others would have nothing to do with him, and he would hardly speak to them. It was an absurd situation. He is well-trained and very capable, but is surrounded by this personality cult which is extremely divisive. He has an aura of spirituality which he uses to obtain power. It will be a catastrophe for the Church to have someone like him in the Apostolic See. He left the Society of Jesus in Argentina destroyed with Jesuits divided and institutions destroyed and financially broken. We have spent two decades trying to fix the chaos that the man left us. [4]

Like all of us, Francis has feet of clay; he is a sinner; there are things in his past that he regrets. As Francis himself now admits:

> My style of government as a Jesuit at the beginning had many faults. That was a difficult time for the Society: an entire generation of Jesuits had disappeared. Because of this I found myself provincial when I was still very young. I was only 36 years old. That was crazy. I had to deal with difficult situations, and I made my decisions abruptly and by myself. [5]

He is a man who has learnt much by his mistakes; he is a sinner who has grown and thrived through his experience of the Lord's mercy. As he says:

4. Quoted by Paul Vallely in 'He's a Person who's Caused a lot of Problems', *The Tablet*, 10 August 2013: 4

5. *Pope Francis, 'A Big Heart Open to the World', 20*

My authoritarian and quick manner of making decisions led me to have serious problems and to be accused of being ultraconservative. I lived a time of great interior crisis when I was in Cordoba. To be sure, I have never been like Blessed Imelda [a goody-goody], but I have never been a right-winger. It was my authoritarian way of making decisions that created problems. I say these things from life experience and because I want to make clear what the dangers are. Over time I learned many things. The Lord has allowed this growth in knowledge of government through my faults and my sins.[6]

What a Jesuit; what a pope; what a man!

There are many things that his erstwhile critics regret. Having fallen out with many Jesuits in his home province, he enjoyed the favour of Pope John Paul II. There were tensions between him and Fr Pedro Arrupe, the Superior General of the Jesuits at the time of the Jesuit General Congregations which defined the Jesuit mission in terms of faith AND justice. The greatness of Francis has been in his capacity to transcend these differences and to be gracious even to those opposed to his viewpoints after many years of silence and isolation. It was very heartening for Jesuits of all stripes to learn of Francis's Mass at the Gesu Church in Rome on the Feast of St Ignatius on 31 July 2013. He visited the tomb of Pedro Arrupe. Just as he had mentioned Matteo Ricci and Karl Rahner in his earlier visit to the offices of *La Civilta Cattolica*, he mentioned Francis Xavier and Pedro Arrupe in his homily at the Gesu—each time linking an historic and contemporary figure, and each time the contemporary figure being one who had difficult relations with the Vatican from time to time. It is a long time since any pope mentioned Karl Rahner or Pedro Arrupe in a positive light. In his homily for the feast of St Ignatius, Francis said:

I have always liked to dwell on the twilight of a Jesuit, when a Jesuit is nearing the end of life, on when he is setting. And two images of this Jesuit twilight always

---

6. Pope Francis, 'A Big Heart Open to the World', 20.

spring to mind: a classical image, that of St Francis Xavier looking at China. Art has so often depicted this passing, Xavier's end. So has literature, in that beautiful piece by Pemán. At the end, without anything but before the Lord; thinking of this does me good. The other sunset, the other image that comes to mind as an example is that of Fr Arrupe in his last conversation in the refugee camp, when he said to us—something he used to say—'I say this as if it were my swan song: pray'. Prayer, union with Jesus. Having said these words he took the plane to Rome and upon arrival suffered a stroke that led to the sunset—so long and so exemplary—of his life. Two sunsets, two images, both of which it will do us all good to look at and to return to. And we should ask for the grace that our own passing will resemble theirs.[7]

As Catholics we can bring God's blessings to all in our world, even those who have no time for our Church and not much interest in our Lord. Remember how Pope Francis ended his address to the journalists in Rome giving a blessing with a difference. He said:

> I told you I was cordially imparting my blessing. Since many of you are not members of the Catholic Church, and others are not believers, I cordially give this blessing silently, to each of you, respecting the conscience of each, but in the knowledge that each of you is a child of God. May God bless you![8]

Now that is what I call a real blessing for journalists—and not a word of Vaticanese. Respect for the conscience of every person, regardless of their religious beliefs; silence in the face of difference; affirmation of the dignity and blessedness of every person; offering,

7. Pope Francis, Homily, 31 July 2013, at <http://w2.vatican.va/content/francesco/en/homilies/2013/documents/papa-frances-co_20130731_omelia-sant-ignazio.html>. Accessed 2 December 2014.

8. Pope Francis, Address to Members of Communications Media, 16 March 2013, at <http://w2.vatican.va/content/francesco/en/speeches/2013/march/documents/papa-francesco_20130316_rappresentanti-media.html>. Accessed 2 December 2014.

not coercing; suggesting, not dictating; leaving room for gracious acceptance. These are all good pointers for us Catholics helping to form the Church of the twenty-first century holding the treasure of tradition, authority and ritual in trust for all the people of God, including your children and grandchildren, as we discern how best to make a home for God in our lives and in our world, assured that the Spirit of God has made her home with us.

In an address to the Brazilian bishops, Pope Francis warned that we must not yield to the fear once expressed by Blessed John Henry Newman that 'the Christian world is gradually becoming barren and effete, as land which has been worked out and is become sand'. Francis said, 'We must not yield to disillusionment, discouragement and complaint. We have laboured greatly and, at times, we see what appear to be failures. We feel like those who must tally up a losing season as we consider those who have left us or no longer consider us credible or relevant.'

Francis drew upon one of his favourite gospel scenes, Luke's account of the disillusioned disciples on the Road to Emmaus failing to recognise the one who broke open the scriptures to them, then recognising him belatedly in the breaking of the bread:

> Here we have to face the difficult mystery of those people who leave the Church, who, under the illusion of alternative ideas, now think that the Church—their Jerusalem—can no longer offer them anything meaningful and important. So they set off on the road alone, with their disappointment. Perhaps the Church appeared too weak, perhaps too distant from their needs, perhaps too poor to respond to their concerns, perhaps too cold, perhaps too caught up with itself, perhaps a prisoner of its own rigid formulas, perhaps the world seems to have made the Church a relic of the past, unfit for new questions; perhaps the Church could speak to people in their infancy but not to those come of age. [9]

---

9. Pope Francis, Address to Bishops of Brazil, 28 July 2013, at

Asking what then are we to do, Francis answers:

> We need a Church unafraid of going forth into **their**
> night. We need a Church capable of meeting them
> on **their** way. We need a Church capable of entering
> into **their** conversation. We need a Church able to
> dialogue with those disciples who, having left Jerusalem
> behind, are wandering aimlessly, alone, with their own
> disappointment, disillusioned by a Christianity now
> considered barren, fruitless soil, incapable of generating
> meaning.

Francis has shown us that our faith is about much more than Church
and internal Catholic matters. Think just of his visits to Lampedusa
and then to the Jesuit Refugee Service in Rome. He has put a
very strong challenge to the West about our treatment of asylum
seekers—a challenge that hopefully will be heard even in Australia
by the very Catholic Abbott ministry as they consider turning back
the boats.

Lampedusa continues to be a beacon for asylum seekers
fleeing desperate situations in Africa seeking admission into the
EU. Lampedusa is a lightning rod for European concerns about
the security of borders in an increasingly globalized world where
people as well as capital flow across porous borders. That's why Pope
Francis went there on his first official papal visit outside Rome. At
Lampedusa on 8 July 2013, Pope Francis said:

> God is asking each of us: 'Where is the blood of your
> brother which cries out to me?' Today no one in
> our world feels responsible; we have lost a sense of
> responsibility for our brothers and sisters. We have fallen
> into the hypocrisy of the priest and the levite whom
> Jesus described in the parable of the Good Samaritan:
> we see our brother half dead on the side of the road, and

<http://w2.vatican.va/content/francesco/en/speeches/2013/july/documents/papa-francesco_20130727_gmg-episcopato-brasile.html>. Accessed 2 December 2014

perhaps we say to ourselves: 'poor soul…!', and then go on our way. It's not our responsibility, and with that we feel reassured, assuaged. [10]

Then on his visit to the Jesuit Church in Rome he said:

> After Lampedusa and other places of arrival, our city, Rome, is the second stage for many people. Often—as we heard—it's a difficult, exhausting journey; what you face can even be violent—I'm thinking above all of the women, of mothers, who endure this to ensure a future for their children and the hope of a different life for themselves and their family. Rome should be the city that allows refugees to rediscover their humanity, to start smiling again. Instead, too often, here, as in other places, so many people who carry residence permits with the words 'international protection' on them are constrained to live in difficult, sometimes degrading, situations, without the possibility of building a life in dignity, of thinking of a new future! [11]

Some of this sounds like politics! In a homily at a mass in 2013, Francis made it clear that the gospel and politics do mix. Reflecting on the centurion who asked healing for his servant, Francis said that those who govern 'have to love their people,' because 'a leader who doesn't love, cannot govern—at best they can discipline, they can give a little bit of order, but they can't govern.' He mentioned 'the two virtues of a leader': love for the people and humility. 'You can't govern without loving the people and without humility! And every man, every woman who has to take up the service of government, must ask themselves two questions: "Do I love my people in order to serve them better? Am I humble and do I listen to everybody,

---

10. Pope Francis, Homily, 8 July 2013, at
    <http://w2.vatican.va/content/francesco/en/homilies/2013/documents/papa-frances-co_20130708_omelia-lampedusa.html>. Accessed 2 December 2014.

11. Pope Francis, Address, 10 September 2013, at
    <http://w2.vatican.va/content/francesco/en/speeches/2013/september/documents/papa-francesco_20130910_centro-astalli.html>. Accessed 2 December 2014

to diverse opinions in order to choose the best path." If you don't ask those questions, your governance will not be good. The man or woman who governs—who loves his people—is a humble man or woman.' Francis insisted that none of us can be indifferent to politics: 'None of us can say, "I have nothing to do with this, they govern . . ." No, no, I am responsible for their governance, and I have to do the best so that they govern well, and I have to do my best by participating in politics according to my ability. Politics, according to the Social Doctrine of the Church, is one of the highest forms of charity, because it serves the common good. I cannot wash my hands, eh? We all have to give something!' [12]

He then became a little playful in his homily: '"A good Catholic doesn't meddle in politics." That's not true. That is not a good path. A good Catholic meddles in politics, offering the best of himself, so that those who govern can govern. But what is the best that we can offer to those who govern?' He concluded: 'So, we give the best of ourselves, our ideas, suggestions, the best, but above all the best is prayer. Let us pray for our leaders, that they might govern well, that they might advance our homeland, might lead our nation and even our world forward, for the sake of peace and of the common good.'

Our Catholic voice must be heard in season and out of season when it comes to laws and policies impacting on the poor, the vulnerable, and the marginalised—the widow, the orphan and the stranger. We must not be afraid to mix it in the world. It's not as if our Catholic tradition gives us fixed answers to all problems but it equips us with principles and a culture well suited to seeking the good, the true and the beautiful in any situation. We are called in the Ignatian tradition to find God in all things, and to discern God's presence in the life of every person. In his *La Civilta Cattolica* interview, Francis said:

If the Christian is a restorationist, a legalist, if he wants everything clear and safe, then he will find nothing.

12. Pope Francis, Morning Meditation, 16 September 2013, at
    <http://w2.vatican.va/content/francesco/en/cotidie/2013/documents/papa-frances-co-cotidie_20130916_politicians.html>. Accessed 2 December 2014.

Tradition and memory of the past must help us to have the courage to open up new areas to God. Those who today always look for disciplinarian solutions, those who long for an exaggerated doctrinal 'security', those who stubbornly try to recover a past that no longer exists—they have a static and inward-directed view of things. In this way, faith becomes an ideology among other ideologies. I have a dogmatic certainty: God is in every person's life. God is in everyone's life. Even if the life of a person has been a disaster, even if vices, drugs or anything else destroys it—God is in this person's life. You can, you must try to seek God in every human life. Although the life of a person is a land full of thorns and weeds, there is always a space in which the good seed can grow. You have to trust God. [13]

And to cap it all off: on 17 September 2013, Francis was 'in attendance' in a simple white cassock, not presiding and not concelebrating, at the episcopal ordination Mass of the new papal almoner (the official distributor of alms), Archbishop Konrad Krajewski. Francis briefly put a stole around his neck and laid hands on the newly consecrated bishop. You could almost hear the episcopal gasps and see the shock of the liturgists and canon lawyers from here on the other side of the globe! Fasten your seat belts. We are in for an exciting ride with this pope. He is happy to make mistakes. He is happy to go with the flow. But above all, he is so happy in his own skin and in his religious tradition and he exudes the confidence that comes only from knowing that he is loved and forgiven, and not from thinking that he is always right and has all the answers.

-o0o-

POSTSCRIPT: *Shortly after his election, Pope Francis announced the convening of an extraordinary synod of bishops to discuss the pastoral challenges to the family in the context of evangelisation. The bishops'*

---

13. Pope Francis, 'A Big Heart Open to the World', 32

conferences were asked to consult with the people of the Church and complete a detailed questionnaire providing background information for the synod. When the synod convened for two weeks in October 2014, some lay people including married couples accompanied the selected bishops to provide input and reflection. But the bishops were the only synod members with the right to vote. An interim document was published towards the end of the first week of the synod, indicating the issues for discussion and further reflection. At the end of the two week session, the bishops voted on a final document (the relatio synodi) which has now been sent to the bishops' conference for reflection and discussion before the next synod in October 2015.

The genie may be out of the bottle but it is still in the ecclesiastical kitchen. The Vatican has now released the official English translation of the 'relatio synodi', the concluding document from the Synod of Bishops convened by Pope Francis to consider 'pastoral challenges to the family in the context of evangelisation'.[14] The earlier 'relatio post disceptationem' was the punchy and slightly provocative discussion paper put together by Pope Francis's small hand-picked group charged with putting the issues for discussion on the table.[15] That document indicated a novel acceptance of some 'constructive elements' of couples living together without marriage, of the need to welcome homosexuals into the life of the Church, and of the possibility of admitting divorced and remarried people to the Eucharist. The Synod fathers agreed that they wanted to 'offer a meaningful word of hope' to the Church. To do this, they needed to acknowledge that the genie is out of the bottle and that there is a need for a comprehensive rethink by the Catholic Church on its teaching about marriage, sexuality, and reception of the Eucharist.

---

14. *Relatio Synodi* of the Third Extraordinary General Assembly of the Synod of Bishops: 'Pastoral Challenges to the Family in the Context of Evangelization', at <http://press.vatican.va/content/salastampa/en/bollettino /pubblico/2014/10/18/0770/03044.html>. Accessed 2 December 2014.

15. *Relatio ante disceptationem* of the General Rapporteur, Cardinal Péter Erdő, 6 October 2014, at <http://press.vatican.va/content/salastampa/en/bollettino /pubblico/2014/10/06/0712/03003.html>. Accessed 2 December 2014.

The *relatio synodi* is much more than a discussion paper. It is a lengthy committee job cobbling together the many different strands of discussion over the two weeks of the synod. Each of the sixty-two paragraphs was separately voted on by the 180 bishops in attendance who voted. It does not put the genie back in the bottle, but it does revert to much of the old style Vaticanese, trying to confine the genie to the episcopal kitchen. What's refreshing is that unlike synod documents published during the last two papacies, this one actually reflects the divisions and differing perspectives. We are even given the voting figures on each paragraph.

Also published is the official translation of Pope Francis's closing remarks at the Synod in which he speaks of 'moments of desolation, of tensions and temptations'. He lists the 'temptation to hostile inflexibility' which is 'the temptation of the zealous, of the scrupulous, of the solicitous and of the so-called traditionalists and also of the intellectuals'. Then crossing to the other side of the street, he speaks of the temptation to practise 'a deceptive mercy (which) binds the wounds without first curing them and treating them; that treats the symptoms and not the causes and the roots'. This is the temptation of the 'do-gooders', of the fearful, and also of the so-called 'progressives' and 'liberals'. All types were inside the Vatican tent last week and acknowledged as such. But this is still a synod only of bishops—celibate males talking about family life. Even though they have been attentive to some married people invited into their midst, they alone get to vote; they alone shape the final document.

This is all a work in progress. All sides of the hierarchy have put their views, and their views are reflected or at least hinted at in this latest document. The Synod fathers are to reconvene in Rome in a year's time. Their *relatio synodi* is 'intended to raise questions and indicate points of view which will later be developed and clarified through reflection in the local Churches in the intervening year'. Those reflections must not be restricted just to bishops or clergy.

The drafters have done a reasonable job given that all paragraphs attracted majority support, with only three paragraphs attracting less than 2/3 support. Those three paragraphs indicate the real neuralgic points of discussion. They were: the paragraph about the community's care for the divorced and remarried being an expression of the community's charity and not a weakening of its faith and testimony to the indissolubility of marriage; the paragraph requesting further theological reflection on the options of 'spiritual communion' or full sacramental communion for the divorced and remarried; and a very clunky paragraph packed with old Congregation for the Doctrine of the Faith terminology on 'pastoral attention towards persons with homosexual tendencies', abandoning any talk of welcome for committed gays who give mutual aid and precious support to each other.

The *relatio synodi* follows the basic outline of the original *relatio post disceptationem* with three parts on listening, looking, and facing the situation. Listening to the context and challenges of the family in the first part, the synod fathers (with no sense of irony or embarrassment) when reviewing the socio-cultural context, highlight the positive aspect of 'a greater freedom of expression and a better recognition of the rights of women and children, at least in some part of the world'. Dare one add: 'at least in some institutions and in some churches'? They speak also of the importance of affectivity in life and relationships.

Looking at Christ and the Gospel of the Family, they move in the second part from Jesus in the history of salvation to the family as part of God's salvific plan. These deft scriptural surveys are followed by a treatment of the family in Church documents including the 1968 encyclical on birth control *Humanae Vitae* which is unquestioningly espoused twice in the course of this document. The bulk of this second part is devoted to the indissolubility of marriage, the truth and beauty of the family, and mercy towards broken families.

The third part is where the rubber hits the road. The fathers set out pastoral perspectives on 'facing the situation'. They display considerable pastoral sensitivity and deep learning on caring for couples preparing for marriage, couples in the initial years of marriage, couples civilly married or living together, and broken families. But there is no consensus on what to do about the eucharist for the divorced and remarried. And for the moment the welcome mat for gays has been put back in the closet. Then comes what undoubtedly some Synod fathers will think to be a prophetic, counter-cultural discussion on 'the transmission of life and the challenges of a declining birthrate'. Living in a world of 7.2 billion people, and constantly meeting young couples who will try anything including IVF to have a child, I would have liked to have seen some treatment of these sorts of issues under this curious heading. Given the soundings that the synod fathers took with their questionnaire before the synod, I am staggered that they have said that 'we should return to the message of the Encyclical *Humanae Vitae* of Blessed Pope Paul VI, which highlights the need to respect the dignity of the person in morally assessing methods in regulating births'.

We never saw the results of many of the questionnaires before the synod. But I have no reason to think those from countries like Australia and the USA would be all that much different from the German response:

> In most cases where the Church's teaching is known, it is only selectively accepted. The idea of the sacramental marriage covenant, which encompasses faithfulness and exclusivity on the part of the spouses and the transmission of life, is normally accepted by people who marry in Church. Most of the baptised enter into marriage in the expectation and hope of concluding a bond for life. The Church's statements on premarital sexual relations, on homosexuality, on those divorced and remarried, and on birth control, by contrast, are virtually never accepted, or are expressly rejected in the vast majority of cases.[16]

---

16 German Catholic Bishops Conference, Pastoral challenges to the family in the context of evangelisation, 3 February 2014, 2 at
<http://www.dbk.de/fileadmin/redaktion/diverse_downloads/presse_2014/2014-012b-ENG-Fragebogen-Die-patoralen-Herausforderungen-der-Familie.pdf>. Accessed 2 December 2014.

We all have our work cut out for us in the next year if this synod is be truly reflective of the life experience and faith-filled hope of those who commit themselves to making a go of bringing Christ to the world through their work, their commitments to each other, and their children. For the moment, I would not see much pastoral point in sharing this document with the many young people I know who are living together, or with those who are gay or lesbian seeking a homecoming in the Church, or with those who have endured the pain of divorce and the moral angst of remarriage. I think I will be telling them to keep the door open, wait a while, and check back in a year to see how we are going. Francis still has a lot of work ahead of him, and so does the Holy Spirit. It would be a good start if all bishops' conferences were to follow the lead of the Germans and publish the results of the original questionnaire. After all, if we can have the voting results on each paragraph of an interim Synod document on the family, why not some indication of what family members are saying to their lordships in good faith and with open hearts?

2

Scrutinising a Non-Transparent Hierarchy

At the conclusion of the 1998 ad limina *visit by the Australian Catholic bishops, the Vatican issued a statement of conclusions about the Australian Catholic Church. Some concerns were expressed about Australian ideas of tolerance and egalitarianism, suggesting these notions might not totally accord with Roman Catholic ideas about church structures and life style. Most Australians are grateful to live in a society that prides itself on equality and the rule of law. We have an expectation that our social institutions will be conducted fairly and transparently. Pope Benedict's forced resignation of the popular, pastoral Bishop William Morris from Toowoomba in Queensland has upset many Australians concerned about the lack of transparency and due process in the Vatican curia.*

William Morris was bishop of Toowoomba for eighteen years. His book *Benedict, Me and the Cardinals Three*[1] is the story of his forced retirement at the insistence of Pope Emeritus Benedict XVI and at the instigation of three Roman curial cardinals all of whom have now left the Vatican, having passed retirement age.

In the 1960s, I lived for five years in the Toowoomba diocese while attending Downlands College, a boarding school for boys conducted by the Missionaries of the Sacred Heart. At that time, I had regularly to deny any relationship to the then bishop of Toowoomba, William Brennan, who gave very long sermons on hot and cold days much to the displeasure of the Downlands students. I used have to emerge

---

1.   William Morris, *Benedict, Me and the Cardinals Three* (Adelaide: ATF Press, 2014).

from chapel rightly claiming to be from another branch of the family back there in the bog. Some of the key priests who appear in Bill Morris's book also were educated at Downlands. The MSCs had a no nonsense style to them, enjoying their independence from the local bishop while being very dedicated to the pastoral care of people in the far flung country diocese and always attentive to the pastoral requests of the parish priests, a disproportionate number of whom went to Downlands. I remember one MSC arriving unexpectedly at the school mid-year to teach French. It was just after *Humanae Vitae* and he had expressed some reservations while ministering south of the Tweed River.

One of the ex-Downlanders to appear in the book is Bill Morris's Vicar General Peter Dorfield who, true to form as one of the world's most punctilious note takers, provided a detailed account to Bill about his unfortunate meeting with the papal visitator, Archbishop Charles Chaput, who came to the diocese for four days (including Anzac Day) in 2007 to report on the state of the diocese. Chaput told Dorfield that Morris

> was a good, humane and prayerful bishop but innocent and naïve and open to manipulation because of (his) great desire to see good in everyone, and that people had taken advantage of (his) goodness and trust. (He) had been captured, manipulated and misled by a so-called progressive group of priests in the diocese who were in fact 'running the diocese'; as a result of the actions of these priests, (he) had been led astray and now needed to recant, and in effect throw (himself) on the mercy of the Vatican authorities, promising a more orthodox and obedient future.[2]

After discussing Bishop Morris's 2006 Advent Pastoral Letter, Chaput then raised the topic of 'outrageous liturgies' and then made 'a series of denigrating comments about different priests'. When Dorfield had the temerity to defend them, Chaput 'suggested

---

2. Morris, *Benedict, Me and the Cardinals Three*, 91.

it might be time for a new Vicar-General because of (Dorfield's) perceived undue influence over (Morris) as a bishop and (Morris's) personal inadequacies in theological practice'.[3] This gives you some of the flavour of the book. It contains accurate recollections of a sham process instituted in Rome to get rid of Bill Morris at any cost, and regardless of any particular charges.

Speaking with Peter Dorfield in preparation for the launch of Morris' book, I asked him what are the key lessons now for the Church of Toowoomba. He reminded me that Christ's faithful in Toowoomba wanted nothing more than the truth. It is important to remember that William Morris was removed from office; he did not resign. He always displayed the highest pastoral integrity and paid the price for it. He was the consummate team player who planned his pastoral strategies in close consultation with his presbyterate and the various consultative organs he set up in the diocese. As the people of Toowoomba continue to live faithful lives as Catholics, they still hold Bill in high esteem; meanwhile all the people in Rome are now gone. As Peter said, it was 'a poor decision based on poor advice'.

I first met Bill when he was Secretary to Archbishop Francis Rush, Archbishop of Brisbane and President of the Australian Catholic Bishops Conference. Rush and his fellow Queensland bishops had appointed me prior to ordination as their Adviser on Aboriginal Affairs in the wake of controversy between the Queensland Church leaders and the colourful Sir Joh Bjelke Petersen in the lead up to the 1982 Commonwealth Games. Even under Bishop Edward Kelly MSC, the Toowoomba presbyterate were quite engaged on justice issues. I remember spending a week motoring all the way out to Quilpie and back with Peter Dorfield to meet with each deanery to discuss Aboriginal rights. In Toowoomba, we had a formal meeting at the bishop's house followed by a fine meal with silver table service. In Dalby we met at the presbytery and chatted over a meal. In Roma, we gathered on the presbytery verandah over a few beers. And out at Charleville, we had a muster by the river and a fine

---

3. Morris, *Benedict, Me and the Cardinals Three*, 92.

barbie. Pastoral style became more relaxed and theological niceties less relevant the further west you went.

I well recall attending Bill's episcopal ordination in Toowoomba in 1993. It was a very joyous and participative liturgy. Aboriginal Catholics played a central role. Darling Downs farmers presented some of their produce at the altar. Women were spotted on the sanctuary. The formal reading of the Latin papal bull was performed at an earlier ceremony much to the consternation of a handful of conservatives. After the mass, the then papal nuncio, Archbishop Brambilla, called aside the Master of Ceremonies who was the parish priest of Cunnamulla with a fairly laidback style. His Grace detailed the thirty-five liturgical abuses that had occurred. The MC heard him out and then said, 'Yes, we must make sure we get it right next time'. All being well, and Bill avoiding further promotion, next time should have come around in just another twenty-six years.

Shortly after the ordination, I was conducting a day of prayer and reflection for the priests of the Wagga Diocese. Their bishop William Brennan, the nephew of the William Brennan at whose feet I had sat as a schoolboy, had invited me. After lunch, the bishop and I went for a stroll. I said how much I had enjoyed Bill Morris's episcopal ordination. He said with a smile, 'Actually, I prefer the Roman rite'. Even back then I suspect Bill Morris was a target for the 'temple police'.

In 2010 I was honoured to deliver the Concannon Oration, the premier annual Catholic event for intellectual reflection on the faith in the Toowoomba diocese. I knew by this time that there was trouble brewing in Rome for Bill Morris. In the 2009 Spring issue of the priests' newsletter *The Swag*, Fr Jeff Scully, the parish priest of Quilpie and one time Roman classmate of Cardinal George Pell, had written with his characteristic light touch and humour:

> How can a respected leader of a local church be investigated without ever finding the content of the report based on these investigations? Is this not unthinkable in this age of transparency and accountability? I kid you not, Archbishop Chaput's visit did nothing to increase

respect for the way Rome's officials do business. After the Chaput visit, not many Toowoomba people were expecting to find in their mailboxes a wee note from Denver, Colorado, saying how much he enjoyed his visit to our part of the world, how enriching the experience had been for him, and how much he had learnt. Learning did not seem to be part of the exercise.[4]

In the oration, I said, 'As far as we all know, the investigation is ongoing. Is it not time for the open conversation to commence? Is it not time for all of us learn new pastoral ways of being Church before new generations in country areas of Australia are completely denied access to the sacraments?' The MC for the evening was Patrick Nunan, one of Toowoomba's most respected solicitors. He had been school captain of Downlands in my first year there. At dinner, clergy and the legal profession discussed the appalling abuse of process that was occurring in Rome in relation to their bishop. We hatched a plan for putting the spotlight on the administrative abuses being orchestrated from Rome.

Speaking to Jeff Scully in preparation for the launch of Bill's book, Jeff was very upbeat about the new direction of our Church under the leadership of Pope Francis. He said he is confident that whistle-blowers and the disaffected temple police wouldn't get the same inside run in Rome now as they did when they set out to do in the bishop of Toowoomba. Jeff said that he thinks Francis would have the good pastoral sense to refer the matter back to the Australian bishops' conference. He thinks the bishops would need to show some resolve either siding with the whistle-blowers or with their fellow bishop. Jeff insisted that Morris always took advice of his own clergy and his pastoral team. He was a servant of the servants of God who was welcomed and was welcoming from Toowoomba to Birdsville. Under Francis we can be sure that the local church is not just to be treated as a branch office of Rome Central. Jeff recalls how exemplary Morris was in dealing with child sexual abuse. You

---

4.   Jeff Scully, 'A Toowoomba Priest's Plea: What Price Leadership—And From Where?', *The Swag*, Spring 2009: 10, 11.

will recall that he asked Rome to delay his forced retirement until he could deal with the abuse crisis in a Toowoomba school where he had even had the foresight to engage a retired High Court judge to mediate the issue. Rome had other priorities preferring that the diocese be without a bishop while that matter was resolved.

It's been very difficult to work out why Bishop Morris was sacked. It has been a moving feast. At first the concern seemed to be over the third rite of reconciliation and his failure to drop everything and come to Rome when Cardinal Arinze specified. Bill pointed out that he was due in Rome four months after the specified date, so surely things could wait until then. It seems that over time Bill had mended his ways on the third rite to comply with Rome's new strictures. So then there was his Advent pastoral letter of 2006.

We are left confused as to whether Morris was sacked chiefly for what he wrote in that letter, or for what was reported by Chaput in 2007, or for what was reported to Rome by those sometimes described as 'the temple police'. The offending section of his pastoral letter was:

> Given our deeply held belief in the primacy of Eucharist for the identity, continuity and life of each parish community, we may well need to be much more open towards other options of ensuring that Eucharist may be celebrated. Several responses have been discussed internationally, nationally and locally
>
> • ordaining married, single or widowed men who are chosen and endorsed by their local parish community
>
> • welcoming former priests, married or single back to active ministry
>
> • ordaining women, married or single
>
> • recognising Anglican, Lutheran and Uniting Church orders

> While we continue to reflect carefully on these options
> we remain committed to actively promoting vocations
> to the current celibate male priesthood and open to
> inviting priests from overseas.[5]

If he was sacked for what he wrote in his Advent letter about the
possible ordination of women, married priests, and recognition
of other orders 'Rome willing', there would have been no need for
Archbishop Chaput later to make his visit and his report. And let us
remember that Morris had published a clarification of his pastoral
letter on his website saying:

> In my Advent Pastoral Letter of 2006 I outlined some
> of the challenges facing the diocese into the future. In
> that letter I made reference to various options about
> ordination that were and are being talked about in
> various places, as part of an exercise in the further
> investigation of truth in these matters. Unfortunately
> some people seem to have interpreted that reference
> as suggesting that I was personally initiating options
> that are contrary to the doctrine and discipline of the
> Church. As a bishop I cannot and would not do that and
> I indicated this in the local media at the time.[6]

But then again if he was sacked for matters detailed in Chaput's
report, we are left wondering why Chaput being apprised of the
Advent letter and having completed his visit would have told
the Diocesan Chancellor Brian Sparksman how extraordinarily
surprising it would be if Morris were to be sacked. As they drove
back to Brisbane after the visitation, Chaput told Sparksman, 'I
would be astonished if you were to lose your bishop'.[7] The matter
is a complete mess reflecting very poorly on a Church that prides
itself on a Code of Canon Law that provides for the protection of the
rights of all Christ's faithful, including priests and bishops.

---

5. Morris, *Benedict, Me and the Cardinals Three*, 324.
6. Morris, *Benedict, Me and the Cardinals Three*, 354.
7. Morris, *Benedict, Me and the Cardinals Three*, 94

As Jeff Scully has said to me, 'You wouldn't give Bill Morris full marks for preaching but you would give him 11/10 for teamwork'. If Pope Francis were to refer future complaints back to the bishops' conference, we could at least expect greater sensitivity to the pastoral needs and concerns which preoccupied Bishop Morris. There would still be the occasional outrider like Cardinal Pell who erroneously claimed when speaking to an American Catholic news agency that 'the diocese was divided quite badly and the bishop hasn't demonstrated that he's a team player'. [8] That is quite a claim coming from an archbishop whose own auxiliary Geoffrey Robinson had cause to say, 'He's not a team player, he never has been'.[9] I think part of the problem has been that in our Church people have had in mind two separate teams. There is the Roman curia team, and there is the local church team. There are those like Cardinal Pell who have played with the Roman curia team providing exclusive avenues for reporting on the local team, and then there are those like Bishop Morris who have played with the local church team knowing little about the workings of the Roman team. One message of Francis is that it's time to bring both teams together, and the Roman team is not always right.

In *Evangelii Gaudium*, Francis says:

> Here I repeat for the entire Church what I have often said to the priests and laity of Buenos Aires: I prefer a Church which is bruised, hurting and dirty because it has been out on the streets, rather than a Church which is unhealthy from being confined and from clinging to its own security. I do not want a Church concerned with being at the centre and which then ends by being caught up in a web of obsessions and procedures. If something should rightly disturb us and trouble our consciences, it

---

8.   Cardinal George Pell, Interview, Catholic News Agency, 28 May 2011, at <http://www.catholicnewsagency.com/news/cardinal-pell-says-bishop-morris-sacking-a-tragedy-but-also-a-useful-clarification/>. Accessed 2 December 2014.

9.   Geoffrey Robinson, Interview, The World Today, ABC Radio, 14 November 2012 at <http://www.abc.net.au/worldtoday/content/2012/s3632475.htm>. Accessed 2 December 2014.

is the fact that so many of our brothers and sisters are living without the strength, light and consolation born of friendship with Jesus Christ, without a community of faith to support them, without meaning and a goal in life. More than by fear of going astray, my hope is that we will be moved by the fear of remaining shut up within structures which give us a false sense of security, within rules which make us harsh judges, within habits which make us feel safe, while at our door people are starving and Jesus does not tire of saying to us: 'Give them something to eat' (Mk 6:37).[10]

Some of the most heartening remarks out of this entire and profoundly disheartening saga detailed by Bishop Morris have been the public affirmations of some of his fellow Queensland bishops. Ray Benjamin, the long retired bishop of Townsville, joined issue with some of the Catholic press in Australia labeling his brother bishop a heretic. Benjamin wrote:

I was distressed to read that *The Record* has associated Bishop Bill Morris with the ugly word 'heresy', especially coming from a publication which I have known and respected for many years. In what sense could he be demoted to such a level? His thoughts on women as priests, (shared with half the Bishops of the world) were always expressed in humble submission to the Church's authority. At no stage did he ever nominate or encourage any woman towards priesthood. Surely no heresy there. Regarding Bishop Bill's attitude to non-Catholic clergy, we must not find ourselves transported back to the bitterness and name-calling of past centuries. Our Catholic attitude to other church communities has developed in many positive ways. Our popes and senior prelates have, for years now, been regularly visiting and sharing with their non-Catholic counterparts, in prayer, preaching and seeking the truth together. Why is Pope Benedict insisting on attending the upcoming

---

10. Pope Francis, *Evangelii Gaudium*, 2013, #49

Assisi Inter-Faith Conference, against the wishes of his 'safe' advisers? We have a whole Pontifical Council for Promoting Christian Unity, with a cardinal at its head, urging all Catholics everywhere into ecumenical endeavours. Students for our Catholic Priesthood are studying Scripture at the feet of Protestant scholars. With the so-called 'mainstream' Churches we willingly share one another's Baptisms and Marriages as sacred, binding, and life giving. In sixty-two years as a Catholic Priest and Bishop, after some early years of self righteous superiority (of which I am now a bit ashamed), I have come to accept that the vast majority of non-Catholic pastors I meet are truly men of God, committed to a lifetime of humble service, responding not only to the 'vocation' of their communities, but equally responding to the urging of God's Holy Spirit. Who else will care for those waiting Christian communities? In our many ecumenical endeavours, for any Catholic to smile and offer the right hand of welcome and friendship to such good people, while keeping the left hand tightly behind our back, reminding us that they are, after all well-meaning heretics, would, I feel, be more heretical than anything Bishop Morris ever said or even imagined.[11]

After attending the huge farewell mass for Bill Morris in Toowoomba, James Foley, bishop of Cairns wrote to the Toowoomba church leadership team:

The reasons, the causes and the motivations for what has occurred may be known only unto God, Who alone may judge. Consistently and officially it has been stated that neither Bill's own integrity nor his pastoral effectiveness are questioned. The fruits—the proof—of this were palpably evident in Sunday's celebration. Now, after almost two decades attending episcopal testimonials and funerals, I have never witnessed so simple yet profound an outpouring of appreciation

---

11. Raymond Benjamin, Letter to the Editor, *The Swag* (18:8 Summer 2011): 6

and love. As one of the other bishops there observed afterwards: The best way to go may be to get sacked! . . . Never have I been more struck than by the sincerity and depth of Faith at this recent Mass of Thanksgiving. The solid no-nonsense Catholic Faith of the people of the Toowoomba Diocese was un-self-consciously and unpretentiously on display.[12]

Bill's book highlights especially through the process suggested by the group gathered for dinner after the Concannon Oration—a report commissioned from retired Justice William Carter and the subsequent canonical report by Fr Ian Waters—that Bishop Morris was denied natural justice. As William Carter said at the Brisbane launch, 'Scripture abounds with references to justice and to our need to "act justly" in our personal lives. Show me the law or doctrine which exempts the pope and the cardinals three from compliance with this same requirement in the circumstances of a case like this? This is why this book *had* to be written.'[13]

In 2012 on the feast of St Benedict, I was back in the Toowoomba Cathedral for the episcopal ordination of Bill Morris's successor, Bob McGuckin. The presiding prelate was Archbishop Mark Coleridge who was very severe in his homily. He said:

[T]here's one point in the Rule where Benedict abandons moderation and speaks with a quite untypical severity. He is describing the four kinds of monk, and he speaks approvingly of cenobites and hermits, both of whom live under the rule of an Abbot, one in community, the other in solitude. But then he lashes the free-wheelers he calls sarabaites and gyrovagues. These are the wandering monks who submit to no authority but their own and call holy whatever pleases them, moving from monastery to monastery and abusing hospitality

12. James Foley, Letter to Toowoomba Catholic Church leaders, 31 August 2011, in *Horizons*, Toowoomba Diocese, October 2011, 19

13. BJ Carter QC, Book Launch, Brisbane, 19 June 2014 at <http://www.eurekastreet.com.au/uploads/File/14/1406morrisbook_carter.pdf>. Accessed 2 December 2014..

to gratify their own desires at every turn. They are do-it-yourself monks who are a law unto themselves. In the terms we have heard in the Gospel of John, they do not remain in the love of Christ but stay imprisoned in the love of self which, according to St Benedict, is the way of perdition.

. . . .

If a Bishop fails to listen to the words of the Master, he will prove to be a law unto himself, every bit as bad as the wandering monks, or worse since he is the shepherd of the flock.

. . . .

Our own situation is different in many ways, but the Diocese of Toowoomba has known turbulence in recent times. St Benedict points the way forward—not just for the new Bishop but for the entire community of the Diocese. The way beyond all turbulence is a new listening to the voice of Christ at the heart of the Church, a new obedience to the Lord, which alone can guarantee that we remain in his love.[14]

Many of us in that Cathedral felt assaulted and we thought the pulpit was being used to commit another wrong on the ever pastoral William Morris who sat there on the sanctuary, dignified, silent and condemned. These were the fading days of Benedict's papacy. Hopefully under the leadership of Pope Francis we will hear no more homilies like that from our church leaders in Australia, and we will treasure the pastoral insights of bishops like Bill Morris as well as

---

14. Mark Coleridge, Homily, 11 July 2012 at <http://brisbanecatholic.org.au/articles/homily-episcopal-ordination-reverend-robert-mcguckin-sixth-bishop-toowoomba/>. Accessed 2 December 2014. Eight months later, Coleridge told the ABC: 'Certainly, the perception among key people in Rome (and here I don't wish to be unfair on Bishop Morris at all) was that Bishop Morris was trying to say "Yes" and "No" at the same time - that he was, as it were, speaking with a forked tongue. Rome put up with that for quite some years, but it reached the point where this situation was

the theological acumen of popes like Benedict at his best, spared the reckless lack of concern for justice and transparency shown by the three cardinals and some others on the Roman team who simply thought it was time to teach the Toowoomba team a lesson. Mind you, Benedict was well past his prime when he wrote to Morris that John Paul II 'has decided infallibly and irrevocably that the Church has not the right to ordain women to the priesthood.'[15]

It is no longer appropriate for Church hierarchs to claim that notions of transparency, due process and natural justice are antithetical to the hierarchical nature of the Church or to the primacy of the papacy. The primacy is not to be exercised arbitrarily or capriciously; and defenders of the Church will want to go to great lengths to ensure that the papal office is not perceived to be exercised without sufficient regard to the circumstances and evidence of a case. For the pope to be totally free in the appointment, transfer and removal of bishops, he and his flock have to be assured that his curial officials exercise their power to recommend appointment, transfer or removal in a just and transparent manner.

The laity, the religious, the presbyterate and the bishops in Australia are sure to have a heightened twenty-first century notion of justice, transparency, and due process. This heightened notion is a gift for the contemporary Church. As the present royal commission highlights, it is a precondition for the Church's continued institutional existence in this country. It is one of the works of the Spirit. It is not antithetical to the nature of the Church. *Lumen Gentium* puts it well:

> Since the kingdom of Christ is not of this world the Church or people of God in establishing that kingdom takes nothing away from the temporal welfare of any people. On the contrary it fosters and takes to itself,

---

deemed untenable. Bishop Morris simply could not keep saying both "Yes" and "No" - it had to be one or the other.' ABC Religion and Ethics, 'Seeing Christ amid the mess: Reflections on the pope, the Church and the Australian situation', 8 March 2013.

15 Letter of Pope Benedict to Bishop Morris, 22 December 2009, at Morris, *Benedict, Me and the Cardinals Three*, 379.

insofar as they are good, the ability, riches and customs
in which the genius of each people expresses itself.
Taking them to itself it purifies, strengthens, elevates
and ennobles them.[16]

The Church of the twenty-first century should be the exemplar
of due process, natural justice and transparency—purifying,
strengthening, elevating and ennobling these riches and customs
of contemporary Western societies which are the homes and social
constructs for many of the faithful, including those most directly
impacted by the decision to force the dismissal of Bishop Morris.

While there can be little useful reflection and critique of the
final decision of Pope Benedict to force the early retirement of
Bishop Morris, there is plenty of scope to review the processes and
the evidence leading to the submission of the brief for dismissal
provided by curial officials to the Holy Father.

I have followed the Morris saga closely. My one new insight from
reading Bill's book is that he was sacked because he was too much a
team player with his local church. By sacking their local leader, the
Romans hoped to shatter the morale and direction of those who
had planned the pastoral strategies of a country diocese stretched to
the limits as a Eucharistic community soon to be deprived priests in
the Roman mould. I imagine it is still not possible for Pope Francis
to apologise for the wrong done to Bishop Morris and the diocese
of Toowoomba. The Roman Curia and its mindset would at least
have that much of a hold over him. But would not it be a grace
for everyone, including those who perpetrated the wrong if he did?
On your behalf, I do apologise to William Morris in the name of
Christ's faithful here gathered immediately following the feast of
Corpus Christi. I commend the book, urging you to buy it, and I
commend the author to your prayers as he continues to minister as
a bishop in good standing, convinced that 'the Church is at its best
when it is most transparent, when the eyes of justice and the eyes of
the Gospel are so clear that all rights are respected for individuals,
no matter who they are in the community'.

16.　Vatican II, *Lumen Gentium*, Dogmatic Constitution on the Church, 1964, #13.

3

Handing on the Faith

There are more than 700,000 desks in Catholic schools around Australia. Teachers in those schools are rarely priests or religious nowadays. They are professionally trained teachers, lay people with their own families and relationships. These teachers are often the face of the Church for children who do not often go to church and whose parents might not know much about Church teachings. Most dioceses organise an annual event for their teachers to gather, reflect on their faith, and learn more about the Church they serve. This chapter was first composed as the opening keynote address at the conference in the diocese of Sandhurst (based in Bendigo, Victoria) in 2012. 2012 marked the fiftieth Anniversary of the beginning of the Second Vatican Council and the Strike for State Aid in Goulburn NSW in July 1962, both very significant events in the development of Catholic Education. The conference theme was 'Re-imagining the Mission: A Pilgrimage of Faith' and the focus was on Catholic education and social justice, the challenge for Catholic schools in educating young Catholics.

Catholic Education and Social Justice

In the wake of the Australian Federal Government's recent review of educational funding, the Gonski Review, coming fifty years after the Goulburn Catholic School Strike, I offer only two observations on school funding, asking that there be a fair go for all children no matter what class of school their parents might choose for them.

First, I am one of those Australians who is not helped when told by one protagonist of an argument that funding is inequitable when one makes reference to the funds provided by only one level of government. In a federation like Australia, the equity of funding arrangements can be judged only by considering the taxpayer funding received from all levels of government.

Second, funding arrangements need to take into account the heavy lifting done by different schools and networks of schools in providing education services to the neediest students including those with acute learning difficulties and those from families where parents have both few resources and little motivation for providing for the education of their children. There is much talk at the moment about "residualisation" of some state schools that are left to do the heavy lifting especially for children who just do not fit anywhere else in the education system. Schools that perform this heavy lifting deserve a higher level of funding. I make no attempt to quantify what that level should be.

More than thirty years ago, the guru on justice was Harvard Professor John Rawls who wrote a book *A Theory of Justice*. He was in the social contract mould, proposing a simple thought experiment. Imagine everyone is placed behind a veil of ignorance where they do not know what their attributes, interests or place in society will be. In this Original Position, people would then choose a list of suitable arrangements to which they would be bound or with which they would voluntarily comply. Everyone would be entitled to the same list of basic liberties. The key offices in society would be open to everyone without discrimination. The unequal distribution of goods and opportunities would be justified in so far as it assisted the worst off in society to be better off than they would have been if no unequal distribution were permitted.[1] For thirty years, social

---

1. John Rawls, *A Theory of Justice*, revised edition (Cambridge, Mass: Belknap Press, 1999), 53,72. In 1971, Rawls formulated the second principle as: 'Social and economic inequalities are to be arranged so that they are both (a) reasonably expected to be to

philosophers made their mark by agreeing or disagreeing with Rawls.

The philosopher Amartya Sen who won the Nobel Peace Prize for Economics recently published a book *The Idea of Justice*. He gives a simple example of three children and a flute. Bob is very poor and would like to have the flute because he has nothing else to play with. Carla made the flute and wants to keep it. Anne is the only one of the three children who knows how to play the flute and she plays it beautifully bringing pleasure to all who hear her. Who has the best claim to the flute? Sen tells us that the economic egalitarian would give it to Bob. The libertarian would insist that Carla retain the fruits of her labour. Most Australians without a second thought would simply assert, 'Carla made it; it's hers; the rest should stop complaining; if they want a flute they should make their own!' The utilitarian hedonist would give it to Anne. Fortunately we have more than one flute to play for appropriate for education in Australia. The resources are divisible. Sen says, 'that it is not easy to brush aside as foundationless any of the claims based respectively on the pursuit of human fulfilment, or removal of poverty, or entitlement to enjoy the products of one's own labour. The different resolutions all have serious arguments in support of them'.[2] What are the relevant considerations when it comes to distributing the education dollar? Education for the poorest? Education for those who would most profit by it? Education for those who can afford it? These are real tensions for all of us making judgments on formulae for the allocation of scarce education resources.

Vatican II and Catholic Education Fifty Years On

In 2004 when last addressing the Australian Diocese of Sandhurst's Education Conference, I asked, 'What Do Our Students Rightly

everyone's advantage, and (b) attached to positions and offices open to all'. In his 1999 revision, he conceded ambiguity in the phrases 'everyone's advantage' and 'open to all' so he proposed: 'Social and economic inequalities are to be arranged so that they are both (a) *to the greatest expected benefit of the least advantaged* and (b) attached to positions and offices open to all *under conditions of fair equality of opportunity.'*

2.. Amartya Sen, *The Idea of Justice* (Cambridge, Mass: Belknap Press, 2009), 14.

Ask of Us, the Church who are Many Parts, One Body?' I gave nine answers:

1. Take Us Beyond Our Comfort Zones
2. Help Us to Count Our Blessings Without Feeling Guilty
3. Assure Us that the Balance Holds
4. Trust Us and teach Us to Form and Inform Our Consciences as We decide How to Act,
5. Inspire Us and Console Us that there is such a thing as Truth
6. Provide us with the Tools to Critique Our Society
7. Invite Us to Participate in a Church that Speaks to Us of Life, Love, Mystery, Suffering, Death and Hope,
8. Teach Us to Engage in respectful Dialogue in Our Church and in Our Society
9. Put Everything in the Context of Love

I think our students are still asking the same things of us. Back then I copped a little flak from some of our Church leaders for daring to insist on the need for teachers to trust their students and to teach them to form and inform their consciences and to their consciences be true. Just as it is too simplistic to equate following one's conscience with doing what one feels like, so it is too simplistic to equate it with doing what 'Father', the 'Bishops' or the 'Holy Father' has to say. I am quite unapologetic in according primacy to the formed and informed conscience of the individual. Any Catholic taking their faith and Church membership seriously will be very attentive to the teaching office of the hierarchy, especially the pope. But at the end of the day, all of us, whether lay or cleric will have to act according to our conscience before God.

In 2012 the Canadian and US Bishops Conferences issued lengthy pastoral letters on freedom of conscience and religion. Suffice to say, bishops cannot lecture to governments about freedom of conscience unless they also concede to the laity the same freedom within the Church. The Canadian bishops have neatly summarised the challenge to parents and teachers re-imagining the mission of the Church fifty years after Vatican II. They say:

Families and schools are the primary places of formation where young people receive a correct understanding of what is entailed in the right to freedom of conscience and religion. Parents and educators have an especially important task to fulfill in forming the consciences of the next generation in respect for their brothers and sisters of different religions. Their constant challenge is to develop in children a conscience that is truly upright and free: one that can choose what is truly good and right and thus reject what is evil. They have the duty of helping young people conform their conscience to the truth of the moral law and to live in conformity with that truth.[3]

Among the human and Christian virtues acquired in the family, certain ones in particular prepare today's youth to resist the attacks on freedom of conscience that they will inevitably encounter: courage, justice, prudence, and perseverance. This formative work also entails forming citizens ready to call to account any person or institution that would intrude upon their right to freedom of conscience or religion.

My Parish

In preparing these thoughts, I was so bold as to announce to the parishioners where I say mass regularly that I would be addressing this gathering in Sandhurst on the fiftieth anniversary of Vatican II. I asked their advice. Being north of the Murray, many of them did not know where Sandhurst was so I explained that I would be coming to Bendigo.

The overwhelming reaction of the parishioners was one of delight and thanks that they had the opportunity to speak their minds in an atmosphere of trust and acceptance that is the Church. Some thought I was being brave in allowing people to speak their minds.

---

3. Permanent Council of the Canadian Conference of Catholic Bishops, *Pastoral Letter on Freedom of Conscience and Religion*, April 2012, 10, at <http://www.cccb.ca/site/images/stories/pdf/Freedom_of_Conscience_and_Religion.pdf>. Accessed 2 December 2014.

It does not take courage, only trust that the Spirit is alive and active amongst the People of God. Let me share with you some of their thoughts.

> Sometimes I think the laity have just been too lazy, not taking up the challenges and opportunities. Other times, I think the clergy have been too anxious to hang on to power and control. Fifty years on, maybe this is the action of the Spirit as we move backwards and forwards with this movement.
>
> Being a Catholic primary school principal, I know that primary schools are the face of the modern Church. Everyone wants their children educated at a Catholic primary school. Our schools are bursting at the seams. But the parents don't necessarily want to be involved with the Church. There are none of our children here at the regular parish mass. But their parents will be delighted to turn up in droves for first communion and confirmation. The problem is that we are not able to make the liturgy relevant to them. We have a confirmation mass coming up and we are not even allowed to change the reading of the day even though it talks about sex and things that have no relevance to the children.
>
> My concern is with our young people. They have lost their way. The church is not there for them. Our liturgies are too boring for young people. I and most of my siblings still go to mass. But none of my four children do. I am a good parent. Liturgies can be inspirational for young people, and more liturgies should be directed at them.
>
> The Church must not let the government take over all the welfare services telling us how to do things. Some things we know best how to do. The churches should co-operate more together to help those in need.
>
> In 1988, our then archbishop made a commitment to reconciliation and we have celebrated Reconciliation Sunday ever since. This has been a great boost for the diocese. How welcome for us to be asked. A church with

no room for Bishop Bill Morris or the journalist and broadcaster, Paul Collins, is hardly going to be able to fulfil the mission of today's gospel: 'Go into all the world and proclaim the good news to the whole of creation'. Rather than Vatican II, I think we risk going back to Vatican I.

It is time for the women to stand up, and it is time for women to be given their rightful place in the Church. Other Churches have done it. Why can't we? The Church's position and treatment of women is now counter-cultural and has no theological explanation. When the priests are running out, why don't we women take part? Do they think we are not good enough?
The new translation of the mass is a disgrace. It's a wonder that any of us still come.

My daughter-in-law is Religion Education Coordinator at a large Catholic school. She swears like a trooper, hardly goes to mass, and has more spirituality than any one else I know. Why can't we just let them find God in their own way?

We might have read the Vatican II documents when they came out but we haven't really looked at them since. I remember a priest telling us that it would be like the new grass growing. It would first be cut down but then it would shoot again. I guess after fifty years we are just at the stage of the grass being cut down for the first time. We'll have to wait and see what grows back.

Looking Back 50 Years

In 1962, I moved from the Brigidine Convent at Indooroopilly in Brisbane to St Joseph's College, Nudgee Junior, under the care of the Christian Brothers. I was an impressionable eight-year-old and was in grade 3. I well recall one of the brothers taking the class up to the top floor of the school. We gathered outside the chapel in front of the large portrait of our Lady of Perpetual Succour. Brother told us that there were very significant events occurring in Rome. Pope John had convened a Vatican Council. We were instructed to pray for all the bishops because this council would affect the future of the

Church. I have no real recollection of the prayers we offered, and thus I am not in a position to say whether or not they were answered. But like you, I know that things have changed very significantly in the Church and in the world since that group of eight-year-old boys offered prayer and supplication.

Fifty years on, we gather to celebrate as Catholics, confident that the gifts of the Spirit will assist us in proclaiming the Good News to each other, to our fellow believers, and to our fellow citizens no matter what their religious beliefs or none. Let us recall that it was the week of Christian Unity in 1959 when John XXIII gathered with a small selection of his cardinals in the Benedictine chapterhouse beside the Basilica of Saint Paul-Outside-the-Walls when he said:

> This festive occasion, commemorating the conversion of St Paul, has gathered us around the tomb of the Apostle in his illustrious Basilica and offers us an opportunity to confide to your kindness and understanding some of the most noteworthy aspects of apostolic activity which have come to our attention during these first three months of our presence here in Rome in close contact with Roman ecclesiastical society. Our chief concern in the *bonum animarum* and our wish is to see the new pontificate meet the spiritual demands of the present time accurately and forcefully.[4]

The great historian of Vatican II from the 'Bologna School', Giuseppe Alberigo, recalls that Roncalli upon election as pope and on choosing the name John emphasised his commitment to being a good pastor consistent with Jesus' discourse in John 10 on the Good Shepherd. Roncalli said, 'The other human qualities—knowledge, shrewdness, diplomatic tact, organisational abilities—can help the pope to carry out his office, but they can in no way substitute for his task as a pastor'.[5] There at St Pauls Outside the Walls, the new Pope said:

---

4. Pope John XXIII, Address to the Roman Cardinals, 25 January 1959, in *The Pope Speaks*, American Quarterly of Papal Documents, 5 (1959): 398.

5. G Alberigo, *A Brief History of Vatican II* (Maryknoll, NY: Orbis Books, 2006), 3

The cup of misfortune confronting the sons of God and of the Holy Church is filled to the brim by temptations in the material order, which are increased and magnified

by the progress of modern technology - in itself morally indifferent.

All of this—this progress, as it is called—distracts men from the quest for superior spiritual goods and is conducive to a weakening of spiritual energies and to a relaxation of the old discipline and order. As a result, grave obstacles arise to confront the Church and her children in her fight against errors which throughout history have always brought about fatal and evil divisions, spiritual and moral decay, and the destruction of nations.

This most disheartening sight has caused this humble priest (whom Divine Providence singled out, although unworthy, for the exalted mission of the Supreme Pontificate) to make a decision intended to recall certain ancient forms of doctrinal affirmation and of wise arrangements for ecclesiastical discipline. These forms, in the course of Church history, have yielded the richest harvest of results because of their clarity of thought, their compactness of religious unity, and their heightened flame of Christian fervour.[6]

Then 'trembling with a bit of emotion', he announced his intention to hold a diocesan Synod for Rome, and an ecumenical Council of the universal Church, as well as an *aggiornamento* (bringing up to date) of the Code of Canon Law. He thought such initiatives would not only produce 'great enlightenment for all Christian people' but also 'a renewed invitation to our separated sisters and brothers so that all may follow us in their search for unity and grace'. What has happened to our ecumenical spirit? He spoke of 'bringing the modern world into contact with the vivifying and perennial energies of the Gospel'. And this is the invitation to you, the Church of Sandhurst, fifty years on.

---

6. Pope John XXIII, Address to the Roman Cardinals, 25 January 1959, in *The Pope Speaks*, American Quarterly of Papal Documents, 5 (1959): 400.

John O'Malley SJ, the finest contemporary historian of Vatican II writing in the English language has provided us with 'a simple litany' of the changes in church style indicated by the council's vocabulary:

> from commands to invitations, from laws to ideals, from threats to persuasion, from coercion to conscience, from monologue to conversation, from ruling to serving, from withdrawn to integrated, from vertical and top-down to horizontal, from exclusion to inclusion, from hostility to friendship, from static to changing, from passive acceptance to active engagement, from prescriptive to principled, from defiant to open-ended, from behaviour modification to conversion of heart, from the dictates of law to the dictates of conscience, from external conformity to the joyful pursuit of holiness.[7]

I am one who welcomes these changes. I am not one of those Catholics so wedded to the continuity of the tradition as to think that nothing happened at Vatican II, and that we should be back to business as usual as we were when those eight-year-old boys gathered with the Christian Brother around the portrait of Our Lady of Perpetual Succour.

Contemporary Faith

Most parents or grandparents wonder how any practice of the faith is to be handed on credibly to their children and grandchildren. They know that the younger generations are more impressed by actions than by words, and that talk of justice rings hollow with them unless there are structures in place to ensure justice is done, and that talk of God's love rings false unless it is lived through deeds and witnessed by a real sense of transcendence and respect for every person's human dignity elevating the believer above the materialism and power of the world. If the faith is to be handed on to the coming generations, we need to be sure that we, the Church, are not an obstacle but rather a bridge for bringing the modern world into contact with the vivifying and perennial energies of the gospel.

---

7. John W O'Malley, 'Vatican II: Did Anything Happen?', in *Vatican II: Did Anything Happen?*, David G Scholthoven, editor, Continuum, 2007, at 81.

The Czech theologian Tomas Halik sees the Church as the community and the institution which helps to instill a person's original, untested, unreflective faith. It is also the privileged space for the person whose original faith is shaken by life to come to a 'second wind faith' which is at home with paradox, engaged with the world, and accepting of inevitable Church shortcomings. The crisis and severance of faith can have various causes: 'It can be some traumatic disillusionment with those who imparted to us our original faith, or it can be a private drama, in which our original trust and certainties are eclipsed, or just simply a change of circumstances and "mental climate"'.[8] Teilhard de Chardin thought Christianity was in its infancy. Many contemporary thinkers assert that it is obsolete and its time has expired. Halik thinks both may be mistaken. 'Maybe our Christianity is actually going through its midlife crisis, its "*acedia* phase", a time of lethargy and drowsiness.'[9]

Halik quotes Joseph Ratzinger's conversation with the journalist Peter Seewald published under the title *God and the World*. Benedict holds that faith is not like some mathematical formula that can be rationally demonstrated apart from the experiment of life: 'The truth of Jesus' word cannot be tested in terms of theory. The truth of what God says here involves the whole person, the experiment of life. It can only become clear for me if I truly give myself up to the will of God. This will of the creator is not something foreign to me, something external, but is the basis of my own being.'[10] Halik posits God himself placing the 'metaphysical disquiet' of the need to seek meaning within the human heart. God responds to this questioning with God's self-revelation. We then respond in faith with an act of trust and self-surrender 'to that divine sharing, the Word, wherein God gives Himself'.[11]

Halik is not one for the certainties of the catechism or the latest Vatican declaration. The certainty of doctrine and submissiveness

---

8. Tomas Halik, *Night of the Confessor: Christian Faith in an Age of Uncertainty* (New York: Doubleday, 2012), 199–200.

9. Halik, *Night of the Confessor*, 200–1.

10. Halik, *Night of the Confessor*, 210.

11. Halik, *Night of the Confessor*, 212.

to religious authority are no substitute for facing the hard reality of true religious experience. This well connected cleric in good Vatican standing proclaims, 'The religion that is now disappearing has tried to eliminate paradoxes from our experience of reality; the faith we are maturing toward, a paschal faith, teaches us to live with paradoxes'.[12]

Hope, Paradox and Reconciliation

In *Spe Salvi*, his last encyclical, Pope Benedict has written that:

> Redemption is offered to us in the sense that we have been given hope, trustworthy hope, by virtue of which we can face our present: the present, even if it is arduous, can be lived and accepted if it leads towards a goal, if we can be sure of this goal, and if this goal is great enough to justify the effort of the journey.[13]

Recently I was travelling around the Catholic parish of Khompong Thom in Cambodia in company with the parish priest, Thai Jesuit Fr Jub Phoktavi, and Director of UCAN News, Australian Jesuit Fr Michael Kelly. As we drove through the village of Prek Sbeuv, Jub matter-of-factly pointed to Pol Pot's old house. It is an unremarkable house, and if tourists happened to be this far off the beaten track they would have little idea that this was the residence of one of the world's greatest war criminals. I thought back to 1987 when I met a Khmer leader in the Site Two refugee camp on the Thai Cambodian border. I asked him if he could ever imagine a return to government in Cambodia. He looked very sad as he told me how the Khmer Rouge had killed most of his immediate family. He could not trust the Khmer Rouge again. I had the sense that he would find it hard to trust any of his fellow Cambodians ever again in rebuilding his nation from such ruins. Reconciliation was a fashionable textbook concept. Twenty five years later, there is a certain routine to life

---

12. Halik, *Night of the Confessor*, 214.
13. Pope Benedict XVI, *Spe Salvi*, 2007, #1.

in Cambodia, though poverty in the villages is widespread and government corruption legendary. The previous evening I had been asked to address a multi-faith group of NGO and Church workers on faith, justice and public policy.

What could I, a Catholic priest from Australia, say about such matters in a largely Buddhist country devastated by genocide? Whether Christian, Buddhist, or Muslim, faith is about my having, owning and reflecting on a belief system which allows me to live fully with the paradoxes and conflicts of life and death, good and evil, beauty and suffering. It is only fundamentalists who are able to live as if these paradoxes are not real, as if they do not impinge on our sense of self and on our considered actions every day.

By embracing these paradoxes and confronting these conflicts, the person of faith whether inspired by Jesus, Mohammed, or Buddha is able to live an engaged life of faith. I am able to commit myself to others, in love and in justice. I am able to be open to reconciling, or at least being reconciled to, the previously irreconcilable. I am able to accord dignity to all others in the human family, no matter what their distinguishing marks, and regardless of their competencies, achievements or potentialities. I am able to surrender myself to that which is beyond what I know through my senses. I am able to commit myself to the stewardship of all creation.

Some Guideposts for Re-imagining the Mission

We need to foster our contemporary sense of the transcendent and openness to the other, the world and culture that are not all bad. We need to be attentive to the arts and culture, open to ecumenical and interfaith dialogue and mutual learning.

We need to be credible in agitating for justice and dignity for all, espousing not just equality and non-discrimination, but also the common good and the public interest, with a particular eye to the voiceless and those whose claims on us do not enjoy fad status.

We need to celebrate liturgy which animates us for life and mission—being faithful to the routine of life including weekly

Eucharist and daily prayer, being sufficiently educated in our faith and familiar with liturgy to celebrate the big events and sacramental moments of life, attentive to our local cultural reality and part of a universal Church which both incorporates and transcends all cultures. The clunky new translation provides us all with a real challenge, particularly when celebrating marriages and funerals when very few in the congregation know the responses.

Given the shortage of priests and religious in the contemporary Australian church as compared with the situation fifty years ago, we need to provide more resources and opportunities to the laity wanting to perform the mission in Christ's name—lay organisations, public juridic persons, volunteering, better structured opportunities for part time commitment to the apostolate, and provision by religious orders for young people wanting to make a commitment for a few years before marriage and life and work in civic service. The greatest challenge is providing a place in the Church for young women wanting to contribute to the mission. When I stood at that portrait of Our Lady of Perpetual Succour fifty years ago, there were almost 15,000 women religious in the Australian Church. Today there are less than 6,000 and their median age is seventy-four. Only six per cent of them are under fifty. When I joined the Jesuits in 1975, almost half the women religious were aged under fifty.

I caused alarm with some of my fellow Jesuits in 2011 when I gave an interview to a newspaper, *The Good Weekend*, saying:

> I wouldn't be a priest if I was twenty-one today. I am one of the last generations of Irish Catholics whose families made it professionally and were comfortable with the Church. I love being a Jesuit but I can't honestly say I would join now. My religious faith has remained rock solid, but there are times when I feel really cheesed off with the institutional Church, which sometimes treats its lay members and non-members in a too-patronising fashion.[14]

---

14. *The Sydney Morning Herald, The Good Weekend*, 28 May 2011

From here on, it is essential that you the laity affirm and live out the reality that you are the hands, feet, heart, and mind of Christ in the contemporary world and in the contemporary Church. And you need to encourage your children to consider the call to priesthood and, given the later age of marrying and the longer life expectancy, to consider dedicating a couple of years to full time church service before marriage and again after retirement from full time paid employment.

We need to reform our Church structures to be more aligned with contemporary notions of justice and due process. Recently I came across a blog reporting on the dismissal this week of Bishop Francesco Micciché from Sicily who is said to have misappropriated diocesan funds. He claims not to have had access to the report of the Vatican visitation which inquired into his financial transactions. The blog reported that another bishop had been 'toowoombed'. In the case of Bishop Morris from Toowoomba, we know there was absolutely no suggestion of financial or other impropriety. In 2011 the Australian bishops told us:

> We appreciate that Bishop Morris' human qualities were never in question; nor is there any doubt about the contribution he has made to the life of the Church in Toowoomba and beyond. The Pope's decision was not a denial of the personal and pastoral gifts that Bishop Morris has brought to the episcopal ministry ... We are hopeful that Bishop Morris will continue to serve the Church in other ways in the years ahead.[15]

When Bishop Morris went to Rome to meet in person with the Cardinal Leaders of the three relevant Congregations (Cardinals Re, Arinze and Levada), with Archbishop Philip Wilson present in support on 19 January 2008, Cardinal Re wrote:

---

15. Letter by Archbishop Philip Wilson, President, Australian Catholic Bishops Conference to Bishop Brian Finnigan, Administrator, Diocese of Toowoomba, in Morris, *Benedict, Me and the Cardinals Three*, 418–9.

> Bishop Morris is a person of integrity in morals, a man of good will and other gifts. He can continue to do much good, but the right role for him is not that of Diocesan Bishop of Toowoomba.
>
> He should be given another assignment, with special duties. With this in mind, the Holy Father asks the Metropolitan Archbishop of Brisbane and the President of the ACBC to help find the most appropriate responsibility in which Bishop Morris can continue to effectively serve the Church elsewhere in Australia, while obviously being assured of financial security for a suitable living.[16]

Now that a new archbishop has been appointed in Brisbane and a new bishop appointed in Toowoomba, let us hope that Bishop Morris might be given an appropriate episcopal task to which to dedicate his splendid pastoral gifts.

The process for dealing with Bishop Morris has been a disgrace. The people of Toowoomba still do not know why he was sacked, and we are all still waiting for a public credible explanation of the reasons for his dismissal. Are we really to believe that it was for having the temerity to point out that people overseas are talking about women's ordination? Fr Jack Mahoney SJ, a former principal of Heythrop College and author of the highly acclaimed *The Making of Moral Theology: A Study of the Roman Catholic Theology*, recently published a new book *Christianity in Evolution* in which he says things like: 'Dispensing with the idea that Christian priesthood involves ordaining a man to act "in the person of Christ" by offering his atoning sacrifice to God removes whatever ground there was for restricting ordination to the priesthood to men and for excluding women.'[17] One of the most respected pastoral theologians in the English Church is Professor Nicholas Lash from Cambridge. He writes in a recent issue of *The Tablet*:

---

16. Cardinal Re's notes of meeting in Morris, *Benedict, Me and the Cardinals Three*, 351.

17. Jack Mahoney, *Christianity in Evolution: An Exploration* (Washington DC: Georgetown University Press, 2011), 147.

> When, for example, Pope John Paul II announced that
> the Church had no authority to ordain women to the
> presbyterate, and that the matter was not to be further
> discussed, two questions immediately came to mind:
> first, how does he know? (that is to say: what were the
> warrants, historical and doctrinal, for his assertion?);
> secondly, what theological note should be attached to
> his assertion? In view of the fact that, so far as I know,
> the question has never, in the Church's history, come
> up for serious and close consideration, that note cannot
> be very high up the scale. From which it follows that
> his further instruction that we must not discuss it lacks
> good grounds.[18]

All Bishop Morris said in his pastoral letter of 2006 was that people overseas were talking about this sort of thing. They were, they are, and they will be. So why the need to sack not the theological agitators but the occasional pastoral bishop who merely points out that these things are being discussed? These issues are being discussed by people who love the Church and care passionately for its future.

You will recall that the Vatican appointed the American Archbishop Charles Chaput to conduct the formal visitation of the Toowoomba Diocese. Bishop Morris remains adamant that Chaput never shared with him the proposed contents of his report. Archbishop Chaput is adamant that he did. Five months after Chaput submitted his report, Morris was presented with an unsigned list of grievances from the Vatican. Seeking a way forward in charity and in truth, on 4 April 2012, I told *ABC Radio National*:

> So from here in order to clear the air one thing
> that would be possible is Archbishop Chaput could
> provide Bishop Morris with the detail of what he says
> he discussed with Bishop Morris in Toowoomba and
> specifically, he would be able to provide a list of the
> matters of concern and we would be able to see whether
> they tallied with the matters that were then listed in the

18. Nicholas Lash, Letter to the editor, *The Tablet*, 28 April 2012: 17

unsigned, anonymous document of September of 2007. The specific list of allegations included amongst other things a demonstrably false statement namely that no priests had been ordained in the last eight years. Well four had been ordained. It also contained the false statement that deacons were being used to replace priests. There were no deacons in the diocese. Now there is no way that Chaput could have provided that information. So, after the Vatican had Chaput's report, they were still proceeding with a list of allegations against Morris which were inaccurate and therefore could not have been drawn from Chaput's report.[19]

Bishop Morris did write at considerable length to Archbishop Chaput, and in a highly respectful and fraternal tone. On 16 April 2012, Archbishop Chaput responded. To be fair to Chaput, I will quote his breath taking response in full:

> Bishop Morris, your imagination is in 'over-drive'. I did share everything with you. I did not keep any notes after sending the report to Rome. How would I—or anyone—ever respond to your questions from memory? You are involved in an exercise of self-justification that is obscuring the truth and good reason. I will pray for you.[20]

This is what still passes for due process and pastoral care in the Roman Church. As Christ's faithful we have to insist on something better. And with greater transparency, we will get something better. Of course, we must continue to show due deference and respect to our bishops, our shepherds. But when they abuse even their own like this, we should ask for better, in Christ's name.

As Catholics, we accept that the pope ultimately has full authority to appoint, transfer or dismiss bishops. Therefore any

---

19. ABC Religion and Ethics Report, Transcript, 4 April 2012 at <http://www.abc.net.au/radionational/programs/religionandethicsreport/the-sacking-of-bishop-morris3a-the-plot-thickens/3932946#transcript>. Accessed 2 December 2014.

20 Morris, *Benedict, Me and the Cardinals Three*, 242.

person recommending an appointment, transfer or dismissal to the pope is obliged to act in a manner such that the ultimate action of the pope could not be or be seen to be capricious, arbitrary, or prejudiced. Any person recommending a dismissal must accord due process and natural justice; otherwise the denial of same will infect the pope's action. Why could Archbishop Chaput not simply have reviewed his report, repeating to Morris the key points, especially given that he claims to have already shared everything? Why would he not do what he could to refresh Bishop Morris's memory, bringing satisfaction to all those concerned that Morris has been denied natural justice?

Pope Benedict commenced his encyclical *Caritas in Veritate* with the words:

> Charity in truth, to which Jesus Christ bore witness by his earthly life and especially by his death and resurrection, is the principal driving force behind the authentic development of every person and of all humanity.[21]

Charity in truth should also be the principal driving force behind all dealings with each other within our Church. If only we were more committed to charity and truth, we the members of Christ's faithful would be able to be more trusting of Vatican moves in relation to Bishop Morris, in relation to the women religious in the USA, in relation to the Girl Scouts in the USA, and in relation to theological training in the Church in Ireland. If only we were more committed to charity and truth, we would have been so much better in confronting the horror of child sexual abuse within our Church. Fr Kevin Dillon a priest from Geelong, near Melbourne, recently asked, 'If Christ was lying in this Church bleeding, would we say, "Can we afford to heal him?" Well, Christ is in this church, bleeding. Not from wounds inflicted from Roman soldiers but from wounds inflicted from within. Victims first; true justice; genuine compassion.'

---

21   Pope Benedict XVI, *Caritas in Veritate,* 2009, #1.

Conclusion

If we as the People of God rejoicing in the name 'Catholic' are to bring the modern world into contact with the vivifying and perennial energies of the gospel, we need to ensure that our Church is an exemplar of the noblest values espoused by people of all faiths and none. We need to recommit ourselves to charity, justice and truth both within our own structures when dealing with each other, and in all our dealings with those outside the membership of our Church, especially those who differ with us conscientiously about the moral challenges of the present age.

We need to examine afresh our belief in 'a love or compassion which is unconditional—that is, not based on what you the recipient have made of yourself—but as one based on what you are most profoundly, a being in the image of God'. The Canadian Catholic philosopher Charles Taylor sums up the challenge as 'a difficult discernment, trying to see what in modern culture reflects its furthering of the Gospel, and what (in modern culture reflects) its refusal of the transcendent'.[22] Thus exercised, we might bring even the young into engagement 'with the vivifying and perennial energies of the gospel'. Re-imagining our mission among the young in our care, let's take to heart Pope Benedict's observations in *Spe Salvi*:

> We need the greater and lesser hopes that keep us going day by day. But these are not enough without the great hope, which must surpass everything else. This great hope can only be God, who encompasses the whole of reality and who can bestow upon us what we, by ourselves, cannot attain. The fact that it comes to us as a gift is actually part of hope. God is the foundation of hope: not any god, but the God who has a human face and who has loved us to the end, each one of us and humanity in its entirety. His Kingdom is not an imaginary hereafter, situated in a future that will never

---

22   Charles Taylor, A Catholic Modernity?, in *Dilemmas and Connections* (Cambridge USA: Belknap Press, 2011), 185.

arrive; his Kingdom is present wherever he is loved and wherever his love reaches us. His love alone gives us the possibility of soberly persevering day by day, without ceasing to be spurred on by hope, in a world which by its very nature is imperfect. His love is at the same time our guarantee of the existence of what we only vaguely sense and which nevertheless, in our deepest self, we await: a life that is 'truly' life.[23]

If we offer our students anything less, a Church they perceive to be marked by hollow rhetoric, empty sacramentality, and authoritarian tradition will rightly disappoint them. As teachers and pastors to the young, I invite you to be bold and confident in proclaiming the love in your hearts, the hope in each other, and the faith in our Church. Thanks for your witness and commitment thus far. I hope and pray that you will be energised during these days together so that you might 'go into all the world and proclaim the good news to the whole of creation'.[24]

---

23 Pope Benedict XVI, *Spe Salvi*, 2007, #31.
24 Mark 16:15

4

Making Room for Aborigines in the Church

In 1982, the year that Queensland hosted both the Commonwealth Games and the International Expo, I was appointed adviser to the Queensland Catholic Bishops on Aboriginal Affairs. The international media spotlight was on Queensland's treatment of the first Australians. In 1985 when Prime Minister Bob Hawke announced proposals for national land rights, I took up an appointment as adviser to the Australian Catholic Bishops Conference. In 1986, Pope John Paul II met with Aborigines and Torres Strait Islanders in Alice Springs. I then worked with a group of Aboriginal and Torres Strait Islander Catholics who proposed the National Aboriginal and Torres Strait Islander Catholic Council (NATSICC). In 2006, I looked back on what a catalyst John Paul's visit had been.[1]

The National Aboriginal and Torres Strait Islander Catholic Council (NATSICC) invited people to gather in Alice Springs between 2 and 7 October 2006 to celebrate the anniversary of the meeting between Pope John Paul II and the Aboriginal and Torres Strait Islander people twenty years ago. The theme of the 2006 triennial NATSIC Conference was 'Dreaming from the Heart'. A mass was held in Blatherskite Park, the same place at which the pope met with Australia's indigenous peoples in 1986. Since 1 May 2005 when NATSICC Councillors left St Mary's Cathedral in Sydney with Message Sticks, in company with a NATSICC youth councillor, parishes, schools and deaneries throughout Australia have been

---

1   A version of this chapter was first published as 'Dreaming from the Heart of Australia Twenty Years On' in *The Australasian Catholic Record* 83/3 (2006): 274

receiving the NATSICC Message Sticks, reflecting on the place of Aborigines and Torres Strait Islanders in the life of the Australian Church and in Australian society.

In 1986, the national Aboriginal committee preparing the papal visit to Alice Springs had composed a special prayer for the event:

Father of all, you gather us the Dreaming.
You have spoken to us through our beliefs.
You then made your love clear to us in the person of Jesus.
We thank you for your care.
You own us, you are our hope.
Make us strong as we face the problems of change.
We ask you to help all the people of Australia
to listen to us and respect our culture.
Make the knowledge of you grow strong in all people,
so that you can be at home in us,
and we can make a home for everyone in our land. Amen

The day before the pope's arrival in Alice Springs on 29 November 1986, the local Alice Springs community was excited and proud to be hosting the pope at his most Australian of meetings. The Murdoch stable of Northern Territory newspapers was laying the groundwork for a great celebration. The *Centralian Advocate* proclaimed, 'Welcome!', and noted that the pope's visit to the Centre 'is expected to hit world headlines'. The local journalists took pride in the fact that foreign journalists expected 'the Alice Springs celebration to be the highlight of the pope's Australian tour'.[2] The *Centralian Advocate's* editorial noted, 'The pope is a man of peace, so let us show him (and the world through the eyes of the media) that we also are people of peace. It is not a day for demonstrations for land rights or against Pine Gap'.[3] On the day of the pope's arrival in the Territory, the Darwin based *Northern Territory News* carried an editorial which was reflective and respectful of the Church's

---

2   *Centralian Advocate*, 28 November 1986.
3   *Centralian Advocate*, 28 November 1986.

contribution to life in the Territory. It reviewed the contribution of the early missionaries and then turned attention to the contemporary situation':

> Then the new missionaries took over. God was replaced by the State, the Bible by the Land Rights Act, brotherhood by separation and division, free will by dependence.
>
> This pope's time in Darwin and Alice Springs will be regrettably brief. But the message he brings is timeless, a message that is not confined just to adherents. He brings warmth, a human cry for the simplicity of a touch or the warmth of a smile in this complicated and politicised country.[4]

The meeting at Blatherskite Park was remarkable. I was invited to accompany a busload of people from Kununurra and Turkey Creek in the Western Australian Kimberley because they did not have their own priest with them. The community leaders gave me a screen-printed red T-shirt which depicted their Dreaming. We all wore yellow head bands, and waited patiently for the pope's arrival. He had been delayed by the breakdown of his Mercedes Popemobile which was unsuited to the hot conditions. Workers resorted to throwing iced water over the engine but failed in their attempts to get the vehicle running. Eventually the pope arrived on the park's caterpillar dreaming track in the back seat of a plain white Australian Ford sedan which was more becoming than the foreign vehicle. There had been months of planning and negotiation about this meeting on the Yipirinya dreaming track. People came from all over Australia.

There had been some consternation early in the planning because a major mining company had donated the offices for the papal visit. But Aboriginal leaders were assured that the pope's message would not be qualified because of the generosity of the corporate sector. A week

---

4   *Northern Territory News*, 29 November 1986, Editorial.

prior to the visit, there was unresolved conflict between the church's national advisory committee of Aborigines and Islanders preparing the visit and the local Aboriginal community. The committee wanted only Aboriginal and Islander children to have access to the ceremony area where the Pope would be welcomed. But they heeded the call of the local Elders with the result that Alice Springs children of all races who shared in the local Dreaming were permitted to participate. The Alice Springs Mayor said, 'It's wonderful. The Aboriginal people are doing the right thing. It's not the locals that have caused any problems. It's people from the south who wanted to segregate the races.'[5] The tension between the local church community and national Aboriginal church leaders evaporated by the time the pope kissed the tarmac at Alice Springs airport. He was welcomed by eight traditional owners who greeted him in the Arrernte language. Among the group were the late Wenten Rubuntja and Charles Perkins.

Protocol dictated that the pope could not be attired in the Aboriginal colours. But Vatican rubrics gave way to local custom when the pope was presented on the dreaming track with a crocheted stole and beanie in black, red and yellow. Being the consummate performer on the international stage, John Paul graciously received the gift and wore the accoutrements for some distance along the path of the dreaming track. Then Louise Pandella from the Nauiyu Community at Daly River made her way to the barrier and handed her baby Liam to the pope. The pope held Liam up to the cameras which captured one of the iconic shots of John Paul II. When I rose at 4 am in Minneapolis nineteen years later to watch the papal funeral, the major US television networks used the photo several times during the course of the broadcast.

Along the dreaming track, the pope met the nation's most respected Aboriginal leaders who presented him with a shield inscribed with an aspirational message. The Director of the Alice Springs based Central Land Council, Patrick Dodson, who had left the priesthood, respectfully stood in the background to spare His Holiness any embarrassment. The pope received numerous other

---

5   *Sunday Territorian*, 23 November 1986

gifts including a copy of the 'Our Father' in the local language of the Stradbroke Island people who had been the first indigenous Australians to receive Catholic missionaries. While the pope was still on the dreaming track, I was approached by a throng of international media who asked my opinion of the pope's speech. Not having heard it, I was in no position to answer. The journalists had read copies on the papal jet once they had taken off from Darwin and they regarded the pope's comments on land rights as very hot news. For many of the international journalists, this was to be the big story of the pope's Australian visit. Fr Dennis Madigan was accompanying the press entourage and he had informed the media that I was the adviser to the Australian Catholic Bishops, as I was. A Vatican official on the plane had told them that I had written the speech, but I had not. After my pleading ignorance of the speech's content, the media throng gave me a copy and I was able to confirm that I had not written the speech. As an adviser to the bishops' conference, I was pleased to have provided some input. And yes, I was very agreeably surprised by the strength and simplicity of the pope's remarks about the entitlement of Aborigines and Torres Strait Islanders to their lands and about their place in the life of the Church.

At the end of the dreaming track, the pope then made his way up to the stadium while threatening storm clouds were gathering on the horizon. Behind the pope was a mural by Wenten Rubuntja depicting the caterpillar dreaming and the mountain gaps around Alice Springs. As the pope completed the lengthy speech, he took a large gum branch, reached into a clay coolamon which later would be used in the Alice Springs church for baptisms, and blessed the people with water. It was at that moment that the lightning sounded and the heavens opened. All of us in the crowd were convinced that grace and nature were one and indivisible at that moment in the red centre of the great south land of the Holy Spirit. The *Centralian Advocate* reported that 'as an electrical storm was threatening the gathering of about 4,000 people, most of the thunder was coming from the podium'.[6]

---

6   *Centralian Advocate*, 3 December 1986.

The pope later confided to Bishop Ted Collins, 'I think the people prefer meeting me rather than listening to me. But I had to say it all because otherwise it could not be published'. The mainstream media picked up the pope's remarks about land rights, self-determination and reconciliation. But he put even more demanding challenges to the Australian church when he enunciated the place of indigenous Australians in the life of the church and when he outlined the relationship between Christian faith and Aboriginal culture and religious tradition.

The pride, excitement and reflectiveness of the local Murdoch media evaporated overnight with the *Sunday Territorian* brandishing the headline: 'Pope's Shock Land Rights Call'. The editorial carried the headline, 'Pope Falls into Land Rights Trap'. It claimed:

> Pope John Paul II entered Australian politics yesterday with a thump that will reverberate across the nation.
> For many people his demand for immediate national land rights—one of the most sensitive issues confronting Australians—will have destroyed in one day the enormous good will generated by a warm and intelligent Pope, a man of the people who came to unite and has ended creating further division and racial tension.
> Unwittingly and regrettably, His Holiness has fallen into the trap.
> He has compromised the Church which cannot avoid being treated just like any other political institution.
> Australia does not need liberation theology. [7]

Aboriginal leaders praised the speech. Wenten Rubuntja said the pope had 'filled a vacuum at a national political level'. Pat Dodson said, 'The main point about it is that the Pope, an international figure, and spiritual leader, has focused clearly on the fundamental injustices'.[8] The Executive Director of the Northern Territory Chamber of Mines said it was 'unfortunate the pope commented

---

7   *Sunday Territorian*, 30 November 1986, Editorial.
8   *Centralian Advocate*, 3 December 1986.

on such a sensitive and highly emotional issue'.[9] Sir Joh Bjelke-Petersen reassured everyone that the pope was not speaking about Queensland because his State was 'leading Australia on the land rights issue'.[10]

Twenty years on, Aborigines and Torres Strait Islanders still take great heart from the speech. Parishes and schools which have been passing on the Message Sticks have had cause to reflect on developments with land rights, reconciliation and self-determination, the place of Indigenous Australians in the Church, and the relationship between Christian faith, Aboriginal culture and Catholic practice in the light of the pope's speech.

Land Rights

At Alice Springs, Pope John Paul II said:

> Let it not be said that the fair and equitable recognition of Aboriginal rights to land is discrimination. To call for the acknowledgment of the land rights of people who have never surrendered those rights is not discrimination. Certainly, what has been done cannot be undone. But what can now be done to remedy the deeds of yesterday must not be put off till tomorrow. [11]

In 1986, there was a patchwork quilt of land rights legislation in Australia. But there was still no recognition of Aboriginal land rights in Western Australia, and Aborigines had title only to the Aboriginal reserve lands in Queensland. In March 1986, the Hawke government had put national land rights in the 'too hard' basket. There was no way that the Hawke government would acquire compulsorily one square inch of land from Premier Brian Burke in Western Australia.

---

9   *Northern Territory News,* 1 December 1986.
10   *Sydney Morning Herald,* 1 December 1986.
11   Pope John Paul II, Address to Aborigines and Torres Strait Islanders, Alice Springs, 29 November 1986, #10 at <http://www.vatican.va/holy_father/john_paul_ii/ speeches/1986/november/documents/hf_jp-ii_spe_19861129_aborigeni-alice-springs-australia_en.html>. Accessed 2 December 2014.

Western Australian governments of both political persuasions had always been sensitive to the demands of the mining industry which was wary of land rights legislation requiring miners and explorers to expend time and money on negotiations with traditional owners whose identities and land claims were often contested and uncertain. The Burke government had proposed its own modest land rights legislation but it failed to pass, not satisfying either the Aborigines or the mining companies.

In 1985, Eddie Mabo had stepped onto the national stage lodging a claim in the High Court of Australia to his traditional lands in the Torres Strait. The Bjelke-Petersen government attempted to short circuit the litigation by passing a law which would extinguish retrospectively any such rights as of 1879, and with no compensation payable. The government claimed that this law was necessary to avoid limitless research work and endless argument in the courts about mere matters of history.

In 1992, for the first time in the history of the federation, the High Court of Australia had to determine whether the common law of Australia recognised Aboriginal native title. Six of the seven High Court judges held that the assertion of sovereignty by the British crown did not necessarily extinguish all native title rights to land, and that native tile rights could still exist on those lands which had not been alienated by the crown to another person and which had not been dedicated by the crown to some public purpose. In the past, these native title rights could be, and were, readily extinguished by action of the crown. But after 1975, state governments would need to show that they were not acting contrary to the Commonwealth's *Racial Discrimination Act*. So, if Aborigines had maintained their connection with the land from European settlement until 1975, the law would now protect their surviving rights in the same way that the rights of an ordinary freeholder were protected.

This decision then required a legislative response from the Commonwealth Parliament. Prime Minister Paul Keating steered the *Native Title Act* through Parliament. The Parliament also legislated for an Indigenous Land Fund which received payments from Consolidated

Revenue for a decade and which is now a self-perpetuating fund for the purchase of lands on the open market. The intention was that those indigenous Australians fortunate to retain their connection with their traditional lands would now have their title protected, and those who were the descendants of the dispossessed would be able to access the fund for lands given in partial compensation for past losses.

Soon after the Howard government's election in 1996 with a commitment to wind back the *Native Title Act,* the High Court, by a narrow majority of 4–3, ruled in the *Wik* Case that native title could co-exist on some pastoral leases. The Howard government legislated an extensive amendment to the *Native Title Act* in 1998. Senator Brian Harradine held the balance of power in the Senate and he set out to avoid the prospect of a race based, double dissolution election, while at the same time insisting that the Howard legislation comply with minimum standards of fairness and non-discrimination. John Howard has described *Mabo* as a decision 'based on a good deal of logic and fairness and proper principle'.[12]

Reconciliation and Self Determination

Having attested the moral claim of Aborigines and Torres Strait Islanders to their land rights, John Paul II went on to say:

> The establishment of a new society for Aboriginal people cannot go forward without just and mutually recognized agreements with regard to these human problems, even though their causes lie in the past. The greatest value to be achieved by such agreements, which must be implemented without causing new injustices, is respect for the dignity and growth of the human person. And you, the Aboriginal people of this country and its cities, must show that you are actively working for your own dignity of life.[13]

---

12 (1996) CPD (HofR) 345; 6 May 1996. Again on 26 June 1996, John Howard told Parliament: 'I have always regarded the *Mabo* decision itself as being a justified, correct decision. I have stated that on a number of occasions.' (1996) CPD (HofR) 2791.

13 Pope John Paul II, Address to Aborigines and Torres Strait Islanders, #11.

In 1988, Australia celebrated the bicentenary of the establishment of the colony of New South Wales, the great caesura of history in this land. 25 January 1988 marked the bicentenary of the last day on which Aborigines enjoyed uninterrupted occupancy of the Australian continent for tens of thousands of years. The next day marked the bicentenary of European settlement founded upon the progressive dispossession of the indigenous inhabitants. During 1988, there were strong calls for a treaty between Aborigines and other Australians. Prime Minister Bob Hawke and his minister Gerry Hand even joined key Aboriginal leaders in signing the Barunga statement which was a commitment to negotiate a treaty. John Howard was at that time Leader of the Opposition and he said that a country could not make a treaty with itself.

In preparation for the bicentenary, the leaders of the major Australian churches issued a series of statements on national reconciliation, the first of which called for reconciliation with Aboriginal Australians, suggesting that our politicians pass a bipartisan resolution to that effect when the new Parliament House was to be opened by the Queen on 9 May 1988. There were political problems, with the result that the Hawke government proposed the substance of the churches' resolution as the first item of business in the new Parliament House on 23 August 1988, but without support from the Opposition parties. Renewed efforts at a bipartisan approach resulted in the parliament's unanimous support for the institution of a Council for Aboriginal Reconciliation which had a ten year mandate to assist reconciliation at local and national levels, investigating the need for agreements between indigenous communities and government, and between indigenous groups and other Australians. The highpoint of the Council's work was the 1997 Reconciliation Convention chaired by Patrick Dodson. The Governor General and his wife, Sir William and Lady Deane were hailed as the nation's first couple of reconciliation. The Convention received the heart rending *Bringing Them Home* Report written by Sir Ronald Wilson and Michael Dodson. Following a recommendation of the Report, National Sorry Day was instituted on 26 May 1998 to recall the memory of those who suffered the effects of forcible separation. In 2000, one million Australians joined in bridge marches to mark their commitment to reconciliation.

In 1989, the Hawke government had instituted ATSIC, a bold initiative aimed at giving Aboriginal Australians a well-resourced national voice and a self-determining organisation for making key decisions about the allocation of resources for Aboriginal communities. This Aboriginal and Torres Strait Islander Commission was run by a board of commissioners most of whom were elected from regional councils which in turn were elected by Aboriginal and Islander voters. In 2004, ATSIC was abolished and the Howard government decided to appoint the National Indigenous Council which provides advice to government on indigenous policy issues.

The Place of Indigenous Australians in the Church

Even those who doubted the competence or wisdom of a Polish pope's speaking about land rights and self-determination for indigenous Australians had to concede his unique role in enunciating the model of Roman Church required in Australia. At Alice Springs, John Paul II said:

> The Church herself in Australia will not be fully the Church that Jesus wants her to be until you have made your contribution to her life and until that contribution has been joyfully received by others.[14]

In the years prior to the pope's visit, the Australian Bishops' Committee for Aborigines would meet twice a year at the regular bishops' conferences held at Kensington, Sydney. As their adviser, I would meet with them—a group of white clergy meeting to discuss the church's mission to Aborigines. The preparation for the pope's visit became a highly collaborative enterprise with Aboriginal leaders taking the lead in the church as well as in their own communities. Kaye Mundine who escorted the pope up the dreaming path assured

---

14   Pope John Paul II, Address to Aborigines and Torres Strait Islanders, #13.

the bishops gathered in Alice Springs that the pope fully supported an initiative for greater Aboriginal involvement in the structures of the Church.

In January 1989 the first National Conference of the Aboriginal and Islander Catholic Councils took place in Cairns. An indigenous working party funded by the Church with representation from every State was set up. In 1992, NATSICC was established. Since then, the Bishops' Committee for Aborigines always meets in company with executive members from NATSICC which is an advisory body to the Australian Catholic Bishops Conference. Through NATSICC, Aborigines and Torres Strait Islanders have been assured greater involvement and greater representation in national church events and activities. NATSICC prepares the liturgy for the annual Aboriginal and Torres Strait Islander Sunday. NATSICC ensures regular indigenous participation in World Youth Day. Indigenous church leaders like Elsie Heiss (NATSICC Councillor, NSW Representative) not only lead their local worshipping community with the assistance of visiting priests. They also organise the Church's local indigenous initiatives and co-ordinate national Church responses to indigenous issues. There are now local and State Aboriginal Catholic bodies such as Sydney's Aboriginal Catholic Ministry all over Australia. When people gathered in Alice Springs to mark the twentieth anniversary, they were welcomed by the local Alice Springs Church community, Ngkarte Mikwekenhe, which traces its origins and inspiration to the pope's visit.

The pope's statement about Aboriginal involvement in the life of the church was more radical than anything he said about land rights. The Australian church mindset had long been one of wonderment about how much more 'we', the non-Aborigines, would need to give 'them', the Aborigines. Now the question became how much the rest of us would receive, and receive joyfully, from Aboriginal and Islander Catholics. This question has stood as a haunting refrain for those many parishes which do not have many, if any, Aborigines in their pews, and for those Catholic schools which have fewer Aborigines per capita than the State schools in their areas.

With the reducing number of priests and religious, dioceses have reduced their commitment to the provision of full time chaplains to Aboriginal communities. There has not been a new generation of priests to emerge like Michael Hayes, Ted Kennedy, Pat Mullins, Michael Peters and Bryan Tiernan who ministered tirelessly with charismatic leadership amongst Aborigines in the towns and cities. Neither is there a new generation of those like John Leary, Anthony Peile, Ray Heaven and Michael McKelson who ministered for years on end in remote Aboriginal communities. The OLSH sisters and the St John of God sisters no longer have the young novices able to commit themselves to lives of service in the Kimberley or in the Northern Territory. It will be a long time before there is another generation of sisters such as Anne Gardiner, Tess Ward, Stella Bryant and Pat Rhatigan.

There are now three married Aboriginal deacons in the Darwin diocese. But the celibacy requirement for Catholic priests militates against young Aboriginal men following in the pioneering path of Patrick Dodson to ordination and priestly service in Aboriginal communities. Aboriginal Anglican bishop Arthur Malcolm once wisely observed: in the Anglican communion, those Aborigines suitable for ordination usually take some years to settle, by which time they have married and started raising their children. Unlike the Anglican and Uniting Churches, and unlike the many Pentecostal sects which have appeal in Aboriginal communities, the Catholic Church now has neither indigenous priests nor enough other priests available for full time service in remote Aboriginal communities.

The Relationship between Christian faith, Aboriginal Culture and Catholic Practice

At Alice Springs, Pope John Paul II addressed the major theological challenge of contemporary evangelisation across the cultural divide:

> That Gospel now invites you to become, through and through, Aboriginal Christians. It meets your deepest desires. You do not have to be people divided into two

parts, as though an Aboriginal had to borrow the faith and life of Christianity, like a hat or a pair of shoes, from someone else who owns them. Jesus calls you to accept his words and his values into your own culture. To develop in this way will make you more than ever truly Aboriginal.[15]

The hunger in the contemporary Australian Church for spirituality which is grounded in the land and which is attentive to the fullness of human history in this part of the world has often been sated by those Aboriginal Christians who have shared their art, their prayer life, and their lives with other Australians. In the last twenty years, many Aboriginal and Islander Catholics have visited parishes to 'tell their story' of faith. One of the highlights of the 1991 World Council of Churches Assembly in Canberra was the exhibition of Aboriginal Art and Spiritualty convened in the High Court of Australia by Sister Rosemary Crumlin and Anthony Knight. The centrepiece of the exhibition was George Mung Mung's *Madonna and Child* that is now a national icon. George died the week before the opening of the exhibition by the Governor General, and his son Patrick came from Turkey Creek with Hector Sandaloo who both then featured in the documentary *The Serpent and the Cross*. When Hector was leaving Canberra, Sister Rosemary accompanied him to the airport. Rosemary said, 'As Hector walked so graciously, slowly and with such poise to the plane, I was left in no doubt who are the custodians of this country'. At Warmun community in Turkey Creek, Wirrumanu community at Balgo Hills, and at Nauiyu Community on the Daly River, Aboriginal artists have produced the finest art informed by their Aboriginal Dreaming and by their Catholic heritage. In recent years, the Melbourne Aboriginal Catholic Ministry produced the 'Invisible No More' exhibition and the Queensland groups produced 'Jesus through Black Eyes'. Richard Campbell's *Black Madona* and Stations of the Cross adorn the Reconciliation Church in La Perouse.

Smoking ceremonies are now regular introductions to significant liturgies throughout the country even if no Aboriginal person

---

15   Pope John Paul II, Address to Aborigines and Torres Strait Islanders, #12

is present. Matthew Gill from Wirrumanu and Miriam Rose Ungunmerr from Daly River have produced Stations of the Cross which have inspired generations of Australian Catholics. Miriam has augmented her art with writings on *Dadirri*, the spirit of stillness and silence bespeaking God's presence in the land and waterholes. Elsie Heiss attested the nationwide involvement of Aboriginal and Islander communities in such initiatives when she informed the Oceania Synod in Rome:

> The Aboriginal and Torres Strait Islander People celebrate the Sacraments of the Church in a way that is culturally appropriate, but we do not change the mass, despite the fact that some people still believe that we do magic and sorcery. The sacraments such as baptism, Communion, Confirmation, Marriage and Burial are all celebrated with a celebrant of the Church. We do, however, add our special smoking purification ceremony, and carefully selected artifacts and symbols to strengthen our culture and identity. In Sydney in 1995 at the Beatification of Mary MacKillop, the Holy Father himself was part of a purification smoking ceremony.[16]

Since 1994, the Catholic Church has been in full partnership with the Anglican and Uniting Churches in the provision of ministry training programs at Nungalinya College in Darwin and through Wontulp-Bi-Buya in Queensland. Aboriginal people are able to leave their communities for theological and ministry training programs, with follow up in the home worshipping communities. Aboriginal Elder Betty Pike from Melbourne offered this reflection on the pope's speech in 2005 when speaking to the National Aboriginal and Torres Strait Islander Ecumenical Commission:

> This speech was like a blue print for an initiation into a New Dreaming for the future, for all Australians to create together, using some aspects of our Aboriginal

---

16   Elsie Heiss, 'Synod for Oceania: intervention by Mrs Elsie Heiss, Aboriginal Catholic Ministry, Archdiocese of Sydney', in *Nelen Yubu* 71 (1999): 3–4

culture as the cornerstone. Somehow, the cornerstone has been misplaced. It needs to be rediscovered and given its rightful priority, otherwise we are a nation not built on rock but on sand. It is time now to let go of our fears and begin with the cornerstone of Hope and the underlying wisdom of our ancestors who as stewards and guardians of the land kept it sustainable for thousands of generations. It is time for a re-examination of the western beliefs of the mechanistic reductionism that has dominated not only the world but the Churches.[17]

No one would claim that the pope's speech at Alice Springs was a determinative catalyst accelerating the positive developments and putting a brake on the negative reversals in Australian church and society these last twenty years. But this speech still embodies the noblest shared aspirations of Aboriginal Catholics and those wanting to see Aborigines take their place in the Australian Church. The speech undoubtedly painted too rosy a picture of the role of the missionaries, glossing over the failings including assimilationist mindsets and the evil of sexual abuse. Only recently has the church come to appreciate its past failings in adopting assimilationist methods such as removing children from their families and placing them in dormitories, and in using English exclusively rather than local languages. The speech gives too optimistic a reading of the prospects of Aboriginal Australians taking their rightful place in the church without the likelihood of Aboriginal priests or bishops in the foreseeable future. The speech too simplistically glosses over some of the disconnection between Christianity and some of the core beliefs and practices of traditional Aboriginal religions.

It has been very helpful to have the pope offer the encouragement that there need not be any conflict between Christian faith and Aboriginal culture. But Aboriginal culture is often founded on religious beliefs that find and express God's self-communication

---

17 Elizabeth Pike, 'Hope Built on the Dreaming', National Council of Churches of Australia, 2005 at <http://www.ncca.org.au/files/Natsiec/Pike_Hope_built_on_the_dreaming.pdf>. Accessed 2 December 2014.

outside of Christ and the Church's seven sacraments. I recall a funeral of a well-respected Aboriginal leader in the Kimberley. After the Church service, the Elders took the body for ceremony that was no place for the priest or other outsiders. No participant presumed that the religious business had been confined to the church and that all that occurred thereafter was purely cultural. The body and its bearers moved seamlessly from one religious world to another, the bearers and the onlookers respecting the sacred space of each world.

The abiding grace of the pope's speech is incarnated in those words in which he reverenced the Aboriginal identification with country and the daily Aboriginal reality of suffering and marginalisation. With papal reverence, he touched the deep Aboriginal sense of belonging, embracing the hope in their suffering. He conceded in the spoken word and by his charismatic presence that the Dreaming is real, sacramental and eternal. He retold the story of Genesis in Aboriginal voice. He relayed the calls of the post-exilic prophets to the contemporary powerbrokers and poor of Australia. He spoke poetically of things he knew not, knowing that those listening had endured the flames:

> If you stay closely united, you are like a tree standing in the middle of a bush-fire sweeping through the timber. The leaves are scorched and the tough bark is scarred and burned; but inside the tree the sap is still flowing, and under the ground the roots are still strong. Like that tree you have endured the flames, and you still have the power to be reborn. The time for this rebirth is now![18]

Everyone present knew that he understood, and more than many who had spent a lifetime in this place. In recent years, the NATSICC Conference has taken up themes like 'Culturally Enriched through the Gospel', 'Holy Spirit in this Land' and 'The Time for Rebirth is Now'. Returning to country with their Message Sticks and taking to heart the pope's message, NATSICC councillors and all Aboriginal

---

18   Pope John Paul II, Address to Aborigines and Torres Strait Islanders, #8.

and Torres Strait Islander Catholics have good reason to recall their Dreaming and the pope's message at Alice Springs, now years further along the caterpillar track of Rubuntja's painting that now hangs in the Alice Springs Church of Our Lady of the Sacred Heart.

-oOo-

In October 2013, Aboriginal leader Miriam Rose Ungunmerr invited me to launch her Foundation at St Mary's Cathedral in Darwin. Miriam, a renowned artist whose design features on my ordination vestment: (shown on the back cover of this book), was the first Aboriginal principal of a school in the Northern Territory. She has been the chairperson of her community's local government council.

I was honoured and humbled as a whitefella from the south to be invited to be Patron of the Foundation dedicated to furthering the work and vision of Miriam Rose Ungunmerr. Celebrating mass before the launch, I recalled that I first came into the Darwin Cathedral in 1981 with Bishop John O'Loughlin MSC. He rounded out the tour of the cathedral by taking me down to the crypt and showing me where he was to be buried. And that's where he lies today. At that time there was no significant Aboriginal art work in the Cathedral. But in pride of place was Czech artist's Karel Kupka's Aboriginal *Madonna and Child*. 'Jolly' O'Loughlin, as the bishop was known, had taught my father at school. He had also taught Brian Sweeney, a Brisbane based man familiar with the arts. One evening, the bishop had visited Sweeney's home in Brisbane and admired the portraits that Sweeney had commissioned of his children. The bishop told Sweeney how good it would be to have a fine portrait of an Aboriginal Madonna in the new cathedral he was planning for Darwin. Returning to the north on the lookout for an artist, O'Loughlin then met the travelling Karel Kupka on the Tiwi Islands. On learning that Kupka was a Catholic, he commissioned him to do the work. Today that iconic painting is complemented by the stained glassed windows replicating the artwork of Aboriginal artists—Larrakia being joined by artists from Nguiu, Palarumpi, Nauiyu, and Santa Teresa. The art that now surrounds a visitor to the Cathedral tells the story of Aboriginal participation and self-determination.

After my tour of the Cathedral in 1981, I then accompanied a carload of Missionaries of the Sacred Heart down to Daly River where the Jesuits had first established a mission ninety-nine years previously. That was the first of many visits over the following decades. Each time I went I admired Miriam's stations of the cross in the Church of St Francis Xavier and I was captivated by the pulpit painting she did. With her permission, I photographed it and my mother then made a splendid tapestry of the pulpit painting that is the centrepiece of my 1985 ordination vestment. I still wear that vestment for special occasions such as the annual NAIDOC mass and family celebrations. Other priests and bishops have worn it for major Aboriginal liturgical celebrations. For three decades I have admired Miriam as an artist, an educator, a community leader, a spiritual contemplative and as a friend.

One of the advantages of flying on the Australian budget airline, Jetstar, through the night from Sydney is that you have little to do but think and pray. As I made this journey to Darwin, contemplating Miriam Rose's vision and all that her community has endured and celebrated in the previous thirty-two years, I was consoled at the thought that her vision in the midst of turbulence, *dadirri* in the midst of noise and turmoil, has always been CLEAR:

C: culture and Church
L: local leadership and expertise
E: education
A: art
R: reconciliation, recognition and respect

A short word about each.

Culture and Church: I recall the baptismal celebration of the feast of the Epiphany in 1987 down at Nauiyu Nambiyu. We spent about a week planning the baptism of twelve kids using traditional symbols including the water ceremony to welcome newcomers to country, the firesticks, the smoking, and the ti-tree bark to heal and make strong. Miriam has always drawn strength from culture and church no matter what the internal tensions.

Local leadership and expertise: There are many Aboriginal foundations the length and breadth of Australia now. What's distinctive about the Miriam Rose Foundation is that it is primarily focussed on the community of Nauiyu Nambiyu, then taking the learnings from there and applying them to other communities. The board draws on the expertise and disciplines of Territory locals who have a long time connection with Miriam, her community and her church. They are committed to being universal and inclusive, while drinking from their local wells that have sustained them in the wet and in the dry.

Education: Miriam was the first Aboriginal principal of a community school in the Northern Territory. She has always been passionate about education as the leg up for her mob. Just look at her grand maternal pride at the achievement of Latisha Marranya who will graduate from the Loreto high school in Adelaide. We watched Latisha's home made video which exudes self-knowledge and self-confidence in the two worlds of which she is a part.

Art: Miriam has always seen art as a medium for telling the story, for keeping the culture strong, for building community, and for giving expression to the deepest Aboriginal aspirations about country, the Dreaming, and finding a place in the swirling changing world of Aboriginal community life intersecting with all those outsiders who come for meetings every day.

Reconciliation, recognition and respect: At the time of the bicentenary in 1988, Miriam did some fantastic paintings emphasising the theme of these three Rs. One, for the National Aboriginal and Torres Strait Islander Catholic Council Conference, was hung in the Cathedral in Cairns after the conference. Another for an international theology conference held in Hobart used hang in the Cathedral here until it was vandalised and stolen. We lost one of the great national treasures of art and spirituality. But Miriam was not bitter. She has continued to reach out in a spirit of reconciliation, gently but firmly asking due recognition, and humbly evincing the respect due to the first Australians who as she says are "caught up in a whirlwind, having to make do with what's left of our culture."

We all know that one of the strong inspirations for Miriam wanting to establish this Foundation was the death of her beloved nephew Liam aged just twenty-two. The world knew Liam's face as a baby but the world knew little of his story thereafter. As a baby he evinced the warmest expressions of love and admiration from strangers across the globe who saw him on their television sets. As a young man, he found no place of belonging in the world. He had no sense that he was being held as he experienced the whirlwind of life in Aboriginal Australia. In November 1986, Pope John Paul II came to Alice Springs, met Aboriginal people from across Australia, walked the dreaming track, donned the Aboriginal colours of black, red and yellow, and then held up baby Liam handed him by Liam's mother, Louise. The photo became an international icon. Coming into adulthood, Liam found himself all alone with nowhere to go, nowhere to belong, and nowhere to be held.

Miriam knows that Liam's journey has been travelled in far too many Aboriginal families. She invites us to get aboard and make a difference with a CLEAR vision: culture and Church, local leadership and expertise, education, art, reconciliation, recognition and respect.

We were privileged at the launch to hear the singing of the Nauiyu children who left home early in the morning to be present at the event. We look forward with hope to their journeys along new songlines etched out with the help of this Foundation and all of you gathered here in good faith this morning. We trust and pray that they will all find themselves lovingly held and belonging in the years to come. The logo speaks to them of the rock of security and the hand that is holding them in the midst of the whirlwind.

5

Dealing with Child Sexual Abuse

In June 2014, after the Royal Commission into Institutional Responses to Child Sexual Abuse conducted a hearing into the Catholic Church's defence in the Ellis v Pell *case, I addressed a large group of lawyers in Sydney on the topic 'Moral Leadership in Difficult Circumstances' asking, 'Do lawyers have too much say?'[1]*

I am one of those Australian Catholics who rejoices in my identity involving what the Archbishop of Canterbury, Rowan Williams, calls 'multiple affiliations'. I am a member of a hierarchical Church with a long tradition and a strong sense of authority. I am also a member of a robust pluralist democracy that prides itself on the rule of law. I am one of those Australian Catholics who came out before the Royal Commission into Institutional Responses to Child Sexual Abuse saying that the Church needed help in order to put its house in order so that children might be as safe as possible in our institutions. The offence rates in our Church seemed to be higher than in equivalent churches, and the fact that we were more involved with vulnerable children did not seem to provide a complete answer.

The announcement of a federal royal commission did not bring me unalloyed joy. I had lived through the Royal Commission into Aboriginal Deaths in Custody. I remember being in the office of a federal minister the week that commission was announced. We agreed that the death rate of Aborigines in custody being ten times the national average was directly related to the imprisonment rate

---

1. A version of this address first appeared in *The Canonist* 5 (2) (2014): 227-235

of Aborigines being ten times the national average. The underlying causes for high indigenous imprisonment rates were not the sort of agenda items that would be solved by a royal commission. Lots of research was undertaken. Lots of public hearings were held. Lots of state police were put through the wringer. Lots of previous deaths and half-baked coronial inquiries were scrutinised. Lots of recommendations were made. Indigenous imprisonment rates are higher today than they were before the royal commission was convened. I am one of those lawyers who knows that royal commissioners may have extensive legal powers of inquiry but they have very limited capacity to influence outcomes.

When dealing with child abuse, we all know that the real points of intersection are with state police forces and state child welfare departments. There has to be real buy-in by them and their political masters if a royal commission is to deliver real results. State agencies still carry memories of the Aboriginal deaths royal commission and know that there is no magic panacea on offer. On 16 June 2014, Commissioner McClellan convened a roundtable of state agencies and stakeholders to discuss Working with Children Checks. Understandably the Commission would like a uniform national approach on this routine mechanism. I understand the Catholic Church was the only one at the table to indicate unqualified acceptance. Progress on a national approach was so slight that the Commission having issued a media release about the forthcoming roundtable did not issue one after it to report progress.

We have seen lots of bishops and leaders of religious groups appearing before the royal commission. We are yet to see any state premier, minister, or departmental head appear. When the Commission decided on a special case study on the *Ellis* v *Pell* litigation, I thought it would be an opportunity for some very detailed learnings about the litigation process. As I said on ABC Radio National at the time, it was very disappointing but not surprising that the Commission having decided to grill the parties to the litigation and their solicitors, left the barristers well alone—the very lawyers who made the decisions about how to conduct the litigation and who carried through with four days of cross-examination of Mr Ellis which everyone now agrees was inappropriate. In the name of transparency and justice, let's put all players under the spotlight. That's what a royal commission is supposed to do.[2]

I come to the issue of institutional responses to child sexual abuse with a strong and unqualified commitment to do and endorse all that can be done to make all social institutions safer for children in the future. I remain agnostic about how much can be achieved by this federal royal commission, in addition to what might be achieved by implementing the learnings from the more modest local initiatives such as the Victorian parliamentary inquiry and the Cunneen Inquiry. Those of us in the Catholic Church have to accept that there will be some anti-Catholic sentiment at play in some organs of the mass media. That comes with the turf. If anything, it should heighten our commitment to transparency, justice and compassion.

Considering my allocated topic 'Moral Leadership in Difficult Circumstances: Do Lawyers Have Too Much Say?', I have four key take-home messages. Lawyers need to assist clients while the clients discern how to maintain their public image of mission and their commitment to their core business, even when engaged in litigation or in a royal commission. The Commission needs to clarify what it actually has power to change or recommend, and to focus its activity more on looking for lessons rather than blame for the past so that procedures might be improved in future. Lawyers need to contribute to a clearer resolution of the legal issues at hand being separated out from the political and media maelstrom that accompanies a commission of this sort. We all need to help and encourage the Church hierarchy to be on the front foot in the public square explaining our mission, past mistakes, and future commitments.

I wonder whether there is more that legal advisers could have done to help witnesses such as Cardinal Pell in their appearance before

---

2. Discussion on legal ethics, ABC Radio National, Saturday Extra, 29 March 2014 at <http://www.abc.net.au/radionational/programs/saturdayextra/legal-ethics/5352252>. Accessed 2 December 2014.

the royal commission. I have no doubt that the lawyers for the Truth Justice and Healing Council would have given robust advice to His Eminence about the likely public perception of the stance he took in the witness box. And of course the Cardinal is very much his own man. The commission is not a court of law. Pell was in the witness box for 2.5 days. He is a senior leader of a Church committed to what he calls the 'new evangelisation'. What a splendid opportunity it could have been to appear on the nation's TV screens over those three nights not as a leader dumping on his underlings and then making a belated apology but as a leader standing tall, apologising at the outset, wearing the responsibility for his curial officials, and affirming without reservation the commitment to protecting children and to acting transparently, justly and compassionately. It could have been a tangible instance of the new evangelization. Instead, it led the esteemed church historian Fr Edmund Campion to opine at the launching of Kieran Tapsell's book *Potiphar's Wife* at the Catholic Institute of Sydney on 27 May 2014: 'Let me just say that on the royal commission that on Monday 24th March I watched Cardinal Pell being questioned in the royal commission and I woke up at 4.40 the next morning and thought, "It's too disgusting, the way he threw his men to the wolves to protect himself." I thought of his men: John Davoren, John Usher and Michael Casey; and I'm sure that those who write about the royal commission will be giving that particular ineptitude a lot of coverage.'

It could have been all so different if His Eminence had been convinced to be on the front foot from the beginning, apologising for those things which warranted apology, and being seen to be committed to justice, transparency and compassion. Welcoming the Victorian parliamentary report, the cardinal had admitted past mistakes by the Melbourne archdiocese during his time as auxiliary bishop there. Signaling his first tentative change of approach, Pell wrote:

> The report details some of the serious failures in the way the church dealt with these crimes and responded to victims, especially before the procedural reforms of

the mid 1990s. Irreparable damage has been caused. By the standards of common decency and by today's standards, church authorities were not only slow to deal with the abuse but sometimes did not deal with it in any appropriate way at all. This is indefensible.[3]

It is only part of the story to lay blame at the feet of deceased church leaders. The opaque hierarchical structure of the Catholic Church leaves many people wondering about the clerical culture inside the church and its lack of transparency and accountability. In preparation for his pending appearance at the royal commission in March 2014 investigating how the Catholic Church had earlier contested fiercely allegations of child sexual abuse trying to block any successful legal claim in the courts, Cardinal Pell admitted the need for a change of approach. He wrote: 'Whatever position was taken by the lawyers during the litigation, or by lawyers or individuals within the archdiocese following the litigation, my own view is that the church in Australia should be able to be sued in cases of this kind.'[4]

The Australian Catholic Church with the forced scrutinies of the state has been assisted in getting back to its mission and basic values, espousing truth, justice, compassion and transparency. As an institution, it has been dragged kicking and screaming. In his written statement to the royal commission, the cardinal was upfront in apologising for the sexual abuse which Mr. John Ellis had undoubtedly suffered when he was a child at the hands of a priest. He wrote: 'I acknowledge and apologise to Mr Ellis for the gross violation and abuse committed by a now deceased priest of the Sydney Archdiocese. I deeply regret the pain, trauma and emotional damage that this abuse caused to Mr Ellis.'[5]

Under cross examination, he had to admit that he, his advisers and his staff had fallen well short of the standards expected of a

---

3. Cardinal George Pell, *Sunday Telegraph,* 16 November 2013.
4. Cardinal George Pell, Witness Statement to Royal Commission into Institutional Responses to Child Sexual Abuse, 24 February 2014, Exhibit 8-0014, tendered on 24 March 2014, 25.
5. Pell, Witness Statement to Royal Commission tendered on 24 March 2014, 2

model litigant, let alone a Christian organisation. He admitted to the vast chasm between Christian decency and the tactics employed in pursuing Ellis in the courts. Having blamed various members of his staff for earlier errors and omissions, he was anxious to exculpate his lawyers who had acted on instructions and perhaps with insufficient supervision. He said:

> I believe in a legal sense there was nothing done that was improper, and any reservations I might have about particular stands of our lawyers, I would not want to suggest that they did anything improper. But from my point of view, from a Christian point of view, leaving aside the legal dimension, I don't think we did deal fairly (with Ellis).[6]

Cardinal Pell then made a long awaited apology to Ellis, not just for the initial and sustained sexual abuse Ellis suffered at the hands of a deviant priest but also for the hurt that had been inflicted on him by the Church ever since he had sought compensation and closure. He said:

> As former archbishop and speaking personally, I would want to say to Mr Ellis that we failed in many ways, some ways inadvertently, in our moral and pastoral responsibilities to him. I want to acknowledge his suffering and the impact of this terrible affair on his life. As the then archbishop, I have to take ultimate responsibility, and this I do. At the end of this grueling appearance for both of us at this Royal Commission, I want publicly to say sorry to him for the hurt caused him by the mistakes made and admitted by me and some of my archdiocesan personnel during the course of the *Towards Healing* process and litigation.[7]

---

6.   Cardinal George Pell, Transcript of Evidence, Royal Commission into Institutional Responses to Child Sexual Abuse, 26 March 2014, 6494
7.   Pell, Transcript of Evidence, Royal Commission, 27 March 2014, 6705

The cardinal's long time critics found fault with his mode of delivery. He did not even look at Mr Ellis who was sitting directly in front of him. If only the apology had been made at the beginning of his testimony. And if only it were the repetition of an earlier apology given at the time when it became apparent that the litigation had gone off the rails in the sense of having taken the Church a long way from its mission and focus on the new evangelisation.

The Cardinal's personal standing and the Church's reputation would stand higher today if he had not only received robust advice but also been convinced to follow it—advice that his primary objective before the royal commission was to indicate a desire to co-operate fully so that future abuse might be avoided and to communicate a message of truth, justice, healing and transparency. This would not entail going soft on one's underlings where they may have fallen short or failing to engage robustly with the commission in pursuit of truth. Lawyers and advisers should always be asking their church clients: How do you want to be heard and seen? What is your core business? Is litigation or testimony at a royal commission conducted in this fashion consistent with your mission?

In future cases like *Ellis*, the Church must provide a legal entity to sue or else the head of the Church organisation being sued (a diocese or a religious congregation) should provide the plaintiff and the court with a legally enforceable assurance that he or she personally will discharge any judgment debt. The Church organisation conceding that a priest or religious is in a position akin to employment should not challenge the assertion that a priest or religious is an employee for the purposes of any damages claim. The Church organisation should comply with a model litigant protocol along the lines of those adopted by governments. Having taken these steps, any church organization is entitled to plead and fight its case consistent with the law.

The royal commission has been too focused on financial compensation for victims. Doing so, it has set up unreal expectations for victims and their supporters and set impossible questions for some of the witnesses. The relevant causes of action are negligence, vicarious liability and non-delegable strict liability.

Under Australian law as most recently set down by the High Court in 2003, there are limits to the extent to which an organisation will be vicariously liable for the criminal wrong of one of its employees sexually abusing a child. And there are very few, if any, instances in which the law would find a non-delegable strict liability going beyond the limits of vicarious liability. The commission is clearly anxious to expand the realm of vicarious liability, much in the way that the courts in the United Kingdom and Canada have done.

There is little point in asking witnesses about this, let alone asking church leaders. It is not a matter for the commission. It is a matter for the High Court. Theoretically, one might postulate the commission recommending a very detailed statutory template for adoption by all state parliaments delimiting when an employer would be vicariously liable for his employee's criminal wrongs. But this is no matter for legislation. And the prospect of getting buy-in from all state parliaments on a matter so complex is very remote. The statute would need to cover Lindsay Fox's truck driver stopping at an intersection and deciding to biff the slow driver in the Ford Focus, as well as the errant teacher who assaulted a child in a classroom or in a dormitory.

In its line of questioning on vicarious liability, the royal commission sometimes gives the impression that it is seeking to make liability co-extensive with the admitted wrongdoing or failing of an employer. But the thing about vicarious liability is that it concerns liability where the employer is not in the least at fault, there being no proven negligence. The courts determining the limits of vicarious liability are concerned to determine the justice of redistributing damage in light of what seems fair given the scope of the enterprise of the employer. With all respect to the commission, I think this line of questioning put to Fr Jim Spence was misconceived:

> Do you think that conventional rules about vicarious liability really have a place to play in that environment? It is not concerned with the church's

training or the failure of the individual as such, but without the church and its whole structure and the invitation which is made to people to come and participate in its activities, the opportunity for a priest to abuse would just not be available, would it?

The issue is whether the church should, even though it is but one person in the church who may have been the abuser—whether because the church in its whole being, its whole structure, says, 'Please come to us. We will care for you. We will provide for you in a variety of ways', and without that invitation, which is not made by the individual priest; it is made by the whole church, without that invitation, that person would not be in a position to be abused by the priest. Do you understand that?

People are saying to us, 'Well, in those circumstances, how can it be that the church can say, "We don't, as a church, have a responsibility, firstly to acknowledge and apologise for the wrongdoing, but also to make redress, which includes financial redress, for what has happened"'?[8]

Ultimately, this will be a matter for the High Court, and not for Justice McClellan. I am pleased that it will remain with the High Court given the egregious error His Honour made in his cross-examination of Cardinal Pell about the prospect of a person insuring himself against future criminal activity on his part. Maria Gerace, counsel for Mr Ellis had asked, 'Does Catholic Church Insurances insure a priest for criminal conduct?' Pell answered, 'No, and it's a moot point whether they can insure somebody for criminal conduct.'

Justice McClellan then took over, floating the possibility that it could be done. Here is the transcript with McClellan asking the questions and Pell answering:

8.   James Spence, Transcript of Evidence, Royal Commission into Institutional Responses to Child Sexual Abuse, 10 December 2013, 2664–5.

Q. Cardinal, the criminal conduct we're talking about is
   a deliberate tort; you understand that?
A. That's a deliberate legal offence.
Q. No - well, it's that, but it's also a civil wrong.
A. Yes.
Q. I mean, if you hit someone in the street, you may
   commit a criminal assault, but you will also be liable
   in the civil law for assault. Do you understand?
A. I understand that now.
Q. There's no reason why the insurer couldn't provide
   insurance for a civil wrong, could it?
A. I simply don't know, but if you say that they can,
   good.
Q. They often do.
A. Good.[9]

McClellan floated the idea of self-insurance against future criminal
activity, not Pell. Australia's Fairfax press, their letter writers and
columnists had a field day fulminating that Pell's espousal of such
insurance showed that he just did not get it.[10] But it was McClellan,
not Pell, who did not get it, and after months of thinking about the
matter. His Honour has been over-reaching himself on this issue of
liability and insurance, an issue about which he is powerless to act
in any event. I note that the commission with its elaborate media
machine issued no correction once the Fairfax presses started to
run against Pell.

There has been one other line of persistent questioning in
the royal commission which I find unpersuasive, at least in part
because there has been a failure to concede the unlikelihood that
the commission will be able to achieve its desired result. Church
personnel are regularly grilled about their failure to report a
paedophile to the police even though the victim now an adult could
do so and has decided not to and has asked church personnel to

---

9. Pell, Transcript of Evidence, Royal Commission, 27 March 2014, 6667.
10. See Elizabeth Farrelly, 'Exit Cardinal Pell, with a bombshell', *Sydney Morning Herald,* 3
    April 2014, and Desmond Manderson, 'Cardinal George Pell Just Doesn't Get it With
    Child Abuse', *Canberra Times,* 5 April 2014.

desist from doing so. This was a matter that came to prominence in the Victorian parliamentary inquiry. The Victorian Parliament has responded by inserting Section 327 in the *Crimes Act*. The Act was amended by the *Crimes Amendment (Protection Of Children) Act 2014* which now provides in s. 327(2):

> Subject to subsections (5) and (7), a person of or over the age of eighteen years (whether in Victoria or elsewhere) who has information that leads the person to form a reasonable belief that a sexual offence has been committed in Victoria against a child under the age of sixteen years by another person of or over the age of eighteen years must disclose that information to a member of the police force of Victoria as soon as it is practicable to do so, unless the person has a reasonable excuse for not doing so.

Section 327(5) provides:

A person does not contravene subsection (2) if—

(a) the information forming the basis of the person's belief that a sexual offence has been committed came from the victim of the alleged offence, whether directly or indirectly; and

(b) the victim was of or over the age of 16 years at the time of providing that information to any person; and

(c) the victim requested that the information not be disclosed.

I can understand that counsel assisting or the federal commissioners might not much like this new Victorian provision. But they could at least acknowledge its existence when cross-examining witnesses about the best way to proceed in such cases. And they ought concede that as a federal commission they will have a very uphill battle trying to convince the Victorian parliament to change this new law. If it were a law passed in 1954 without the benefit of recent inquiries, then that would be a different matter. But a 2014 law passed after consideration of the vexed issue by a parliamentary committee advised by a criminal lawyer of the competence of retired Justice Frank Vincent AO is another matter.

Lawyers and church advisers should be urging church leaders to be more proactive, on their front foot in the public square. Consider the response to the Cunneen Report. More than three weeks after the Cunneen Report had been published, the faithful and the Australian community had heard nothing from the ACBC (Australian Catholic Bishops Conference) in relation to two key matters, even in the wake of the damning statement to parliament by Barry O'Farrell who was the premier who commissioned the inquiry.

The first key matter was that the Report found that there was sufficient evidence warranting the prosecution of a senior church official. Not a word has been said in response to this by the ACBC, and no senior church official is known to have stepped aside from his duties and obligations.

The second key matter was that the Report was critical of some former practices of the secretary of the ACBC (Fr Brian Lucas, a good friend of mine) and that the ex-premier was very condemnatory of him, seeking the ACBC's removal of him as 'a worthwhile first step'. Barry O'Farrell told Parliament:

> The report further states that from 1993 Father Brian Lucas possessed information, including admissions of sexually abusing children, that would have been of interest to police and would have facilitated a police investigation of (Fr) McAlinden, and that Bishop Michael Malone, head of the diocese from 1995 to 2011, was aware from 1995 that McAlinden was reported to have abused children and had admitted to such conduct, yet he also failed to bring the matter to the attention of police. This is behaviour that would be inexcusable and unacceptable in anyone, but I find it unbelievable, abominable and, frankly, unchristian when it is found amongst so-called 'men of the cloth'. This criminal inaction was never justifiable on the grounds of avoiding a church scandal.[11]

---

11. Barry O'Farrell, New South Wales Legislative Assembly, Hansard, 17 June 2014, 29645–6.

There was no detailed response offered to the public by the ACBC which blandly indicated its ongoing support through a spokesperson, not a bishop, informing the Murdoch press: 'There had been careful consideration of the entire report. The report did not make adverse findings as to the credit nor did it recommend any action be taken with respect to Father Lucas.'

That's not the point. It was not Commissioner Cunneen's job to say what the Church should do in light of criticisms she made of Fr Lucas's *modus operandi*. Her job was to consider whether any prosecution was warranted. Imagine if a commission of inquiry had made critical and adverse remarks about the modus operandi of a corporate CEO or CFO but said there were no grounds for prosecution. From the corporation's point of view, would that be the end of the matter? No. The corporation would provide the shareholders and public with a response to the criticisms admitting those that were accurate, correcting those that weren't and explaining those that were now unrepeatable in light of renewed procedures. This is the sort of advice the ACBC needs to hear, and not just from people behind the scenes like me.

There is a growing public perception that the hierarchy is paralysed, and that the senior church official referred to by Commissioner Cunneen is not helping by remaining at his post as if nothing had happened and as if there is no need for action unless and until formal charges are laid. There is a perception that the Church does nothing unless and until the State acts and proscribes. This has very adverse consequences. For example, I think that ex-premier O'Farrell was intemperate and unjust in his treatment of Bishop Bill Wright, the bishop of Maitland-Newcastle who in his press conference on 3 June 2014 was honest, humble, transparent, apologetic and realistic—the sort of leadership the Church so desperately needs at the moment. Wright had decided that his clergy who had been named adversely would be stood aside until a process could be instituted to determine their future. O'Farrell told Parliament: 'On the day the report was made public Bishop Wright issued a statement that suggested the report would be scrutinised, its findings taken on board and action taken. Yet last week, despite the damning exposition by the commission of Monsignor Hart's lack of action in 1993, Bishop Wright simply stood him aside from advisory positions in the diocese. As a response to such a damning inquiry it was completely underwhelming—more a sign of spin than a response to the grave sins of omission'.[12]

I presume the ACBC is powerless to respond to O'Farrell's slight on one of their members, given its own failure to address publicly the other two matters raised. Even people like me are powerless to respond in the public square. Because the first question will be: 'What about the unnamed senior church official? What should he do? What about Fr Lucas? What should he do?'

In the next two years with this royal commission, the Catholic Church needs to be more proactive, more on the front foot, more unashamedly committed to truth, justice, transparency and compassion, regardless of what the royal commission might recommend and regardless of the continuing barbs of those sections of the media that are anti-Catholic. We must have the confidence that in the end the truth will out and that we have nothing to fear but fear itself. Moving forward in hope with a commitment to assist and protect vulnerable children, the church needs fearless legal advisers to keep reminding church leaders about the fine ideals of scripture and the Church tradition which should animate, inform and shape every public utterance no matter how adverse the circumstances to personal self-interest.

-o0o-

In September 2014, the Royal Commission into child abuse in institutions was granted an extension. The challenges to the Church of a five-year federal royal commission are considerable.

The Royal Commission into Institutional Responses to Child Sexual Abuse has been granted its sought two-year extension. It will run for

---

12. Barry O'Farrell, New South Wales Legislative Assembly, Hansard, 17 June 2014, 29646.

five years. That is appropriate. I predicted on the night Julia Gillard announced the commission that it would take five years to do its work. I told Emma Alberici on ABC *Lateline*: 'I think a commission of the breadth that the Prime Minister has announced, if it was to be anything more than broad brush, but if it were to have the particularity that we were looking for with state inquiries, I think it will take at least five years.'[13] I am still worried about this extended federal royal commission—and that is not because I am a Catholic priest afraid of what the commission might discover in the bowels of my Church. I have long been an advocate for State assistance to the Church in this area, concerned that the Church could not do it alone. All church members, and not just the victims who continue to suffer, need light, transparency and accountability if the opaque injustices of the past are to be rectified.

With the Commission's case study in August 2014 into the Melbourne Response, much of the media focus was on Cardinal Pell, as it was during the case study on the John Ellis case in March 2014. For some time, many Australians, myself included, had wondered how Cardinal Pell was not in a position when an auxiliary bishop in Melbourne between 1987 and 1996 to know much, if anything, about the extent of child sexual abuse by his clergy and to do much, if anything, to address the issue. On 21 August 2014, Cardinal Pell told the Royal Commission that, prior to his becoming Archbishop in August 1996, he 'had no knowledge of any criminal behaviour that was not being dealt with' and that he was 'not even sure to what extent (he) would have been privy to matters that might have been criminal but were being dealt with by the Vicar General.'[14] He told the Commission: 'I wasn't in the direct line of authority before I was Archbishop. I was an Auxiliary Bishop with no responsibility in this area.'[15] In his written statement to the commission, he said, 'When I took office (as Archbishop in 1996), it was my view

---

13. ABC *Lateline*, Transcript, 12 November 2012, at < http://www.abc.net.au/lateline/content/2012/s3631260.htm >. Accessed 2 December 2014.
14. Pell, Transcript of Evidence, Royal Commission, 21 August 2014, C4525.
15. Pell, Transcript of Evidence, Royal Commission, 21 August 2014, C4525.

that the arrangements in the Archdiocese for responding to and assisting victims of child sexual abuse were insufficient to ensure a compassionate, effective and consistent response. I thought there needed to be clearly documented procedures for dealing with complaints.'[16] So he had quickly come to know there was a very major problem, when before he was oblivious and seemingly lacking in curiosity. He went on to state: 'I was very conscious, around the time that I became the Archbishop of Melbourne, that there was a growing awareness of the issue of child sexual abuse, and of the fact that such offences had been committed by clergy and Church personnel. There was understandable attention being paid to the issue in the media and in public debate.'

This evidence highlights two problems. First, there was the institutional problem of clericalism that infected the Catholic Church at least until 1996. A bishop as competent as (now) Cardinal Pell was able to be oblivious to the problem and to lack curiosity about how it was being handled in his archdiocese even though he occupied for nine critical years what most of us would see as the position of 2IC—second in charge. He was after all not just any auxiliary bishop. As an auxiliary bishop, he was already a member of the Vatican's Congregation for the Doctrine of the Faith, and thrice appointed Vatican Visitor to various overseas seminaries. It is not too worldly to observe that he was always known to be going places up the Catholic hierarchy, and he has. He was seen by the Roman authorities as one of our best. He was the Vatican's Australian 'go to' bishop. Second, there was the broader societal problem that in those days such oblivion was not restricted to high ranking, ever promoted clerics. As a community we did not know enough about the issue, and we did not do enough to respond. It was not just the Catholic bishops. The royal commission with time to conclude its task in a timely manner should be able to help the Church and the whole Australian community in its commitment to truth, justice, compassion, and healing.

---

16. Cardinal George Pell, Witness Statement to Royal Commission, 7 August 2014, tendered on 21 August 2014, Exhibit 16-0009, 6.

This brings me to my longstanding fear about a national inquiry of this sort in our Australian federation. Justice McClellan and his fellow commissioners have to do more to bring the States and Territories to the table and to get real buy-in by all governments. The mainstream media have been very neglectful of this part of McClellan's challenge.

In the same week that this royal commission was granted an extension, we saw the disastrous consequences with another royal commission which failed to take account of the role of State governments. The Royal Commission into the Home Insulation Program produced a report which is a dog's breakfast. The mainstream media has been oblivious to the report's glaring shortcomings, focusing more on the party politics of the blame game. That royal commission concluded that the commonwealth when administering the program should not have relied on the States to implement their own occupational health and safety laws, their own employment training requirements or their own building regulations.

The Commissioner, Mr Ian Hanger QC, reported, 'To rely on the State and Territory regimes to police their respective workplace health and safety laws seems to me to have been misguided, as those regimes are largely reactive. That is, when an incident happens the workplace health and safety regulators or electrical safety regulators investigate, report and, if appropriate, take enforcement action. What was, in my view, required of the Australian Government with the HIP (Home Insulation Program) was the provision of some preventative measures to attempt to mitigate some of the obvious workplace health and safety risks endemic to the HIP.'[17] And yet, the Commission went on to suggest that the Commonwealth should have considered having the states, rather than the Commonwealth, implement the whole program.

The regrettable deaths of the four young men working on the Home Insulation Program were the result of problems in

---

17. Ian Hanger QC, Report of the Royal Commission into the Home Insulation Program, 2014, 33.

administration at the commonwealth AND state levels and in delayed, poor communication between commonwealth AND state officials, especially in the State of Queensland where three of the four men worked and died. In reaching his bizarre conclusions, the royal commissioner, received little help from government. He observed: 'With very few exceptions, the public servant witnesses chose not to make any submissions. Quite extraordinarily, in my view, the Commonwealth chose not to make submissions when given the opportunity to do so. It made some desultory submissions in reply to the submissions of the pre-existing insulation business owners and the State of Queensland.'[18] A royal commission set up to investigate only the Commonwealth Government, especially when receiving inadequate co-operation from the Commonwealth Government, was bound to provide an inadequate and flawed report.

When investigating child abuse, the commonwealth royal commission needs to be very attentive to, and scrutinising of, state governments, especially their police forces and their child welfare departments. They are the key agencies which intersect with institutions where child abuse has occurred or is likely to occur. Justice McClellan will not be able to provide a national blueprint for the future protection of children unless there is real and forced buy-in by the states. The omens are not good. When the most appalling instances of child sexual abuse by a South Australian public servant came to light in August 2014, the South Australian government moved immediately to set up its own royal commission. The South Australian commission is to report on many matters including:

> The assessment, by relevant authorities, of persons who work and volunteer with children in the custody and/or under the guardianship of the Minister
> Management, training, supervision and ongoing oversight of persons who work and volunteer with children in the custody and/or under the guardianship of the Minister

---

18. Hanger, Report, 14.

The reporting of, investigation of and handling of complaints about care concerns, abuse or neglect of children cared for in the custody and/or under the guardianship of the Minister.[19]

These are the very matters within Justice McClellan's federal remit—agreed to by all governments, including South Australia. There was not the national political will to insist that the corrupted South Australian agency be subjected to the same national spotlight as has been, and quite rightly, Cardinal Pell. McClellan now has the time and the money to do a comprehensive report. State police forces and state child welfare agencies must be put under the national spotlight, and state governments need to make detailed submissions as to how they can improve their agencies for the protection of children. Otherwise McClellan risks becoming another Hanger.

-o0o-

After Cardinal Pell's second appearance before the Royal Commission, I reviewed his evidence concluding that the Church should accept liability for all abuse by clergy occurring before 1996 without contesting issues such as vicarious liability.

In August 2014 the Royal Commission into Institutional Responses to Child Sexual Abuse turned its spotlight on the Melbourne Response, the protocol adopted by the Catholic Archdiocese of Melbourne after George Pell became the Archbishop of Melbourne in 1996. Much of the media attention was on Cardinal Pell's video link appearance from Rome where he is now overseeing Vatican finances as Prefect of the Secretariat for the Economy. His critics understandably fixed on his comments about the common law,

---

19. Draft Terms of reference for South AustralianInquiry at <http://yoursay.sa.gov.au/ mediaWWWIWIWIW1siZiIsIjIwMTQvMDgvMDUvMDVfMTRfNTFfNzE0X0 RyYWZ0X1Rlcm1zX29mX1JlZmVyZW5jZS5wZGYiXV0/Draft%20 Terms%20of%20Reference.pdf > Accessed 2 December 2014.

vicarious liability and the liability of truck owners for the wanton criminal act of any truck driver. This is the third time Cardinal Pell has appeared and been cross-examined about his role as a bishop in overseeing church attempts to put right the tragic consequences of child sexual abuse perpetrated by church personnel, including priests. As a result of his three appearances, there is now greater clarity about past practices, as well as greater precision about the unanswered questions for those seeking a better and safer future for all children in all institutions, including the Catholic Church.

Reviewing Cardinal Pell's evidence, I have concluded that we Catholics need to accept moral responsibility and legal liability for all child sexual abuse committed by clergy prior to 1996, regardless of what might be the moral or legal position after 1996 when improved measures for supervision and dismissal of errant clergy were put in place. Ultimately, the High Court of Australia will be asked to reconsider the law of vicarious liability. But in relation to any abuse occurring before 1996, there is no way that we can argue that we had structures in place which gave priority to the well being of vulnerable children. That is why we are collectively responsible as a social institution. Reviewing Cardinal Pell's evidence I have also concluded that he made a fair fist of trying to fix things after he became archbishop in 1996. Credit should be given where it is due, even though we are yet to hear why he decided not to co-operate with the other Australian bishops in drawing up a more robust national protocol. I have no doubt that further improvements can be made, both to the Melbourne response and the national protocol *Towards Healing*. Hopefully Justice McClellan and his fellow commissioners will be able to provide a politically achievable blueprint for all institutions.

1996 was a significant year, and not just because that was when George Pell took over as Archbishop of Melbourne. It was the year that all Australian bishops agreed to major changes aimed at correcting past failures to deal adequately with child sexual abuse in clerical ranks. It also happens to be the year that the Irish bishops adopted new procedures which have helped to stem abuse there. Everyone, including church leaders realised that there was a real problem and that it required urgent action different from the *ad hoc* measures which had been put in place and tried over the previous decade.

On his appointment as archbishop, Pell wasted no time and spared no expense engaging the top end of town to design a scheme for redress and the provision of counselling services for those victims reporting sexual abuse by a church official. Before acting, Pell had discussions with Jeff Kennett, the Victorian premier, and Richard McGarvie, the governor. He consulted people like Sir James Gobbo and QCs Charles Francis and Joe Santamaria. The protocol was finalised in close consultation with the Victorian Police and with the Victorian Solicitor General. He set up a panel to oversee the administration of the protocol. Membership was not confined to Catholics. The chair of the panel has always been an outstanding lawyer: first, Alex Chernov, later the Victorian governor; David Habersberger later a Supreme Court judge; Sue Crennan later a High Court judge; and now David Curtain QC, one time Chairman of the Victorian Bar Council. These are not the sort of people you retain if you are wanting to engage in cover up or if you are wanting to maintain a secret Vatican approach at odds with contemporary community values. There can be no doubt that everyone has been on a steep learning curve and that Pell and his fellow bishops since 1996 have been keen to learn the lessons.

But prior to 1996, things were a mess. For nine of those years, Pell was an auxiliary bishop in Melbourne. Only his archbishop was superior to him in the archdiocesan power structure. Pell told the 2013 Victorian parliamentary inquiry, 'When I was Auxiliary Bishop of Melbourne I was not a part of the system or procedures for dealing with paedophilia'.[20] By 1988, he like anyone else attentive to media reports was aware that there was a problem and that there were 'terrible situations, for example, in Canada'. In 1988, Pell's superior, Archbishop Sir Frank Little had set up a confidential subcommittee

---

20. Family And Community Development Committee, Victoria Parliament, Inquiry into the handling of child abuse by religious and other organisations, *Transcript*, 27 May 2013, 7.

to deal with abuse complaints. Membership included a couple of clergy, a barrister and a psychiatrist. Pell says he knew nothing of their deliberations. In 1993, a Pastoral Response Office (PRO) was set up in the archdiocese. Pell says, 'Prior to my appointment as Archbishop, I had little if any involvement with the PRO'.[21]

As an auxiliary bishop, Pell was responsible for one of the three zones into which the archdiocese was divided. He was charged with monitoring the priests in that zone. For example there had been complaints about an alleged abuser in his zone, Fr Searson. Pell told the Victorian inquiry:

> There were two police investigations into Searson, I think in 1989 and 1991. They were inconclusive. The Catholic Education Office got the lawyers Minter Ellison to evaluate what was done and whether it was done properly, and they were still unable to pin anything on the man. He was not a pleasant man. He denied everything and anything. In the Searson matter I certainly acted on that, and this is one case where we consistently tried to do the right thing . . .
>
> I met on at least two occasions with groups of teachers from Searson's school. One was in 1989 and the other one was in 1991 or 1992. I think it was after the second meeting I asked the curia about it. It was mentioned that the Catholic Education Office had been investigating these things—I certainly did not do nothing; I certainly did. I was sent back to Searson to tell him to follow the protocols correctly, because people were saying he was misbehaving.[22]

Later as archbishop, Pell suspended Searson from all parish duties. Ultimately Searson pleaded guilty to a physical assault of children but no sexual abuse was ever proved.

---

21. Pell, Witness Statement to Royal Commission, 7 August 2014, 5.
22. Family And Community Development Committee, *Transcript*, 27 May 2013, 16.

In his sworn statement to the royal commission in August 2014, Cardinal Pell said, 'During the period in which I was Auxiliary Bishop from 1987 to 1996, I did not myself have any direct responsibility for handling issues relating to child sexual abuse. It was not my role to assist Archbishop Little in managing these matters.'[23] He told the Commission, 'I wasn't in the direct line of authority before I was Archbishop. I was an Auxiliary Bishop with no responsibility in this area.'[24]

What we Catholics have to accept is that, at least until 1996 when the new protocols were introduced, we were part of a social institution so hazily structured that not even one as savvy as Cardinal Pell was expected to know or do anything conclusive about alleged child sexual abuse, regardless of how high he had escalated the ecclesiastical pyramid. He had been a priest in Ballarat where abuse was rampant, rector of the Melbourne seminary when abuse in some of the Melbourne parishes was frequent, and then auxiliary bishop for nine years when clerical sexual abuse was being constantly discussed in the mainstream media. Conceding that there was 'significant truth' in the suggestion that a 'systemic cover-up allowed paedophile priests to prey on innocent children', Pell told the Victorian parliamentary inquiry:

> Nobody would talk about it; nobody would mention it. I certainly was unaware of it. I do not think many persons, if any, in the leadership of the Catholic Church, knew what a horrendous, widespread mess we were sitting on. I have sometimes said that if we had been gossips, which we were not, and we had talked to one another about the problems that were there, we would have realised earlier just how widespread this awful business was.[25]

If only Pell and Little had the occasional responsible conversation, rather than a gossip, about these matters, how different things

23. Pell, Witness Statement to Royal Commission, 7 August 2014, 5.
24. Pell, Transcript of Evidence, Royal Commission, 21 August 2014, C4525.
25. Family And Community Development Committee, *Transcript*, 27 May 2013, 14.

might have been before 1996. If only Pell and the clergy on Little's subcommittee had met for the occasional discussion, and just over a cup of tea. If only Pell had decided to seek out the PRO members in order to get a better understanding of the matters which were being raised in the media. The Church has not judged him to have failed in his duty as a bishop for knowing and doing little before 1996. The Church has promoted him as one of our finest bishops who could not be expected to have known or done anything more before 1996.

We have to accept that the institution until at least 1996 was structured so opaquely as to work against the interests of vulnerable children. The inner sanctum of an archdiocese in those days could be so fortified and so exclusive as to shield a competent auxiliary bishop from alleged abuse by a priest in the bishop's allocated monitoring zone. That fortification was not put in place and maintained with a care for children. It was maintained without sufficient regard for the well being of vulnerable victims whose interests were secondary to the name of the Church and the protection of its clergy. This is the shocking moral consequence of Cardinal Pell's evidence, and now we all as Church must accept the blame, committing ourselves to transparency and accountability in the Church so that this sort of thing can never happen again. We, and not just the deceased bishops who occupied the inner sanctum, must accept responsibility for the harm suffered by those who would not have suffered but for the existence of such a fortified, exclusive inner sanctum. We can do this, and should do this, even while acknowledging the exhaustive work done by our leaders like Cardinal Pell who have worked to clean up the unholy mess since 1996, making the Church safe for children. Whatever the High Court ultimately rules about abuse occurring after 1996, we need to wear the rap for everything that went on before 1996 when the procedures in place were hazy, porous and totally inadequate.

On this difficult topic, there will always be those who question my motivation as a Catholic priest and there will be those who remain convinced that I lack compassion for victims. Nothing I say will change their minds about me, the Church or abuse issues. I accept that. I hope and pray that this royal commission can help provide a safe environment for all children in Australia and some further healing and justice for those who have been victims of sexual abuse, especially those who were children violated by members of the Catholic Church in positions of trust. That is why I write on this issue. It is why I was one of the church people calling for some state intervention before the royal commission was established.

There are moral questions to consider and legal questions. By addressing the legal questions, we are not leaving morality and compassion at the door. But we are needing to enter the chamber of reason and legal analysis, before re-emerging and asking in moral terms what we should do and for what should we be responsible.

In law, the perpetrator is of course liable for his wrong (and it usually is a male). The bishop or superior is also liable if he (and it nearly always is a male) is negligent in relation to the perpetrator. That negligence will relate to the failure adequately to train, supervise, correct or suspend someone later proven to be a perpetrator. There may be circumstances in which the bishop or superior would be vicariously liable for the wrong committed by the perpetrator. Vicarious liability arises when the supervisor has NOT been in any way personally negligent, but when it is appropriate to hold the supervisor or the organisation responsible for the wrong committed because the wrong was committed as part of the enterprise to which the supervisor or organisation is committed. To date, the High Court of Australia in three decisions has said that vicarious liability does not usually attach to a school authority overseeing the activity of a teacher, even a teacher in a single teacher country school for primary school children. Since these High Court decisions, there have been developments in the law in the UK courts more in harmony with previous decisions in Canada which extend the range of vicarious liability.

I am suggesting that regardless of what the High Court might decide in the future about vicarious liability, church authorities when sued for child sexual abuse prior to 1996 (and that is most of the present cases) should accept that they were negligent in their supervision of any perpetrator because, on the uncontested evidence of Cardinal Pell, there was prior to 1996 a system of training, appointment, supervision and dismissal of priests which was such a mess and so disregarding of the well being of children that there was no expectation that even an auxiliary bishop in an Archdiocese would be able to know or do anything to rectify abuse.

I readily concede that there were many of us church members, especially laity, who knew nothing and could do nothing about these issues at the time, in part because of the clericalism and lack of transparency in the church hierarchy. But, in justice, if a victim chooses to sue 'the Church' for abuse by a priest or other church official, 'the Church' ought provide the victim with a legal entity to sue, backed with the guarantee that the entity will be able to pay any judgment debt. The money will come from 'Church funds' which will be money largely given by laity who knew and could do nothing about the committed and proven abuse. It is in that sense that I say that we, the Church, are responsible and should accept legal liability. Morally, we should accept collective responsibility as the local Church. I in no way want to suggest that this makes it the personal moral fault of unknowing laity. But from here on, we are all on notice that we have a right and a duty to call our hierarchy to account on this issue because in the end we do wear the rap collectively—morally and legally.

There will continue to be discussion at the royal commission about compensation and reparation schemes which spare victims the need to litigate their claims in court and which provide authorities (including churches) with greater certainty about financial liabilities for alleged but unproven or unadmitted claims of abuse. Everyone concedes that it is best that victims be spared having to prove that abuse occurred. But as a backdrop, there must always be recourse to the courts if a claim is disputed.

It is far too simplistic to claim that the Catholic Church in Australia did nothing prior to 1996 or prior to 2013 to deal with these issues. There is no doubt that the Australian Catholic Bishops Conference (ACBC) started addressing this issue seriously in 1988, seeking the best advice available nationally and internationally. The first makings of a national protocol were agreed to in 1992. This is the real significance of Cardinal Pell's evidence. As a bishop, he attended the ACBC from 1987 onwards. From 1990, he was a member of the Congregation for the Doctrine of the Faith (CDF) regularly attending meetings in Rome, and thus presumably hearing details about the problems in Canada and the USA. Our now most promoted bishop was party to all these discussions for nine years but back home in his own diocese, he and his archbishop never discussed the issue and the particulars of local wrongdoing. He never sought to be brought into the loop with archdiocesan personnel charged with dealing with this mess and human tragedy. He was part of an institution, and was being constantly promoted in an institution, which did not put the interests of vulnerable children first. If it had, any auxiliary bishop, and especially a highly competent and favoured one, would have been across the local particulars seeking a better way. That did not happen until 1996. So prior to 1996, we must all collectively wear the rap. This is my sad conclusion from reading His Eminence's evidence on the three occasions he has taken the oath on this issue.

6
Bringing the Church to the World

In 1995, I had the good fortune to study at the Georgetown Law School in Washington DC. A fellow Jesuit Kevin Quinn was a young law professor there. In 2011 he was inaugurated as the President of another Jesuit university, Scranton. He invited me to deliver the occasional address for his inauguration. I spoke about 'A Jesuit Perspective on Making Human Rights and Religion Friends, Not Foes'.

I note that Scranton University was founded in 1888 by Most Rev William O'Hara, the first Bishop of Scranton, and that one of the chief benefactors of late has been a Brennan, and thus the imposing presence of Brennan Hall here on the campus. Being a Brennan and my mother an O'Hara, I am delighted to be invited to the other side of the world to honour your new university president, Fr Kevin Quinn SJ, though any blood relationships to your founders or benefactors might need to be traced back to The Bog. Your motto *Religio Mores Cultura* grounds all our reflections upon ourselves and upon the world that we serve.

In Australia, Downunder in the southern hemisphere, it is spring. Before coming here I took a stroll past your US embassy in Canberra, the Australian national capital. Your embassy is a very imposing, fortressed Georgian red brick complex. To quote the embassy blurb: 'The observer is provided a glimpse of the charm and stately beauty of Colonial Williamsburg that was a fountainhead of liberty and freedom in the life of the new American republic.' On the fence of the embassy, the golden spring sunlight at dusk was illuminating the almost 3,000 small flags placed commemorating those who died in that tragic event of 9/11 ten years ago, including more than 300 foreign nationals from more than fifty countries, ten of whom were Australians. The sea of Stars and Stripes was dotted with flags of other nations whose nationals had perished alongside yours. America's greatest onshore tragedy has reverberated throughout the world. Here at Scranton, your links to 9/11 are not just to New York City and the Capitol but also to Shanksville, 250 miles from here, where United Airlines Flight 93 came down.

Ten years on, our societies are still wrestling with finding the balance between individual human rights and national security in this new global configuration. While espousing religious freedom, we know that some express their religious beliefs with contempt for others, and we face afresh the limits on religious freedom and freedom of conscience. The relationship between religion, culture and morals is freshly contested.

Your friends from other lands hope and pray that the American mix of idealism and pragmatism will ensure that your ideals are strengthened through this reconfiguration, and your pragmatism rewarded with workable protections for all in the community. Recently, President Obama wrote to the Australian Prime Minister saying, 'In the decade since the attacks, we have had no more steadfast partner than Australia in our effort to defeat terrorists in Afghanistan, in Bali, in the Middle East and in South East Asia'. Like all friends, let us hope we can learn from each other even critically, and not just support each other uncritically as we confront the great moral quandaries and challenges of our age.

I am one of those Jesuits from elsewhere in the world who has profited much from knowing American Jesuits and their collaborators both onshore and offshore. One of my very formative life experiences was spending a few months in a large refugee camp on the Thai Cambodian border in 1987. There were 100,000 Khmer in Site II camp. I went to look at the human rights situation there.

On arrival, one of my housemates, American Mary Sutphin, warned me as I was about to drive off in a car: 'Be careful, it takes a while to get used to driving on the wrong side of the road.' I replied: 'Mary, I've never driven on any other side of the road.' Though we speak the same language, we come from very different backgrounds and life experiences. The authorities were not minded to admit a Jesuit lawyer into the camp for the purpose of scrutinising human rights violations. So I was assigned to teach a management course to the refugees. My mentor was an American Jesuit, Ron Anton. He armed me with an American management textbook. Being one page ahead of the students with Management 101, I asked them to list those resources that were plentiful, relatively scarce, and rare—pointing out that management was largely focused on the best harnessing of relatively scarce resources.

They were able to list only two plentiful resources in the camp—air and human beings. Everything else, including the water was rare and had to be rationed, and usually corruptly. There was nothing relatively scarce to manage. We had to revise the textbook fairly radically for local conditions.

A very charismatic French Jesuit Pierre Ceyrac headed our Jesuit Refugee Service team. One day the shelling and exchange of fire came close to the camp and all us volunteers were called out. Having headed out of the camp, our convoy of NGO vehicles was lined up stationary on a remote Thai country road. In the opposite direction came Fr Pierre in his old beat up Toyota. He was smoking his French cigarettes, demanding entrance to the camp. The UN and Thai authorities were unwilling to admit him, but he insisted. He stayed the night. The rest of us did not get back inside the camp for some days.

The Georgetown Medical Team members were furious with Fr Pierre—and for good reason. They said he could give no practical help in the camp if it were to be shelled. And if he were injured, there would be a risk that the international NGOs including the doctors would not be allowed back into the camp for weeks. With a French existential hunching of the shoulders, he surmised: 'What else could I do? I had to be with the women and children.'

He had accompanied the refugees for ten years. He did not want to abandon them in their hour of need. His presence that night was almost sacramental. It transformed the quality of his presence to the refugees on all those other days when the shelling was far distant. Fr Pierre was right. So too was the Georgetown medical team.

I have been a regular visitor to Jesuit universities in the US. One of things I enjoy most about you Americans is that you love conversation and public disputation about contested moral and ethical issues. You are relentless in your inquiry into whether Fr Pierre was more right than the Georgetown Medical Team. You concede that there might be another side of the road on which to drive. You are open to adapting your management principles to previously unimagined real life situations. But in all these instances, it requires dialogue and the risk that your critics will think you are too fixated on 'process' and 'status'—two words that always give you away, whatever your accents. You often think the law must require an answer to political and moral quandaries.

I first met your new President Fr Kevin Quinn SJ at Georgetown Law Center where we were both mentored by Frs Bob Drinan SJ and Ladislas Orsy SJ, having been inspired by the writing of Fr John Courtney Murray SJ who wrote:

> The spiritual order of society is founded on truth—on the true view of man, his dignity, his duties and rights, his freedoms and obligations. This order must be brought into being under fidelity to the precepts of justice, whose vindication is the primary function of the public power as well as the primary civic duty of the citizenry. This order needs to be animated and perfected by love; for civic unity cannot be achieved by justice and law alone; love is the ultimate force that sustains all humans living together. Finally, this order is to achieve increasingly more human conditions of social equality, without any impairment of freedom.[1]

I think that quote of Murray could keep most of us going for a lifetime, or at least for three or four years study at Scranton. To me, Drinan was the epitome of the modern American Jesuit committed to the faith that does justice—passionately active on the international stage

---

1   John Courtney Murray, 'The Problem of Religious Freedom' in *Religious Liberty: Catholic Struggles with Pluralism*, edited by Leon Hooper (Louisville: Westminster/ John Knox Press, 1993), 176–7.

espousing human rights, testing the limits of church involvement in politics at home, and not afraid of conflict. Orsy had that refined European touch but with a fierce independence, turning church teaching about human rights and human dignity back on the Church itself, insisting on due process within the life of the Church community. In his latest book, Orsy proposes 'that in the quadrangle of every university a monument should be erected dedicated to the "Anonymous Inquiring Students" who keep the teachers' minds fresh'.[2] That might be the first building project for President Quinn!

Having known Fr Quinn at Georgetown and at Santa Clara, I am delighted to come as a visitor and to honour him at his inauguration as Scranton president by reflecting on human rights and the contemporary challenge offered by Fr Adolfo Nicolas SJ, current Superior General of the Jesuits, who has urged Jesuit universities to promote depth of thought and imagination, re-discovering universality, and being places of learned ministry which mediate between faith and culture.

In Mexico last year many of us gathered from Jesuit universities around the world under the leadership and inspiration of the late Fr Paul Locatelli SJ to hear Fr Nicolas put before us three major challenges in response to what he calls the pervasive 'globalisation of superficiality' by which we can be 'overwhelmed with such a dizzying pluralism of choices and values and beliefs and visions of life, then one can so easily slip into the lazy superficiality of relativism or mere tolerance of others and their views, rather than engaging in the hard work of forming communities of dialogue in the search of truth and understanding'. Fr General told us:

> First, in response to the globalization of superficiality, I suggest that we need to study the emerging cultural world of our students more deeply and find creative ways of promoting depth of thought and imagination, a depth that is transformative of the person. Second, in order to maximize the potentials of new possibilities

---

2   Ladislas Orsy, *Receiving the Council: Theological and Canonical Insights and Debates* (Collegeville: Liturgical Press, 2009), x.

of communication and cooperation, I urge the Jesuit universities to work towards operational international networks that will address important issues touching faith, justice, and ecology that challenge us across countries and continents. Finally, to counter the inequality of knowledge distribution, I encourage a search for creative ways of sharing the fruits of research with the excluded; and in response to the global spread of secularism and fundamentalism, I invite Jesuit universities to a renewed commitment to the Jesuit tradition of learned ministry which mediates between faith and culture.[3]

So how can those of us inspired by the Jesuit tradition help to make human rights and religion friends, not foes? How can we form communities of dialogue in the search of truth and understanding about human rights and their limits, and about the place of religion in the State and in society? The trouble with much human rights discourse is that it is too readily reduced to assertions just about individual rights and non-discrimination. Human rights discourse needs to be more subtle when it comes to a conflict of rights situation or when the law is having to consider the public interest or the common good as well as individual liberties. In the public square, human rights discourse is usually conducted against a backdrop of presumed atheism and without much serious consideration for the rights of religious freedom and conscience.

The challenge to the contemporary Jesuit university is: providing a truly Catholic ambience where every intellectual idea about human rights can be examined from all sides, espousing human dignity in the light of the Church's tradition. Human rights and religion can only enhance each other when studied and lived in a vibrant Jesuit university committed to learning, service and research. Their friendship can be cultivated even in the midst of culture wars.

---

3   Adolfo Nicolas, 'Depth, Universality, and Learned Ministry: Challenges to Jesuit Higher Education Today', Address to the 'Networking Jesuit Higher Education: Shaping the Future for a Humane, Just, Sustainable Globe' Conference, Mexico City, 22 April 2010 at <http://www.scu.edu/scm/winter2010/shapingthefuture.cfm>. Accessed 3 December 2014.

Many citizens wanting to contribute to the shaping of law, public policy, and conversation in the public square come to the task with their own comprehensive worldview. For some, that view is shaped not just by their culture and intellectual peers but also by their religious tradition and beliefs. Just because they do not often talk about such tradition and beliefs outside their own circle of family and friends does not mean that these tradition and beliefs are left at home once the individual steps into the public square. When launching his foundation on 'Faith and Globalisation', the retired British Prime Minister Tony Blair observed that his former press secretary, Alastair Campbell, was fond of saying, 'We don't do God'. Blair clarified that Campbell 'didn't mean that politicians shouldn't have faith, just that it was always a packet of trouble to talk about it'.[4]

Whether or not our comprehensive worldview is shaped by religious influences, it informs the development of values that the individual expresses and lives out in their own specific cultural context. From those values, one is able to articulate principles which underpin informed and considered decision making about laws, public policies and public deliberation on contested social questions.

We can practise politics, that art of compromise in the public square where laws and policies are determined in relation to the allocation of scarce resources or in relation to conflicts where there is no clear resolution either in principle or by the exercise of legitimate authority. Public policy can include the allocation of preferences by the State extended to individuals who can avail themselves of state benefits while avoiding state burdens. Laws can include the dictates of the State enforceable against individuals who fail to comply voluntarily.

A year or so ago, to the disapproval of some of my family and friends I agreed to appear on television with the ubiquitous atheist and now deceased Christopher Hitchens. As I said to family and

---

4 Tony Blair, Launch of the Tony Blair Faith Foundation, 6 June 2008 at <http://www.tonyblairoffice.org/speeches/entry/video-tony-blair-speech-on-the-launch-of-the-tony-blair-faith-foundation/>. Accessed 3 December 2014.

friends at the time, it is part of my day job. Someone has to do it. Something crystallised for me that night when a young member of the television audience said:

> Hello Comrades. Can we ever hope to live in a truly secular society when the religious maintain their ability to affect political discourse and decision making on issues such as voluntary euthanasia, same-sex unions, abortion and discrimination in employment?[5]

The TV compere and Hitchens were clearly *simpatico* with this approach, as were many in the audience, but I was dumbstruck, wondering how can we ever hope to live in a truly democratic society when secularists maintain their demand that people with a religious perspective not be able to claim a right to engage in the public square agitating about laws on issues such as voluntary euthanasia, same-sex unions, abortion and discrimination in employment? We have just as much right as our secularist fellow citizens to contribute in the public square informed and animated by our worldview and religious tradition. We acknowledge that it would be prudent to put our case in terms comprehensible to those who do not share that worldview or religious tradition when we are wanting to win the support and acceptance of others, especially if we be in the minority. But there is no requirement of public life that we engage only on secularist terms. And we definitely insist on the protection of our rights including the right to religious freedom even if it not be a right highly prized by the secularists.

One of my US role models, Fr Bryan Hehir put it well when reflecting on John Courtney Murray's mode of engagement in the public square. Hehir said:

> I am deeply interested in, but not yet convinced by, the argument that a more explicitly theological style of assertion, using religious symbols to interpret and adjudicate justice claims, is more appropriate to the

---

5   ABC, *Q&A*, Transcript, 1 October 2009 at
      <http://www.abc.net.au/tv/qanda/txt/s2695716.htm>. Accessed 3 December 2014.

questions faced by the Church in the United States today. To specify both my interest and my scepticism, it is necessary to distinguish the need for shaping 'the mind of the Church' (as a community and an institution) regarding social questions from the task of projecting the perspective of the Church into the societal debate about normative questions of social policy.[6]

Hehir concluded:

In brief, faced with both greater interdependence and an expanding framework of human-rights claims, I do not think we can do better than the style of public discourse found in *We Hold These Truths* and *Pacem in Terris*.[7]

The Oxford academic John Finnis in his book of essays *Religion and Public Reasons* identifies three types of practical atheism: that there is no God, that God is unconcerned with human affairs, and that God is easily satisfied with human conduct or easily appeased or bought off.[8] He reminds us that 'neither atheism nor radical agnosticism is entitled to be treated as the "default" position in public reason, deliberation and decisions. Those who say or assume that there is a default position and that it is secular in those senses (atheism or agnosticism about atheism) owe us an argument that engages with and defeats the best arguments for divine causality.'[9] Though it might be prudent and strategic to suggest that religious accommodationists carry the onus of persuasion in a public square with a secularist prejudice, might there not be a case for arguing that the representatives of the more populist, majoritarian mindset in the public square need to be more accommodating of religious views?

---

6   Quoted in David Hollenbach, 'Theology and Philosophy in Public: A Symposium on John Courtney Murray's Unfinished Agenda', in *Theological Studies* 40 (1979): 700 at 710–1.

7   Quoted in Hollenbach, 'Theology and Philosophy in Public', 712.

8   John Finnis, *Religion and Public Reasons* (Oxford: Oxford University Press, 2011), 124.

9   Finnis, *Religion and Public Reasons*, 45.

Professor Finnis, a Catholic but making a point equally applicable to all faith communities, says:

> Outside the Church, it is widely assumed and asserted that any proposition which the Catholic Church in fact proposes for acceptance is, by virtue of that fact, a 'religious' (not a philosophical, scientific, or rationally grounded and compelling) proposition, and is a proposition which Catholics hold only as a matter of faith and therefore cannot be authentically willing to defend as a matter of natural reason.[10]

For Finnis, much of what John Rawls in his *Political Liberalism* describes as public reason can be equated with natural reason. Whereas Rawls would rely only on an overlapping consensus not wanting to press for objective reality of right and wrong, Finnis would contest that the only content of an overlapping consensus would be that which can be objectively known through natural reason.

In 2008 the Archbishop of Canterbury Rowan Williams gave an insightful address at the London School of Economics pointing out that rights and utility are the two concepts that resonate most readily in the public square today. But we need concepts to set limits on rights when they interfere with the common good or the public interest, or dare I say it, public morality—the concepts used by the UN when first formulating and limiting human rights sixty years ago. These concepts are no longer in vogue, at least under these titles. We also need concepts to set limits on utility when it interferes with the dignity of the most vulnerable and the liberty of the most despised in our community. Addressing the UN General Assembly to mark the anniversary of the *UN Declaration of Human Rights* (UNDHR), Pope Benedict XVI said:

> This document was the outcome of a convergence of different religious and cultural traditions, all of them motivated by the common desire to place the human person at the heart of institutions, laws and the

---

10   Finnis, *Religion and Public Reasons*, 114–5.

workings of society, and to consider the human person
essential for the world of culture, religion and science...
(T)he universality, indivisibility and interdependence
of human rights all serve as guarantees safeguarding
human dignity. [11]

It would be a serious mistake to view the UNDHR stipulation and
limitation of rights just as a western Judaeo-Christian construct.
Then again it would be hard to envisage its formulation without a
deep drawing on the western Judaeo-Christian tradition engaged
intelligently and respectfully with other traditions. It is fascinating
to track the different ways in which the drafting commission dealt
with the delimitation of rights in the UN Declaration. Ultimately
Article 29 provided:

Everyone has duties to the community which enables
him freely to develop his personality.
In the exercise of his rights, everyone shall be subject
only to such limitations as are necessary to secure due
recognition and respect for the rights of others and
the requirements of morality, public order and general
welfare in a democratic society.

So here in the heart of the modern world's most espoused
declaration of human rights came an acknowledgment that we all
have duties and not just rights, duties to the community which,
perhaps counter-intuitively, enable us to develop our personalities.
At the Commission, it was said that 'morality' and 'public order'
were 'particularly necessary for the French text, since in English,
"general welfare" included both morality and public order'.[12] At one
stage it was suggested that the term 'public order' was too broad,
permitting the grossest breach of human rights by those committing
arbitrary acts and crimes in the name of maintaining public order.

---

11 Pope Benedict XVI, Meeting with the Members of the General Assembly of the
United Nations Organisation, 18 April 2008 at <http://www.vatican.va/holy_father/
benedict_xvi/speeches/2008/april/documents/hf_ben-xvi_spe_20080418_un-visit_
en.html>. Accessed 3 December 2014.

The commission considered the substitution of 'security for all' for 'public order', similar to the 28th article of the American Declaration of the Rights and Duties of Man, but decided to stay with the more jurisprudentially certain European term 'public order'. But also we have the acknowledgment that individual rights might be limited not just for the preservation of public order and for the general welfare of persons in a democratic society, but also for morality— presumably to maintain, support, enhance or develop morality in a democratic society. Sixty years later, these words of limitation might not sit with us so readily, but they still have work to do.

Once we investigate much of the contemporary discussion about human rights, we find that often the intended recipients of rights do not include all human beings but only those with certain capacities or those who share sufficient common attributes with the decision makers. It is always at the edges that there is real work for human rights discourse to do. On one of my recent trips to Cambodia, I met a woman concerned for the well being of a handful of children who had both cerebral palsy and profound autism. There are more than enough needy children in Cambodia. It is not surprising that religious persons often have a keen eye for the neediest, not only espousing their rights but taking action for their well being and human flourishing. Speaking at the London School of Economics on 'Religious Faith and Human Rights', Rowan Williams, the Archbishop of Canterbury boldly and correctly asserted:

> The question of foundations for the discourse of non-negotiable rights is not one that lends itself to simple resolution in secular terms; so it is not at all odd if diverse ways of framing this question in religious terms flourish so persistently. The uncomfortable truth is that a purely secular account of human rights is always going to be problematic if it attempts to establish a language

---

12 Erica-Irene A Daes, *The Individual's Duties to the Community and the Limitations on Human Rights and Freedoms Under Article 29 of the Universal Declaration of Human Rights*, UN Doc. E/CN.4/Sub.2/432/Rev.2, 1983, 72

of rights as a supreme and non-contestable governing concept in ethics.[13]

No one should pretend that the discourse about universal ethics and inalienable rights has a firmer foundation than it actually has. Williams concluded his lecture with this observation:

> As in other areas of political or social thinking, theology is one of those elements that continues to pose questions about the legitimacy of what is said and what is done in society, about the foundations of law itself. The secularist way may not have an answer and may not be convinced that the religious believer has an answer that can be generally accepted; but our discussion of social and political ethics will be a great deal poorer if we cannot acknowledge the force of the question.

Once we abandon any religious sense that the human person is created in the image and likeness of God and that God has commissioned even the powerful to act justly, love tenderly and walk humbly with their God, it may be very difficult to maintain a human rights commitment to the weakest and most despised in society. It may come down to the vote, moral sentiment or tribal affiliations. And that will not be enough to extend human rights universally. In the name of utility, the society spared religious influence will have one less impediment to limiting social inclusion to those like us, 'us' being the decision makers who determine which common characteristics render embodied persons eligible for human rights protection. Nicholas Wolterstorff says, 'Our moral subculture of rights is as frail as it is remarkable. If the secularisation thesis proves true, we must expect that that subculture will have been a brief shining episode in the odyssey of human beings on earth.'[14]

---

13 Rowan Williams, *Religious Faith and Human Rights,* London School of Economics, 1 May 2008, at <http://rowanwilliams.archbishopofcanterbury.org/articles.php/1161/ archbishop-religious-faith-and-human-rights#Lecture >. Accessed 3 December 2014.
14 Nicholas Wolterstorff, *Justice: Rights and Wrongs* (Princeton: Princeton University Press, 2008), 393.

Robert Drinan who taught me at Georgetown was a Jesuit priest and lawyer who had served ten years in Congress before the Vatican finally got its way, insisting that he resign. Drinan first met the Kennedy clan in 1964. He joined a group of leading moral theologians down at the Kennedy compound at Hyannis Port. His biographer Raymond Schroth says 'they hoped to come up with a stance on abortion acceptable to both Catholic teaching and the public at large'.[15] A decade before *Roe* v *Wade*, this group proposed 'that the translation of a rigorously restrictive ethic of abortion into law was unlikely to be enforceable or achieve its positive goals without significant social evils'. The issue was to dog Drinan all his public life. Before going into public life, Drinan tried to clear a path about the legal and moral complexities of abortion. Writing in *Theological Studies* in 1970, he said:

> This author has no easy solutions or ready options for the Catholic legislator, jurist, or spokesman on the question of abortion and the law. Perhaps the central issue was described in the reasoning of John Courtney Murray, SJ, who, while not addressing himself to the question of abortion, wrote as follows about the criminal law: 'The moral aspirations of law are minimal. Law seeks to establish and maintain only that minimum of actualized morality that is necessary for the healthy functioning of the social order . . . It enforces only what is minimally acceptable, and in this sense socially necessary . . . Therefore the law, mindful of its nature, is required to be tolerant of many evils that morality condemns.'[16]

A strong opponent of the Vietnam War, Drinan had become interested in running for Congress. His great backer was Jewish

---

15 Raymond A Schroth, *Bob Drinan: The Controversial Life of the First Catholic Priest Elected to Congress* (New York: Fordham University Press, 2011), 80.

16 Robert Drinan: 'The Jurisprudential Options on Abortion', Theological Studies, 31 (1970): 149–169. On 4 June 1996, long after his departure from Congress Drinan decided to publish an opinion piece in the *New York Times* in support of President Bill Clinton's veto of the *Partial Birth Abortion Ban Act*. Church leaders went ballistic.

businessman Jerome Grossman who knew Drinan to be a good friend of Israel. Grossman thought Drinan would deliver 'the Catholic vote' for the Democratic Party in Massachusetts. Drinan needed to convince his religious superiors in Rome. There has been a long running controversy whether Drinan did have approval to run from the then Superior General Pedro Arrupe. Arrupe properly left the matter for determination by the Jesuit superiors here in the US. Schroth says:

> It is reasonable to conclude . . . that Arrupe did not want Drinan to run. In fact, Arrupe said publicly on several occasions that, although he strongly urged Jesuits to fight for justice, he did not think they should participate in partisan politics as candidates for office, that the party politician priest would not be free to be the priest-prophet.[17]

Each of the five times he came up for re-election to Congress, Drinan had first to renegotiate the permission from his superiors. Time ran out in 1979 after Pope John Paul II had insisted that priests not serve in government in Nicaragua. Finally it was the pope who insisted that the Jesuit superiors instruct Drinan not to run for a sixth term. Drinan who had spent much time as Congressman agitating international human rights, having moved the first motion of impeachment against President Nixon for the unauthorised bombing of Cambodia on 31 July 1973, accepted the decision and said:

> I am grateful to have had these opportunities as a moral architect. I can think of no other activities more worthy of the involvement of a priest and a Jesuit. I am proud

---

At the insistence of the New England provincial of the Jesuits, he retracted almost a year later, stating, 'I withdraw those statements and any statement that could be understood to cast doubt on the church's firm condemnation of abortion—a doctrine that I today accept.' (see Schroth, *Bob Drinan*, 331).

17 Schroth, *Bob Drinan*, 121.

and honoured to be a priest and a Jesuit. As a person of faith, I must believe there is work for me to do which somehow will be more important than the work I am required to leave.[18]

Drinan confided to a young Jesuit that he was 'hurt, bitter and confused'.[19] Looking back on his congressional career, even his friends would concede that he was not always the greatest political strategist. For example, the bombing of Cambodia was not the issue on which the American people would move to impeach their president. His long time friend, House majority leader Tip O'Neill said, 'Morally, Drinan had a good case. Publicly, he's always been proud that he was the first member of Congress to file for impeachment. But politically he damn near blew it.'[20]

In 1995, I first met Robert Drinan in Johannesburg, South Africa. The US government had funded his trip there and he was giving a round of lectures on human rights. I then attended his international human rights course at Georgetown. After treating any topic, he would turn to me in a half mocking tone and ask, 'And how do you deal with this down under, in Australia?'

Initially, I thought he was an American imperialist convinced that the United States always found the best way of addressing any human rights question. While the US had the answers, the rest of us were playing catch up. But over the course of the semester, I realised that Drinan, who had travelled the globe extensively, had no preconceived notion about the best way. Much depended on the local circumstances. There were principles to espouse and to act upon in the search for any solution.

Senator Edward Kennedy and House Speaker Nancy Pelosi were the chief political mourners at his funeral. The preacher Fr John Langan SJ observed:

---

18 Schroth, *Bob Drinan*, 312.
19 Schroth, *Bob Drinan*, 313.
20 Schroth, *Bob Drinan*, 210.

Any society built on the practice of rights is not so sweetly transcendent as the holy mountain of feasting and joy which Isaiah summons up for us; it is not so intimately and delicately responsive as the virtue of charity or *agape* which St Paul commends to us. But it is essential to the realisation of the common good in a world which is marked by enormous human diversity and intermittently intense social conflict. It is a reality which protects those of us who are neither beasts nor angels from our own worst impulses and from the harms which others would do to us. It is not the realm of the best but of the imperfect good and the necessary.[21]

In her eulogy Nancy Pelosi said; 'Father Drinan lived and legislated according to the expansive view of the gospel, believing that it had something to teach about the whole range of public policy, from war and peace to poverty and justice to how we treat our children and parents. It was because of his faith that he was one of our greatest champions of human rights.'[22]

Schroth asks:

To what degree had Drinan answered the question: Can a priest successfully be an elected politician? Drinan would say yes. The pope said no. Jerome Grossman . . . says today that the answer is no—the roles are basically incompatible. Except for Drinan. He was a special case, chosen for a special mission—to stop the Vietnam War. He did a great job, said Grossman, but he should be the last of his kind.[23]

This Australian Jesuit lawyer agrees. I am one Jesuit lawyer who learnt much from Bob Drinan in his strivings to bridge the gap

---

21 John Langan, Homily, Gonzaga Church, Washington DC, 1 February 2007, at <http://americamagazine.org/issue/604/other-things/splendidly-himself>. Accessed 3 December 2014.

22 Nancy Pelosi, Eulogy for Robert Drinan, 1 February 2007, at <http://www.democraticleader.gov/newsroom/pelosi-statement-passing-father-robert-drinan/ >. Accessed 3 December 2014.

23 Schroth, *Bob Drinan*, 346.

between idealism and pragmatism—enhancing human rights and respecting human dignity in the midst of cultural, philosophical and religious diversity. He made mistakes; we all do. He was hurt and scarred in the public square; almost anyone who ventures in there is. He maintained a simple faith and a profound pride in the Jesuits; let's hope we can too.

In May 2011, Australian Catholics were treated to the early retirement of one of our most pastoral bishops, William Morris. Overseeing a large country diocese with very few and ageing priests, he knew he needed to provide for the day when there would be not enough priests to celebrate mass. He had written to the diocese indicating that several responses 'have been discussed internationally, nationally and locally' including the ordination of women and the recognition of other churches' orders. He invited discussion while remaining 'committed to actively promoting vocations to the current celibate male priesthood and open to inviting priests from overseas'. When quizzed by the media, he said he 'would ordain single or married women and married men if church policy changed'. The Vatican sent a Visitator who complied a confidential report which has never been shown to the bishop or his consultors. After visitation, all but three priests of the diocese wrote to Rome in support of Morris's pastoral leadership. So too did all the Pastoral Leaders and all members of the Diocesan Pastoral Council.

One of the unfortunate aspects of this affair is that no church official is in a position to inform the people of God about the due process which was followed, the case against the bishop, and the justice of the decisions made by curial officials leading to the recommendation made to the Pope that Morris be relieved of his office as bishop. Anyone questioning the process or decision is placed in the invidious position of being seen as one insufficiently trustful of the papacy. One can be a great defender and advocate for the papacy and still be a strong advocate for due process especially when administrative or judicial type functions by curial officials may result in a pastor being relieved his office without satisfactory explanation to his flock.

In his recent commentary on the *Regulations for the Examination of Doctrines*, Ladislas Orsy says:

The virtue of justice, as integrated with faith, hope and love among Christians, is a powerful factor in forging unity in the community. For this reason, it is never enough to do justice, it must be done publicly. The people should see that justice is done.

Of course, prudence and discretion may require some confidentiality. When it is needed, so be it. But when there are no greater values in jeopardy, openness should be the rule. A trial is never about one single individual: the accused is a member of a community of believers. Whether he is guilty or not, the community nurtured him and suffers with him. It is fair, therefore, that the community should be informed in a prudent manner.[24]

Vatican II's dogmatic constitution on the Church, *Lumen Gentium*, describes the Church as the people of God. Many of the people of God anxious to respect the human dignity of all and to ensure that the Church be as perfect a human institution as possible now think that natural justice and due process should be followed within the Church, while always maintaining the hierarchical nature of the Church and the papal primacy. Of course, there are some who question the papal primacy or the need for an ordained hierarchy, but they are not our concern here. The question for the contemporary Catholic is: can we assent to the teaching of *Lumen Gentium* without having a commitment to due process, natural justice and transparency in Church processes and structures thereby maximizing the prospect that the exercise of hierarchical power and papal primacy will be for the good of the people of God, rather than a corrosive influence on the faith and trust of the people of God?

It is no longer appropriate for Church hierarchs to claim that notions of transparency, due process and natural justice are antithetical to the hierarchical nature of the Church or to the primacy of the papacy. The primacy is not to be exercised arbitrarily or capriciously; and defenders of the Church will want to go to great lengths to ensure that the papal office is not perceived to be exercised

---

24 Orsy, *Receiving the Council*, 100.

without sufficient regard to the circumstances and evidence of a case.

The laity, the religious, the presbyterate and the bishops in some nations are sure to have a heightened twenty-first century notion of justice, transparency, and due process. This heightened notion is a gift for the contemporary Church. It is one of the works of the Spirit. The Church of the twenty-first century should be the exemplar of due process, natural justice and transparency—purifying, strengthening, elevating and ennobling these riches and customs of contemporary Western societies which are the homes and social constructs for many of the faithful, including those most directly impacted by the decision to force the early retirement of Bishop Morris.

While there can be little useful reflection and critique of the final decision of Pope Benedict to force the early retirement of Bishop Morris, there is plenty of scope to review the processes and the evidence leading to the submission of the brief for dismissal provided by curial officials to the Holy Father. Those officials acted primarily on written complaints by a small minority of the faithful and of the presbyterate of the diocese, the report of the Visitator, and the responses provided by Bishop Morris who was unable to cite the complaints or the report. There has been a resulting confusion about the pastoral effectiveness of Bishop Morris. His fellow bishops have been happy to attest publicly to his pastoral gifts. And yet Bishop Morris was led to believe that the visitator's report and the anonymous complaints alleged 'flawed' and 'defective' pastoral leadership.

Due to a lack of due process, natural justice and transparency, the papacy has been harmed, the standing of the Vatican curia has been harmed, the public standing of the Australian Catholic Bishops Conference further undermined, and the confidence of the Australian Church in the public square compromised. The Church cannot credibly proclaim a message of social justice in a pluralist democracy when its own processes fall so demonstrably short of ordinary community standards of justice.

In countries like the United States and Australia, the Church's voice in the public square risks becoming a clashing cymbal. Our fellow citizens are more interested in our actions and structures for justice, rather than our disembodied utterances. This is where a university like Scranton has an abiding mission and task. John Courtney Murray says:

> The public consensus is the property of the *studium*. This is the institution that, together with the Church, stood between the People and the Princes, the men of power who bore the responsibility of using their power in the high service of justice and freedom of the people. It is the function of the University, which has care both for the princes and the people, to see that this duty is wisely performed, chiefly by defining what justice is, and what the freedom of the people requires in changing circumstances. The University assembles these definitions and requirements into the public consensus, whereby the prince's use of his power in respect of the people may be judged, directed and corrected.[25]

Who are the persons of reason to whom both the people and the princes might look for judgment? With his characteristic lack of gender inclusiveness, Murray a man of his times answers with a kernel of eternal truth wrapped in the language of the day: 'all one can say is that they are the men who have a "care", but who are not "interested parties".'[26]

The great Sinologist Simon Leys (Pierre Rykmans) when contemplating Newman's *Idea of a University,* once called to mind Gustave Flaubert when he was writing to his friend Ivan Turgenev: 'I have always tried to live in an ivory tower; but a tide of shit is beating at its walls, threatening to undermine it.'[27] The tide of which he speaks is the torrent of abuse one receives from outside the university about its elitist character as an ivory tower and its non-

---

25 John Courtney Murray, *We Hold These Truths* (New York: Sheed and Ward, 1960), 122.

26 Murray, *We Hold These Truths,* 123.

utilitarian output. Leys thinks we should be unapologetic about our place in the ivory tower of learning:

> Democracy is the only acceptable political system; yet it pertains to politics exclusively, and has no application in any other domain. When applied anywhere else, it is death—for truth is not democratic, intelligence and talent are not democratic, nor is beauty, nor love— nor God's grace. A truly democratic education is an education that equips people intellectually to defend and promote democracy within the political world; but in its own field, education must be ruthlessly aristocratic and high-brow, shamelessly geared towards excellence.[28]

He invokes Zhuang Zi, a Daoist philosopher of the third century BC 'and one of the most profound minds of all time': 'People all know the usefulness of what is useful, but they do not know the usefulness of the useless.'[29] Leys taught Chinese studies to a previous Australian Prime Minister Kevin Rudd when he was an undergraduate. Rudd recalls that Leys stopped midsentence in class one day and asked, 'What are we doing at university?' Having heard the utilitarian responses of his students, Leys said simply, 'We are doing only two things: learning to think, and then thinking'. May the combination of *religio, mores et cultura* sustain you all here at Scranton during the forthcoming Quinn era and may this campus be a privileged place where religion and human rights walk hand in hand for the well being of persons and societies here, faraway downunder, and all places in between. Fr Kevin Quinn, I invite you to take on your mantle of university presidency recalling the words of your beloved, late President at Santa Clara, Paul Locatelli SJ: 'We must challenge the illusion of privilege and isolated individualism. We must bind ourselves emotionally and functionally to others and to the earth.'[30]

---

27 Simon Leys, *The Hall of Uselessness* (Melbourne: Black Inc, 2011), 398.

28 Leys, *The Hall of Uselessness*, 399.

29 Leys, *The Hall of Uselessness*, 399.

30 Quoted by Fr Michael McCarthy SJ in his homily at the funeral of Paul Locatelli SJ on 16 July 2010, at <http://www.scu.edu/scm/winter2010/lastgoodbye.cfm>. Accessed 3 December 2014.

Let this be a campus where religion and human rights have nothing to fear from each other, each being indispensible to truth and the dignity of all.

PART TWO
Amplifying That Still, Small, Voice
... in the World

At Bridges and Frontiers
in the Church and the World

On 16 November 2014 we marked the twenty-fifth anniversary of the assassination of the six Jesuits, their housekeeper and her daughter at the Universidad Centroamerica (UCA) in El Salvador during their dreadful civil war. I was at Boston College where we marked the event with an address by American poet Carolyn Forché who spent years in El Salvador listening to the horrific stories. She spoke about 'A Poet's Journey from El Salvador to 2014: Witness in the Light of Conscience'. She knew Fr Ignacio Ellacuria SJ, the rector of UCA who was the main target of the assassins. He taught her that 'each moment of our life shapes the whole of our life, and that we are not always responsible for what befalls us but we are certainly responsible for our response'. He spoke of the capacity to meet the moment beautifully, and in a manner that honours our deepest human aspirations.

She was a friend of the late, and hopefully soon to be canonised, Archbishop Oscar Romero. She was with him the week before he was assassinated in March 1980. This is how she told the story:

> I met with Monsignor in the kitchen of the convent of the Carmelite Missionary Sisters, where he told me gently that it was time for me to go home, as the situation had become too dangerous, and I was more needed in the United States, in the work of helping Americans to understand the struggle for justice. But I begged him to leave, as his was the first name on the death squads' lists. He seemed so calm that afternoon, tapping his fingers on the Bible he carried with him. I realised I was in the presence of a saint. 'No', he said, 'my place is with my people, and now your place is with yours.'

In the audience was Fr Donald Monan SJ who had been president of Boston College when his Jesuit brothers at his sister university were assassinated. With other Jesuit university presidents from the USA, he went to El Salvador and sat through the trial of the soldiers indicted with the killings. He spent years lobbying US congressmen to withdraw support for the unaccountable military in El Salvador, observing, 'The intellectual architects of this crime have never been publicly identified' or called to account.

When Ellacuria became rector of UCA he said that his country was 'an unjust and irrational reality that should be transformed' and that the university needed to contribute to social change: 'It does this in a university manner and with a Christian inspiration.' When Monan returned from El Salvador, he was fond of telling his students: 'We must do all we can to ensure that freedom predominates over oppression, justice over injustice, truth over falsehood, and love over hatred. If the university does not decide to make this commitment, we do not understand what validity it has as a university, much less as a Christian inspired university.'

The voice of conscience missions the believer not just for service in the Church but most especially for service in the world, not just with commitment to justice in the Church but most especially to justice in the world. This cannot be done without a commitment to laws and policies which do justice, protecting the weak and vulnerable. It is a call to take an intelligent, informed stand in solidarity. In his 2014 address to the Council of Europe, Pope Francis offered his 'heartfelt thanks for your work and for your contribution to peace in Europe through the promotion of democracy, human rights and the rule of law'. Democracy, human rights and the rule of law are not foreign to Christian faith nor hostile to Catholic tradition. Francis put a great challenge to the Europeans, the same challenge which confronts any Christian believer seeking to live in faith, hope and love:

> Throughout its history, Europe has always reached for the heights, aiming at new and ambitious goals, driven by an insatiable thirst for knowledge, development,

progress, peace and unity. But the advance of thought, culture, and scientific discovery is entirely due to the solidity of the trunk and the depth of the roots which nourish it. Once those roots are lost, the trunk slowly withers from within and the branches—once flourishing and erect—bow to the earth and fall. This is perhaps among the most baffling paradoxes for a narrowly scientific mentality: in order to progress towards the future we need the past, we need profound roots. We also need the courage not to flee from the present and its challenges. We need memory, courage, a sound and humane utopian vision.

[The twentieth-century Italian poet, Clemente] Rebora notes, on the one hand, that 'the trunk sinks its roots where it is most true'. The roots are nourished by truth, which is the sustenance, the vital lymph, of any society which would be truly free, human and fraternal. On the other hand, truth appeals to conscience, which cannot be reduced to a form of conditioning. Conscience is capable of recognising its own dignity and being open to the absolute; it thus gives rise to fundamental decisions guided by the pursuit of the good, for others and for one's self; it is itself the locus of responsible freedom.[1]

When popes speak to parliaments or to the United Nations, they demonstrate well how we can transpose our learnings in Church to service in the world. When speaking at the Reichstag, Francis's predecessor Benedict told his countrymen:

For most of the matters that need to be regulated by law, the support of the majority can serve as a sufficient criterion. Yet it is evident that for the fundamental issues of law, in which the dignity of man and of humanity is at

---

1.   Pope Francis, Address to Council of Europe, 25 November 2014 at
     <http://w2.vatican.va/content/francesco/en/speeches/2014/november/documents/
     papa-francesco_20141125_strasburgo-consiglio-europa.html>. Accessed 3 December
     2014.

stake, the majority principle is not enough: everyone in a position of responsibility must personally seek out the criteria to be followed when framing laws.[2]

He went on to say:

> Unlike other great religions, Christianity has never proposed a revealed law to the State and to society, that is to say a juridical order derived from revelation. Instead, it has pointed to nature and reason as the true sources of law—and to the harmony of objective and subjective reason, which naturally presupposes that both spheres are rooted in the creative reason of God.

Benedict then joined issue with the positivist mindset: 'Where positivist reason dominates the field to the exclusion of all else—and that is broadly the case in our public mindset—then the classical sources of knowledge for ethics and law are excluded.' He provided this arresting image of the positivist mindset:

> In its self-proclaimed exclusivity, the positivist reason which recognises nothing beyond mere functionality resembles a concrete bunker with no windows, in which we ourselves provide lighting and atmospheric conditions, being no longer willing to obtain either from God's wide world. And yet we cannot hide from ourselves the fact that even in this artificial world, we are still covertly drawing upon God's raw materials, which we refashion into our own products. The windows must be flung open again, we must see the wide world, the sky and the earth once more and learn to make proper use of all this.

When chairing the National Human Rights Consultation, I arrived in Kalgoorlie, Western Australia for a community

---

2. Pope Benedict XVI, Address to Reichstag, 22 September 2011 at <http://www.vatican.va/holy_father/benedict_xvi/speeches/2011/september/documents/hf_ben-xvi_spe_20110922_reichstag-berlin_en.html>. Accessed 3 December 2014.

consultation accompanied by lawyers and secretariat staff from the Commonwealth Attorney-General's Department. We were to hold a community consultation on human rights at the race track on the afternoon of 12 May 2009. That morning we learnt that many people were gathered at the local courthouse for the resumed coronial inquiry into the death of Ian Ward who had died of heartstroke in the Kalgoorlie Hospital on 27 January 2008. I thought it best that we visit the court in the morning to get a sense of the human rights issues occupying the local community. I insisted that all members of the secretariat keep out of the public eye. On arrival, we encountered an Aboriginal protest outside the courthouse. There was a bevy of media on hand including the Australian national broadcaster's ABC *4 Corners* crew.

Walking towards the courthouse, I heard a cry, 'Hey, Father Frank, over here! You've got to support us mob'. Looking around I saw Ben Taylor, an old Aboriginal friend from Perth whom I had long known in the local Aboriginal Catholic Ministry. He was often accompanying Fr Bryan Tiernan on visits to Aborigines in jail and to Aboriginal families in need around Perth. I was torn. What should I do? I was chairing a national consultation at the request of the Commonwealth Government. I did not want to politicise our presence in town. And I did not want to end up on television or in the newspapers in relation to a much publicised coronial inquiry I knew little about. But then again, I did not want to abandon Ben and his colleagues in their hour of need. I walked across to the group of grieving relatives who were surrounded by protesters including Ben. They all stood in front of an Aboriginal flag. Some were crying out for justice for their deceased loved one. Ben was holding a simple placard which read, 'White Australia has a black history'. I stood with the group, in silence, in solidarity. I then accompanied Ben into the back of the courtroom where we heard the appalling testimony about the last hours of Ian Ward, a respected Aboriginal community leader, an artist, and a traditional owner. He had been picked up for drink driving in Laverton on Australia Day. He was denied bail. He was being transported into Kalgoorlie in the back pod of a prison vehicle. Alistair Hope, the State Coroner found:

> The deceased was transported in the vehicle from Laverton to Kalgoorlie, a distance of approximately 360 kilometres. The deceased was taken on a journey of approximately 3 hours and 45 minutes on an extremely hot day with the outside temperatures being over 40 degrees centigrade.[3]

The air conditioning for the pod was not working. There was very little ventilation in the pod. It had no windows and only very limited airflow.

The Coroner was to find that 'the deceased suffered a terrible death while in custody which was wholly unnecessary and avoidable'.[4] He found that 'the quality of the supervision, treatment and care of the deceased in the hours before his death was disgracefully bad'.[5] He agreed with the prison administrator that the vehicle 'was not fit for humans to be transported in' and that the use of the pod for long distance travel was inhumane. Ian Ward died because of the inhumane way in which he had been transported in suffocating heat.

After hearing some of this evidence, I and my secretariat proceeded to the racetrack for our community consultation on human rights. It was a tame meeting, carrying none of the pathos, anger or disgust of the morning's coronial inquiry. Next morning, I flew from Kalgoorlie to Perth. Next to me sat a lady reading her morning newspaper featuring a photo of the Aboriginal protest outside the courthouse. There was an unmistakable 6'4" white male with them—Fr Frank Brennan. I hoped this would not jeopardise our inquiry. I was pleased to have stood in solidarity with the grieving Aboriginal protesters at the request of my friend Ben. What else could I do? A photo of the protest features on the cover of this book, the same photo judged unacceptable for publication in the report of the National Human Rights Consultation.

---

3   Western Australia Coroner, *Inquest into the Death of Ian Ward* at <http://www.abc.net.au/4corners/special_eds/20090615/ward/ward_finding.pdf>, 3-4. Accessed 3 December 2014.
4   Western Australia Coroner, *Inquest into the Death of Ian Ward*, 5.
5   Western Australia Coroner, *Inquest into the Death of Ian Ward*, 130.

It is now time to consider how in the light of Christian faith and Catholic tradition, the conscientious citizen might amplify that still, small voice in the world. It is time to fling open the windows so that people like Ian Ward might live in justice and peace.

PART THREE
Amplifying That Still, Small, Voice
... in the World

7

Pursuing Human Rights

In 2008–9, I chaired the National Human Rights Consultation established by the Rudd Government. I had long been a fence sitter about the idea of Australia having a national Human Rights Act or Bill of Rights. I had the opportunity to hear first hand from thousands of Australians. After our report was tabled, I addressed various groups about the practical outcomes of the inquiry. This was my address to judges gathered for the 2013 Judicial Conference of Australia Colloquium.

I was privileged to chair the 2009 National Human Rights Consultation with a committee—Mary Kostakidis, Mick Palmer and Tammy Williams, assisted by Philip Flood—with diverse views about how best to protect human rights in Australia. Our report and very detailed appendices are available on the website of the Commonwealth Attorney-General's Department.[1] The Murdoch press was fond of portraying us as a group of likeminded lefties. The diversity of our views however ensured the transparency and integrity of our processes, especially given that we did not reach agreement on our recommendations about a Human Rights Act until five minutes to midnight.

As chair, I was on the record favouring a modest statutory human rights act. But our individual opinions were irrelevant to the task at hand, which was to conduct a public consultation on three questions posed in our terms of reference:

1. See <http://www.ag.gov.au/RightsAndProtections/HumanRights/ TreatyBodyReporting/Pages/HumanRightsconsultationreport.aspx> Accessed 3 December 2014.

Which human rights (including corresponding
responsibilities) should be protected and promoted?
Are these human rights currently sufficiently protected
and promoted?
How could Australia better protect and promote human
rights?

We were asked to identify options that would preserve the sovereignty
of parliament and not include a constitutionally entrenched bill
of rights. In seeking the views of the Australian public on these
questions, we made use of new technologies, conducted community
consultations and received tens of thousands of submissions. I ran
a Facebook page. We hosted a blog and commissioned academics
on opposite sides of the argument to steer the blog debate. We held
three days of hearings which were broadcast on the new Australian
Public Affairs Channel. During the course of our consultation,
various groups ran campaigns for and against a Human Rights Act
in the wake of Australia's ongoing exceptionalism, Australia being
the only remaining country in the British common law tradition
without some form of Human Rights Act. Groups like GetUp! and
Amnesty International ran strong campaigns in favour of a Human
Rights Act, accounting for 25,000 of the 35,000 submissions we
received. My committee did not see itself as having the competence
or authority to distinguish campaign generated submissions from
other submissions. We simply decided to publish the figures and let
people make their own assessments.

   We engaged a social research firm, Colmar Brunton, to run focus
groups and administer a detailed random telephone poll of 1200
persons. The poll highlighted the issues of greatest concern to the
Australian community:[2]

---

2.   Colmar Brunton Social Research, Final Report, National Human Rights Consultation
     – Community Research Phase, September 2009, 40338, 17 at
     <http://www.ag.gov.au/RightsAndProtections/HumanRights/TreatyBodyReporting/
     Documents/NHRCR-AppendixBReport.pdf>. Accessed 3 December 2014.

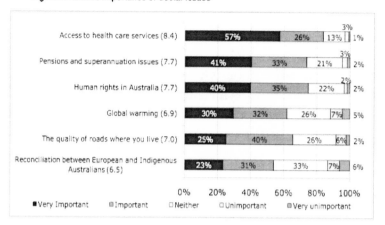

Figure 1. Relative Importance of Social Issues

At community roundtables, participants were asked what prompted them to attend. Some civic-minded individuals simply wanted the opportunity to attend a genuine exercise in participative democracy; they wanted information just as much as they wanted to share their views. Many participants were people with grievances about government service delivery or particular government policies. Some had suffered at the hands of a government department or at least knew someone who had been adversely affected—a homeless person, an aged relative in care, a close family member with mental illness, or a neighbour with disabilities. Others were responding to invitations to involve themselves in campaigns that had been instigated when the Consultation was launched. Against the backdrop of these campaigns, the Committee heard from many people who claimed no legal or political expertise in relation to the desirability or otherwise of any particular law; they simply wanted to know that Australia would continue to play its role as a valued contributor to the international community while pragmatically dealing with problems at home.

Outside the capital cities and large urban centres, the community roundtables tended to focus on local concerns, and there was limited use of 'human rights' language. People were more comfortable talking about the fair go, wanting to know what constitutes fair service delivery for small populations in far-flung places. At Mintabie in outback South Australia, a quarter of the town's population turned out, upset by the recent closure of their health clinic. At Santa Teresa in the red centre, Aboriginal residents asked me how I would feel if the government required that I place a notice banning pornography on the front door of my house. They thought that was the equivalent of the government erecting the 'Prescribed Area' sign at the entrance to their community. In Charleville, western Queensland, the local doctor described the financial hardship endured by citizens who need to travel 600 km by bus to Toowoomba for routine specialist care.

The Committee learnt that economic, social and cultural rights are important to the Australian community, and the way they are protected and promoted has a big impact on the lives of many. The most basic economic and social rights—the rights to the highest attainable standard of health, to housing and to education—matter most to Australians, and they matter most because they are the rights at greatest risk, especially for vulnerable groups in the community.

Which Rights To Protect?

The community roundtables bore out the finding of Colmar Brunton Social Research's 15 focus groups that the community regards the following rights as unconditional and not to be limited:

- basic amenities—water, food, clothing and shelter
- essential health care
- equitable access to justice
- freedom of speech
- freedom of religious expression
- freedom from discrimination
- personal safety
- education.

Many of the more detailed submissions presented to the committee argued that all the rights detailed in the primary international instruments Australia has ratified without reservation should be protected and promoted. Most often mentioned were the *International Covenant on Civil and Political Rights 1966* and the *International Covenant on Economic, Social and Cultural Rights 1966*, which, along with the *Universal Declaration of Human Rights 1948*, constitute the 'International Bill of Rights'.

Some submissions also included the *International Convention on the Elimination of All Forms of Racial Discrimination 1965*, the *Convention on the Elimination of All Forms of Discrimination against Women 1979*, the *Convention against Torture and Other Cruel, Inhuman and Degrading Treatment or Punishment 1984*, the *Convention on the Rights of the Child 1989*, and the *Convention on the Rights of Persons with Disabilities 2006*.

Having ratified these seven important human rights treaties, Australia has voluntarily undertaken to protect and promote the rights listed in them. This was a tension for us in answering the first question. Many roundtable participants and submission makers spoke from their own experience, highlighting those rights most under threat for them or for those in their circle. Others provided us with a more theoretical approach, arguing that all Australia's international human rights obligations should be complied with.

True to what we heard from the grassroots, we singled out three key economic and social rights for immediate enhanced attention by the Australian Human Rights Commission—the rights to health, education, and housing. We thought that government departments should be attentive to the progressive realization of these rights, within the constraints of what is economically deliverable. However, in light of advice received from the solicitor-general, we did not think the courts could have a role to play in the progressive realisation of these rights.

We recommended that the federal government operate on the assumption that, unless it has entered a formal reservation in relation to a particular right, any right listed in the seven international human rights treaties should be protected and promoted.

Is There Sufficient Protection Now?

Colmar Brunton Social Research found that only ten per cent of people reported that they had ever had their rights infringed in any way, while another ten per cent reported that someone close to them had had their rights infringed. Ten per cent is a good figure, but only the most naively patriotic would invoke it as a plea for the complacent status quo. The consultants reported that the bulk of participants in focus groups had very limited knowledge of human rights. Sixty-four per cent of survey respondents agreed that human rights in Australia are adequately protected; only seven per cent disagreed; the remaining twenty-nine per cent were uncommitted.[3]

A total of 8671 submissions expressed a view on the adequacy or inadequacy of the present system. Of these, 2551 thought human rights were adequately protected, whereas 6120 (seventy per cent) thought they were not.

One of the challenges in conducting a public consultation is that respondents with limited education in law and jurisprudence might express internally inconsistent views. We found this to be the case when asking people how best to balance individual rights and the public interest. A majority espoused both that the rights of individuals should always prevail and that public safety and security should always prevail.

There is enormous diversity in the community when it comes to understanding of rights protection. Though two thirds of those who participated in the random survey thought human rights were adequately protected in Australia, over seventy per cent identified three groups in the community whose rights were in need of greater protection.

---

3.   Colmar Brunton, *Final Report*, 6.

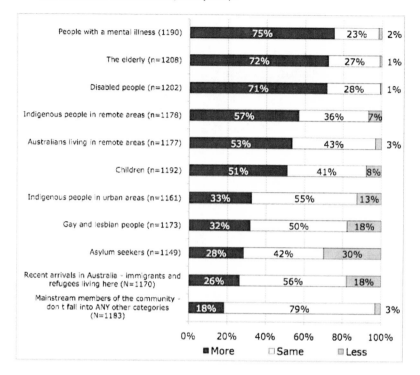

Figure E8. Amount of Protection Required By Groups

The majority of those surveyed also saw a need for better protection of the human rights of those living in remote rural areas. The near equal division of the survey groups when it comes to the treatment of asylum seekers highlights why this issue recurs at Australian elections.

How Can Protection And Promotion Of Human Rights Be Improved?

The committee commissioned The Allen Consulting Group to conduct cost–benefit analyses of a selection of options proposed during the Consultation for the better protection and promotion of human rights in Australia. The consultants developed a set of three criteria against which the potential effects of various options were assessed—benefits to stakeholders, implementation costs and timeliness, and risks. The options evaluated were a Human Rights Act, human rights education, a parliamentary scrutiny committee for human rights, an augmented role for the Australian Human Rights Commission, review and consolidation of anti-discrimination laws, a new National Action Plan for human rights, and maintaining the status quo.

This cost-benefit exercise was our most problematic task. Given the 2013 decision of the federal government to drop a proposed consolidation of anti-discrimination laws, it is salutary to revisit the consultancy report's finding:

> The introduction of consolidated anti-discrimination legislation may pose a risk in terms of future resourcing and the potential for an increase in litigation. However, new legislation does not pose a risk to parliamentary sovereignty and is likely to be strongly supported by the community.[4]

We put forward three tranches of measures to be considered for further protecting and enhancing human rights. I will deal with them in ascending order of controversy and in descending order of broad community endorsement. The government ultimately implemented those measures winning the broadest community endorsement while deciding not to enact a Human Rights Act which, though supported by the majority of people consulted, was supported less strongly than other options.

---

4. The Allen Consulting Group, Analysis of Options Identified During the National Human Rights Consultation, Final Summary Report, September 2009, 20 at <http:// www.ag.gov.au/RightsAndProtections/HumanRights/TreatyBodyReporting/ Documents/NHRCR-AppendixD.pdf>. Accessed 3 December 2014.

Table E10. Most preferred protection option

Option	Most preferred
Parliament to pay attention to human rights when making laws	29%
More human rights education	23%
More Government attention to human rights when developing laws and policies	18%
A statement of principles available to everyone	11%
Legislation by Federal Parliament	10%
None of these	*8%*

Education and culture

At many community roundtables, participants said they didn't know what their rights were and didn't even know where to find them. When reference was made to the affirmation made by new citizens pledging loyalty to Australia and its people, 'whose rights and liberties I respect', many participants confessed they would be unable to tell the inquiring new citizen what those rights and liberties were and would not even be able to tell them where to look to find out. In the report, we noted the observation of historian John Hirst 'that human rights are not enough, that if rights are to be protected there must be a community in which people care about each other's rights'. It is necessary to educate the culturally diverse Australian community about the rights all Australians are entitled to enjoy. 81% of people surveyed by Colmar Brunton said they would support increased human rights education for children and adults as a way of better protecting human rights in Australia.

At community roundtables there were consistent calls for better education. Of the 3914 submissions that considered specific reform options, 1197 dealt with the need for human rights education and the creation of a better human rights culture. This was the most frequent reform option raised. While 45% of respondents in the opinion survey agreed that 'people in Australia are sufficiently educated about their rights', Colmar Brunton concluded:

> There is strong support for more education and the better promotion of human rights in Australia. It was apparent

that few people have any specific understanding of what rights they do have, underlining a real need as well as a perceived need for further education.[5]

The Committee's recommendation that a readily comprehensible list of Australian rights and responsibilities be published and translated into various community languages follows from Colmar Brunton's finding that there was 'generally more support for a document outlining rights than for a formal piece of legislation *per se*'. There was wide support for this idea in the focus groups, and 72% of those surveyed thought it was important to have access to a document defining their rights. More significantly, Colmar Brunton found:

> Many participants were sceptical about the practical value of any legislation, but felt that it at least created a common starting point which people could refer to.
> The Devolved Consultation phase (a set of discussions with vulnerable and marginalised groups in the community, and the bodies that represent and service them) also showed a very strong desire for there to be a formal documentation of rights to which people and organisations could refer.[6]

Sixty one per cent of people surveyed supported 'a non-legally binding statement of human rights principles issued by the Federal Parliament and available to all people and organisations in Australia'. We recommended a readily comprehensible list of Australian rights and responsibilities.[7]

---

5. Colmar Brunton, *Final Report*, 10.
6. Colmar Brunton, *Final Report*, 6.
7. Colmar Brunton, *Final Report*, 10.

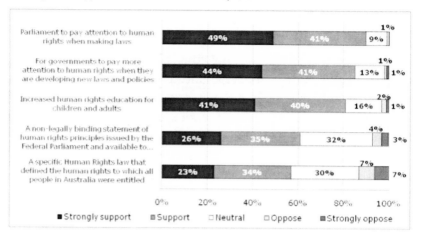

Figure E9. Support Levels for Various Protection Options

During the course of our public consultation, the Murdoch press made a strong claim that existing protections for human rights were adequate and that the occasional shortfall could be rectified by the investigative journalism of credible broadsheets such as their masthead *The Australian*. The public did not share this view:[8]

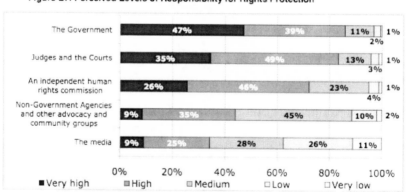

Figure E7. Perceived Levels of Responsibility for Rights Protection

---

8. Colmar Brunton, *Final Report*, 7.

More government attention

The second tranche of proposals for enhancing human rights protection included recommendations for ensuring that commonwealth public authorities could be more attentive to human rights when delivering services and for guaranteeing compliance of commonwealth laws with Australia's voluntarily assumed human rights obligations. We recommended that the Human Rights Commission have much the same role in hearing complaints of human rights violations by commonwealth agencies as it presently has in relation to complaints of unlawful discrimination.

We also recommended an audit of all past commonwealth laws so that government might consider introducing amendments to parliament to ensure human rights compliance, that all future commonwealth bills be accompanied by a statement of human rights compatibility, and that there be a parliamentary committee which routinely reviews bills for such compliance. These measures are fully respectful of parliamentary sovereignty yet are stronger than other models where parliament is able to receive the parliamentary committee report on human rights violations long after the legislation has been passed. We saw no point in window dressing procedures which close the gate only once the horse has bolted.

A Human Rights Act?

The third tranche of our recommendations related to a Human Rights Act. Many Australians would like to see national government take more notice of human rights as they draft laws and make policies. The majority of those attending community roundtables favoured a Human Rights Act, and eighty-seven per cent of those who presented submissions to the Committee and expressed a view on the question supported such an Act. In the national telephone survey, fifty-seven per cent expressed support for a Human Rights Act, thirty per cent were neutral, and only fourteen per cent were opposed.

Our committee did recommend a Human Rights Act which would grant judges the power to interpret commonwealth laws consistent with human rights, provided that interpretation was always consistent with the purpose of the legislation being interpreted. This power would be more restrictive than the power granted to judges in the United Kingdom where parliament has been happy to give judges a stronger power of interpretation because a failed litigant there can always seek relief in Strasbourg before the European Court of Human Rights. Understandably, the English would prefer to have their own judges reach ultimate decisions on these matters, rather than leaving them to European judges. We have no such regional arrangement in Australia.

An Act would give a person claiming that a commonwealth agency had breached their human rights the right to bring an action in court. For example, a citizen disaffected with the commonwealth government's welfare agency, Centrelink, might claim that their right to privacy has been infringed. The court would be required to interpret the relevant Centrelink legislation in accordance with the Human Rights Act. The court might find that Centrelink was acting beyond power, infringing the right to privacy or alternatively, that Centrelink was acting lawfully but that the interference with the right to privacy was not justified in a free and democratic society. It would then be a matter for the parliamentary committee on human rights to decide whether to review the law and recommend some amendment. Ultimately, it would be a decision for the responsible minister and the government as to whether the law should be amended. The sovereignty of parliament would be assured.

Consistent with international human rights law, I acknowledged that economic and social rights such as the rights to health, education and housing are to be progressively realised. Nothing in our recommendations would allow a citizen or non-citizen to go to court claiming a right to health, education or housing. The progressive realization of these rights would be a matter for government and the Human Rights Commission in dialogue. We recommended that some civil and political rights such as the right to life, precluding the death penalty, protection from slavery, torture and cruel and degrading treatment be non-derogable and absolute. Such rights cannot be suspended or limited, even in times of emergency.

Some will argue that there is no prospect of these rights being infringed in Australia, so why bother to legislate for them? The facts that any infringement of these rights would be indefensible and that most Australians hold such rights as sacrosanct created a strong case, in the opinion of the committee, for these rights being guaranteed by commonwealth law.

Most civil and political rights can be limited in the public interest or for the common good or to accommodate the conflicting rights of others. Nowadays the limit on such rights is usually determined by inquiring what is demonstrably justified in a free and democratic society. Under the dialogue model we proposed, courts could express a contrary view. But ultimately it would always be parliament's call. This makes it a very different situation from the US where, under a constitutional model, judges have the final say.

Some politicians have said that they or their colleagues would be too timid to express a view contrary to the judges and thus the judges in effect would have the last word on what limits on rights are demonstrably justified in a free and democratic society. Such timidity is not my experience of Australian politicians. After all, if the contest is about what is justified in a free and democratic society, who is better placed than an elected politician to claim that they know the country's democratic pulse on the legitimate limit on any right?

One of the complex legal questions my committee had to face was whether declarations of incompatibility by a court would be constitutional. We did have an opinion from the Solicitor General (published as an appendix in the Report, after some negotiation within the Attorney-General's Department) advising that they would be constitutional, but that was not the end of the matter. After considering all the complications, our recommendation on 'declarations of incompatibility' read: 'The Committee recommends that any federal Human Rights Act extend only to the High Court the power to make a declaration of incompatibility. (Should this recommendation prove impractical, the Committee recommends alternatively that any federal Human Rights Act not extend to courts the formal power to make a declaration of incompatibility.)'[9]

In the alternative to court declarations we proposed that 'the parties to the proceedings, and perhaps the Australian Human Rights Commission, could be given the power to notify the Joint (Parliamentary) Committee on Human Rights of the outcome of litigation and the court's reasoning indicating non-compliance of a Commonwealth law with the Human Rights Act. It would then be a matter for members of parliament themselves to trigger the processes of the Joint Committee, which could seek the Attorney-General's response.'[10]

After the High Court's decision in *Momcilovic* which dealt with the complications of the Victorian *Charter of Human Rights and Responsibilities Act 2006*,[11] Professor Helen Irving, a long time critic of Human Rights Acts, wrote: 'At the heart of (the Brennan Committee's) recommendations was the adoption of a Commonwealth Human Rights Act empowering the High Court to make "declarations of incompatibility" between a law and a right, as in the Victorian Charter . . . The model proposed by the Brennan committee was unconstitutional.'[12] This was a drastic and misleading misrepresentation of our nuanced position. Some of those we consulted during our inquiry warned that a decision such as *Momcilovic* was on the cards.

An Act empowering the High Court to make such declarations was 'at the heart' of our recommendations only in the sense that our recommendations could have stood without the body of the Act including the heart of court declarations. In the alternative to

---

9. Recommendation 29, National Human Rights Consultation, *Report* (Canberra: Attorney-General's Department, 2009), xxxvii.
10. National Human Rights Consultation, *Report*, 375.
11. *Momcilovic v The Queen* [2011] HCA 34.
12. Helen Irving, 'The High Court of Australia Kills Dialogue Model of Human Rights', *The Australian*, 16 September 2011.

court declarations we proposed what Irving would have to class a heartless body: that 'the parties to the proceedings, and perhaps the Australian Human Rights Commission, could be given the power to notify the Joint (Parliamentary) Committee on Human Rights of the outcome of litigation and the court's reasoning indicating non-compliance of a Commonwealth law with the Human Rights Act. It would then be a matter for members of parliament themselves to trigger the processes of the Joint Committee, which could seek the Attorney-General's response.'[13]

Yes, we followed the solicitor general's advice on constitutionality of 'declarations of incompatibility'. But we thought they might be so problematic and impractical that it might be wiser to do without them.

Government Response

Our elected leaders were able to adopt many of the recommendations in our report without deciding to grant judges any additional power to scrutinise the actions of public servants or to interpret laws in a manner consistent with human rights. In future, they could decide to take the extra step, engaging the courts as the guarantor that politicians and the public service will be kept accountable in respecting, protecting and promoting the human rights of all Australians. Our report sets out how this could best be done— faithful to what we heard, respectful of the sovereignty of parliament, and true to the Australian ideals of dignity and a fair go for all.

In the section of our report dealing with a Human Rights Act, we set out previous attempts to legislate for an Act in Australia and analysed why those attempts failed. We also gave an overview of the statutory models in New Zealand, the UK, Victoria and the Australian Capital Territory. We followed this with a dispassionate statement of the case both for and against an Act. Finally we outlined the range of 'bells and whistles' that could be included in any Human Rights Act. This part of our report stands alone as a useful

---

13. National Human Rights Consultation, *Report*, 375.

resource for anyone undecided about the usefulness or desirability of a Human Rights Act. The intended reader is the person who is agnostic about this question, not altogether convinced of the social worth of lawyers, wanting bang for the buck with social inclusion and protection of the vulnerable in society.

Government decided to put a Human Rights Act on the long finger. But they did legislate to provide for statements of compatibility and for a parliamentary committee on Human Rights, in the *Human Rights (Parliamentary Scrutiny) Act 2011* which came into effect in early 2012. Parliament appointed a ten member Parliamentary Committee on Human Rights which is required to examine bills and legislative instruments 'for compatibility with human rights'. The Committee may also examine existing Acts and inquire into any matter relating to human rights referred to it by the Attorney-General. 'Human rights' are defined to mean 'the rights and freedoms recognised or declared' by the seven key international human rights instruments on civil and political rights, economic, social and cultural rights, racial discrimination, torture and other cruel inhuman or degrading treatment, including the Conventions on women, children and persons with disabilities. Anyone introducing a Bill or legislative instrument to Parliament is required to provide 'a statement of compatibility' which must include an assessment of whether the Bill (or instrument) is compatible with human rights.

The Parliamentary Joint Committee on Human Rights presented eighteen reports to the 43rd Parliament. On 2 December 2014, it presented its seventeenth report to the new parliament which has been in session only one year. Professor Andrew Byrnes has been a much valued external consultant to the committee. The committee has conducted some very detailed inquiries into quite controversial legislative areas. For example, the committee did not baulk at conducting a detailed human rights audit of the *Migration Legislation Amendment (Regional Processing and Other Measures) Act 2012* and the *Stronger Futures in the Northern Territory Act 2012*. Speaking for Harry Jenkins, the robust first Chair of the Committee, Senator Ursula Stephens, also then a member of the committee explained the committee's role to the 2013 Australian Government and Non-Government Organisations Forum on Human Rights:

> A key role of this committee is to assist the Parliament and encourage departments and agencies to consider human rights in a more systematic, rigorous and consistent way. From the beginning, we recognised that this would be an evolutionary process as we all came to grips with the meaning and scope of Australia's human rights obligations and how to apply these obligations in our work.
>
> At the same time we came to appreciate that the committee was not intended to be a quasi-judicial body. The committee recognises that if we are to encourage our fellow parliamentarians, and hundreds of public servants, to become engaged in the consideration of human rights, we must try to interpret rights in a way that makes them real and effective.
>
> At the same time, the committee's deliberations must be underpinned by a sound understanding of the human rights principles engaged by legislation and a robust interpretation of Australia's human rights obligations as expressed in the seven human rights treaties.

By June 2013, the committee had considered 272 bills and 1774 legislative instruments, having also sought further information in relation to 111 bills and 54 instruments. The committee sent advisory letters in relation to a further 456 instruments where the statements of compatibility had fallen short of the committee's expectations. These statistics indicate that the committee is a useful addition to the legislative process enhancing the prospect of human rights compliance without the need for judicial intervention.

So at a national level, neither the executive nor the legislature can escape the dialogue about legislation's compliance with UN human rights standards. Neither can the courts, because of the provisions of the *Acts Interpretation Act* which make reports of the Parliamentary Committee on Human Rights and statements of compatibility relevant in court proceedings determining the meaning of new commonwealth statutes which impinge on internationally recognised human rights and freedoms.

Ultimately Australia will require a *Human Rights Act* to set workable limits on how far ajar the door of human rights protection should be opened by the judges in dialogue with the politicians. We will now have a few years of the door flapping in the Canberra breeze as public servants decide how much content to put in the statements of compatibility, as parliamentarians decide how much public access and transparency to accord the new committee processes, and as judges feel their way in interpreting the laws. There is no turning back from the federal dialogue model of human rights protection.

Six years on from our report and four years into the operation of the new federal human rights framework, the National Human Rights Consultation is still perceived as a failed attempt to enact a federal Human Rights Act. It was nothing of the sort. The committee was faithful to its public trust in providing government and the parliament with accurate information about community perceptions on the protection of human rights. The government responded by adopting the three most popular remedies for enhancing human rights protection: human rights education; statements of compatibility from the Executive; and a parliamentary committee for human rights. The human rights education campaign has now run its course. The new Abbott Government has not indicated any intention to scrap statements of compatibility or the parliamentary committee. When appearing before UN human rights committees, the Abbott Government, like its Labor predecessor, regularly invokes the new parliamentary scrutiny measures with approval and in defence of Australia's commitment to human rights without a Human Rights Act. There is every indication that most Australians are content with this ongoing Australian exceptionalism. It remains to be seen if the new measures are sufficiently robust.

8

Insisting on the Separation of Powers

In 1984, I published my first book Too Much Order with Too Little Law. *It was a study of the street march bans instituted in Queensland by Sir Joh Bjelke-Petersen. I found there was insufficient respect in Queensland for the separation of powers between the Executive government, parliament and the judiciary. Thirty years later, some of the same issues were being debated in Queensland after the election of Campbell Newman's government. In February 2014, I spoke at the annual dinner of the Queensland Law Society against the backdrop of considerable tension between the Executive and the judiciary, amongst speculation that the government was considering the appointment of a new Chief Justice who would be seen to be more accommodating of government. Following that speculation, there was a very bungled government announcement of the appointment of Tim Carmody as the new Chief Justice. Having accepted a longstanding invitation to address the Queensland Council for Civil Liberties on 8 July 2014, I found that I was speaking on the very day of Chief Justice Carmody's swearing in. In January 2015, Campbell Newman's government was voted out of office.*

During this NAIDOC Week, I join with you in acknowledging the traditional owners of the land on which we meet. In doing so, I note that before *Mabo* such an acknowledgement was rare. But since then community attitudes have been informed by the thinking of our High Court which in developing and applying the common law found that Aboriginal Australians had title to land which pre-existed the assertion of sovereignty by the British Crown and which survived that assertion. That is the firmer legal and social foundation for our relating nowadays. It's great to have the opportunity to address you here in the Irish Club, the hearth of those Queenslanders with Irish heritage. Like many of you, I am a descendant from Irish migrants who came here in search of a better life.

I have been asked to address the Council on the comparison between the situation as described in my book *Too Much Order with Too Little Law* and the current developments in Queensland. I have also been asked to comment on the need for a Human Rights Act in this context. I am delighted to be here in Brisbane on the day that your new Chief Justice has been sworn in privately without an official welcome in the Supreme Court. These are difficult times for all Queensland lawyers, including your new Chief Justice, Tim Carmody. These are difficult times for the rule of law here in Queensland. I had cause to reflect on these difficulties a while ago when reading the news of Stephen Keim SC and the complications of his having been offered a government brief in a politically uncontroversial matter in an area of law in which he is known to be expert. Stephen and I first got to know each other when we started secondary school sharing a dormitory in Toowoomba almost a lifetime ago. I have therefore long had cause to watch his career as an independent counsel of the Queensland Bar. On withdrawal of the brief without coherent explanation, I contacted him with a reminiscence.

Forty-three years ago there was a state of emergency declared in this city while an all white Springbok rugby team played against the Wallabies. I was a first year law student at the University of Queensland at the time. On 2 August 1971, the Vice President of the Queensland Bar published a letter in *The Australian* saying:

> The contemporary discussion of law and order has been overlaid with other issues: apartheid and football (as to which there is little disagreement), politics and protest (as to which there will always be disagreement). The fact remains that law and order are essential to a civilised

community . . . When legitimate protest degenerates into unlawful disruption, governments are invited to assume powers of doubtful legality, and to condone unlawful actions by police. When governments do not exercise their powers honestly and fairly and with statesmanship, they invite disruptive expressions of protest. In either case both the rulers and the ruled attack the concept of law and order. Is it not time for both to examine their consciences?

When attending the Bar common room for lunch that day, a senior silk told the Vice President that there was now no prospect of his ever being a judge. That Vice President happened to be my father. Recently a 1973 letter has come to light from Chief Justice Sir Garfield Barwick to Prime Minister Gough Whitlam suggesting eight possible future appointees to the High Court.[1] My father was the only Queenslander on the list, and at a time even before his presidency of the bar here, aged just forty-five. He did end up a judge—being appointed twice by the Fraser government and finally to the chief justiceship by the Keating government. There is a place for conscience and courage in the law, especially when the prevailing political orthodoxy of those who exercise legislative or executive power is contrary to one's deeply considered assessment of human rights and human dignity.

As Chief Justice, Sir Gerard Brennan when speaking at Bond University had cause to observe:

> Montesquieu had pointed out that 'there is no liberty, if the power of judgment be not separated from the legislative and executive powers'. Hamilton, following Montesquieu, described an independent Judiciary as 'the best expedient which can be devised in any government to secure a steady, upright, and impartial administration of the laws'. In this country, the separation of judicial from legislative and executive

---

1.   Letter by Sir Garfield Barwick to Gough Whitlam, 14 September 1973.

power and the separation of the judges from political activity have been rigorously maintained by the High Court. The separation of the political powers from the judicial power and the repositories of those respective powers from one another guarantees not only the independence of the Judiciary but the appropriate responsibility for the exercise of those powers.[2]

He went on to explain:

Responsibility for the state of the law and its implementation must rest with the branches of government that are politically accountable to the people. The people can bring influence to bear on the legislature and the executive to procure compliance with the popular will. But a clamour for a popular decision must fall on deaf judicial ears. The Judiciary are not politically accountable. The Courts cannot temper the true application of the law to satisfy popular sentiment. The Courts are bound to a correct application of the law, whether or not that leads to a popular decision in a particular case and whether or not the decision accords with executive policy.

The second last time there was a new Supreme Court building opened in this city was September 1981. The then Chief Justice Sir Charles Wanstall reflected:

[King] James regarded himself in authoritarian terms as the embodiment of the Divine Right to dictate, but his Chief Justice, Lord Edward Coke, boldly responded to this assertion in words that have become immortal: 'Sire, you are under God and the law.' And so commenced the struggle for the independence of the judges that was won in England in 1701, when the Act

2.　Sir Gerard Brennan, 'The Parliament, The Executive And The Courts: Roles And Immunities', School Of Law, Bond University, 21 February 1998, at <http://www.hcourt.gov.au/assets/publications/speeches/former-justices/brennanj/ brennanj_bond2.htm>. Accessed 3 December 2014.

of Settlement finally established it. Today, the people of Queensland, the inheritors of that fundamental and priceless constitutional principle, will recognise in this simple ceremony its symbolic restatement as their enduring right.[3]

Last time a new Supreme Court building was opened in this city, your now newly retired Chief Justice Paul de Jersey recalled these words of his predecessor on receiving the key to the court from the Attorney-General. The Chief Justice then said, 'This symbolic act thereby emphasizes the independence of the judiciary from the other branches of State authority, the legislature and the executive.'[4]

Back in 1981, there had been controversy here in Queensland, as there has been recently, about the exercise of executive and judicial power. The then governor was not a lawyer, but a very savvy Navy Commodore, Sir James Ramsay. Opening what proved to be a very unsatisfactory court building, he very satisfactorily stated the relevant principle:

> We, in this country today, can be grateful that our predecessors, the colonisers of this land, brought with them and instituted the practices of English law. For it is a dynamic system. It can, and must, and will evolve to solve and meet the changes in social, industrial and international relationships taking place in the world today. 'Law and order' is one of today's important political issues. There is a danger however that we try to achieve too much order with too little law, by bypassing the processes we have inherited from those eight centuries of experience and hard fought battles against tyranny. The people of Queensland look to the law to defend their rights.[5]

3. Quoted by Chief Justice Paul de Jersey, Opening of Metropolitan Supreme and District Courthouse, 3 August 2012, at < http://138.25.65.17/au/journals/QldJSchol/2012/37. pdf>. Accessed 3 December 2014.
4. de Jersey, Opening of Metropolitan Supreme and District Courthouse.
5. Quoted in frontispiece of Frank Brennan, *Too Much Order with Too Little Law* (Brisbane: University of Queensland Press, 1984).

That year I was spending a brief time at the Victorian Bar. Over the previous years while studying theology and philosophy, I spent my vacations coming here to Queensland to appear in the Magistrates' Court defending protesters who had fallen into the web of legal regulations being wrongly applied to thwart public protest at the whim of the then premier. I was briefed to appear because it was difficult for young barristers here to take the briefs because there was a directive within crown law that those appearing were never to receive any government work.

I remember on one occasion running into a mate from law school days who by then was a judge's associate. He is now a respected Supreme Court judge so I will not name him. He told me that he had just been up to crown law trying to fix up his pay. He met a magistrate who unloaded rather freely. The magistrate said that he was tied up in the 'expletive deleted' demonstrator court: 'We have this flash Jesuit from the south who has come putting all sorts of legal arguments which we cannot understand. But that's not the worst of it. When we reject his submissions, he is just so "expletive deleted" polite.' I returned to Melbourne that weekend well-satisfied, though troubled that my advocacy was not sufficient to render comprehensible the points being made about onus of proof and the prosecution's undue reliance on averment provisions.

Reflecting on the experience in the demonstrator court, I wrote my first book, drawing the title *Too Much Order with Too Little Law* from the insightful remarks of the Queensland governor. It was Peter Applegarth writing on the letterhead of the Queensland Council for Civil Liberties who recommended publication of the manuscript to the University of Queensland Press. I was honoured to have the book launched by Bill Pincus then President of the Bar.

Three decades on, Queensland once again has a populist premier who finds some political advantage in skewing the balance between law and order, impugning the integrity and vocation of the legal profession. He has described defence lawyers as hired guns. I understand litigation is now pending. No doubt the Premier will retain the services of competent paid counsel. Following upon the

Premier's claim that defence lawyers 'will see, say and do anything to defend their clients',[6] I was heartened to read the remarks by Justice Peter Applegarth to a jury being empanelled in your splendid new Supreme Court building:

> [T]he lawyers who appear before you in this case and the lawyers who appear in all the cases in this building have high duties, duties to prosecute to the best of their ability, duties to defend to the best of their ability, duties to represent the interests of those who they appear for. But they have higher duties. And they're demanding. And I'm pleased to say that in this country we have, with very rare exceptions, lawyers who will put their duty to the court and their duty to justice higher than the interests of their clients and winning a case.[7]

Undoubtedly there are many challenges confronting our elected leaders in dealing with violent crime and with pathological sex offenders. But long-term sustainable solutions must be based on respect for judicial independence and for the role of the legal profession. Having chaired the National Human Rights Consultation in 2009, I am convinced that Australia's exceptionalism in failing to legislate comprehensively for the protection of human rights will put increasing pressure on the relationship between the three branches of government. Responding to that pressure, our courts are now isolated from courts elsewhere, including those in the United Kingdom which are constrained and directed by Strasbourg and their own Human Rights Act. In the UK, the Tories long concerned about the influence of Strasbourg are no longer suggesting the repeal of their Human Rights Act but the passage of a new Bill of Rights which will include the principles of the European Convention on Human Rights. Our courts are less able to profit from the cross-fertilisation of ideas from other equivalent jurisdictions such as the UK, New Zealand, Canada and the USA.

---

6. *Courier Mail,* 6 February 2014.
7. Supreme Court of Queensland, Transcript, *R v Earel,* 7 February 2014.

At his swearing in, Queensland's most recent High Court Justice, Patrick Keane took some comfort that the Australian judiciary were not a social elite as in some other countries, being drawn from the egalitarian democracy shaped by those Australians of the Depression and War eras who provided selflessly and generously for the education of their children. He invoked Martin Luther King who said, 'The arc of the moral universe is long, but it bends toward justice.' With a touch of nationalistic pride, Keane opined that it bends more sharply in that direction here in this part of the southern hemisphere because of the egalitarianism of our forebears.[8]

When made a life member of the Queensland Bar on 27 February 2014, Keane, as he often does, delved into legal history to make his point:

> When Justice Jeffrey was made James II's chief justice of the King's Bench [in 1683]he adjured his fellow judges:
> 'Be sure to execute the law to the utmost of its vengeance upon those that are now knowne, and we have reason to remember them, by the name of Whigs; and you are likewise to remember the snivelling trimmers; for you know what our Saviour Jesus Christ says in the Gospel, that "they that are not for us are against us".'
>
> This seems to have been the last occasion when it was thought respectable for judges to be told to go about their work in accordance with the wishes of the executive government. It was also the last occasion when the naïve notion that you are 'either with us or against us' was applied to the work of the courts and the legal profession.
>
> The very point of the legal system, and the profession which serves it, is that the profession is not 'either for us or against us': whatever the private opinions of its members may be, in the honourable service of justice, each is obliged to be politically neutral and professionally detached. And that is how it ought to be.

---

8. Justice Patrick Keane, Remarks at Swearing in as Justice of the High Court of Australia, 5 March 2013 at < http://www5.austlii.edu.au/au/other/HCATrans/2013/40.html>. Accessed 3 December 2014.

We should not be unduly agitated by the occasional rocky moment. Things have been a lot worse in times past.

In the challenging times ahead here in Queensland all members of the profession need to take to heart President Margaret McMurdo's comments to newly admitted practitioners:

> As members of the legal profession, together with the assistance of an independent judiciary, you play an institutional role in Queensland's precious democracy. The independent legal profession operates as a check on the abuse of executive power and ensures that every citizen has access to the rule of law which provides equal justice for all, regardless of gender, race, skin colour, religion, sexual preference, power or wealth.[9]

May this continue to be the case in the Sunshine State no matter what the prevailing ethos of executive government or the populism of the parliament. Without the lawyer's independence and attention to conscience, the arc of the moral universe will be skewed away from justice when our elected leaders think they can maintain order without law. Together, performing their respective roles, and respecting the roles of others, elected politicians, unelected judges and professional lawyers can deliver that most valuable social good—justice according to law, for all persons. Despite our differences, we all need to support each other in discerning and then playing our part in the midst of present controversies.

As you who live here know only too well, all is not well here in the Sunshine State. Campbell Newman's government is running a strong 'law and order' line, and there's nothing new in that. Governments often find political advantage in being tough on crime. In the process, they sometimes think something is to be gained by having a go at the judges for being out of touch and for being soft

---

9.   President Margaret McMurdo, Remarks on the Admission of new practitioners, 19 December 2013 at <http://archive.sclqld.org.au/judgepub/2013/mcmurdo191213.pdf>. Accessed 3 December 2014.

on crime, and by taking practical steps to toughen them up. Judges are well used to this sort of commentary and political bravado, getting on with their job of sentencing offenders, ensuring that the sentence matches the crime and the circumstances of the criminal. Fortunately, we Australians live under constitutional arrangements which guarantee, more or less, that executive government is popularly elected with the ministry being drawn from the party or parties enjoying a majority in the lower house of parliament (or in Queensland, the only house of parliament). Our judges are not elected and they enjoy independence from the executive government once appointed, in that they can be dismissed only by vote of the parliament determining proven misbehaviour. The risky part is the judicial appointment process.

The appointment of High Court judges sometimes excites strong political interest because those seven constitutional luminaries have the final say interpreting the division of powers between the Commonwealth and the States. The appointment of state judges rarely excites strong political interest, though often accompanied by lots of speculation and interest in the legal profession. Even the appointment of a state chief justice is usually a matter of only passing interest for the public.

When Jim Spigelman decided to retire as chief justice of New South Wales in 2011, a routine set of consultations with the legal profession took place with the state Attorney-General Greg Smith then issuing a mundane press release announcing the appointment of Tom Bathurst and appending a matter-of-fact CV of the appointee's legal expertise and experience.[10] Bathurst was then sworn in publicly, being welcomed in open court by his fellow judges, members of the legal profession, representatives of government and members of the public.

---

10. Greg Smith, Media release, 13 May 2011 at
    <http://www.justice.nsw.gov.au/Documents/Media%20Releases/2011/130511_CJ.pdf>. Accessed 3 December 2014.

In February 2014, Campbell Newman made the long awaited announcement that Paul de Jersey, your long serving Chief Justice would be your new governor. Campbell Newman said he would take time to appoint a new chief justice, in line with a promise to be more consultative: 'We will be consulting with senior members of the legal profession in Queensland. Obviously I will also be asking His Honour for his opinion and we'll make an announcement when we've undertaken that process. But we're going to listen and we're going to consult.'[11]

Last month, with great fanfare, Campbell Newman appeared at the Supreme Court flanked by Chief Justice de Jersey and his Attorney-General Jarrod Bleijie to announce the appointment of Tim Carmody as Queensland's new Chief Justice. The government described the event as a 'launch' of the new Chief Justice. There is no rule to say that one should just do these things in an understated way by media release as they did in Sydney with the appointment of the eminently qualified and suitable Tom Bathurst. Usually an appointment should just speak for itself. The appearance of the premier, the future governor and the proposed chief justice together at the Supreme Court was novel, providing a picture in stark contrast to the usual separation of powers. Judge Carmody spoke and affirmed that he would be independent as a chief justice: 'I am fiercely independent. If my views happen to coincide with the Government's that is pure coincidence.'[12] By this stage alarm bells were ringing. To me, this was the equivalent of a new archbishop holding a press conference in the cathedral with the papal nuncio and proclaiming his faith in Jesus Christ. True, but why the need to say it? Over the next twenty-four hours, things unravelled badly.

Unlike Tom Bathurst, Tim Carmody was not your usual prospective appointee as chief justice. Except for his close relationship with the Attorney-General and his expressed coincidence of viewpoint with government about law and order issues, there is no

---

11. ABC, *News*, 26 February 2014 at <http://www.abc.net.au/news/2014-02-26/chief-justice-paul-de-jersey-to-be-qlds-next-governor/5285170 >. Accessed 3 December 2014.
12. *Courier Mail*, 12 June 2014.

way that he would be in the mix for consideration. Despite some of the more shrill observations by his critics (and he has had many in the legal profession), this closeness and coincidence of views would not necessarily rule him out of consideration if he had the requisite prudence, experience and learning in the law. He took to the airwaves to defend himself and his appointment. This is unheard of in the Australian system. He revealed on air that not one of the twenty-six serving Supreme Court judges had congratulated him, and that he would have to knock on the door of each of them to determine if they were friend or foe.[13] Imagine, a new chairman of a major corporation like BHP Billiton announcing to the public that he had not been congratulated by any serving board member and that he would now have to take soundings, presumably building alliances and dividing his board into camps. The shareholders would not be happy.

As for Premier Newman's much promised consultation, we will never know if he consulted Chief Justice de Jersey and what was said, and neither should we. This is what made de Jersey's presence at the press conference in his own court building so problematic, given that Newman and Carmody used the press conference to make such self-serving remarks. Peter Davis, then President of the Bar representing the barristers of the State was devastated that either the Attorney General or one of his staff had leaked details of their confidential discussions to others including Carmody even before the decision had been made to appoint him. Davis wrote to all the barristers saying, 'The Bar Association ought to be involved in the process of appointment of judges. That is done through the President. As I have no faith in the integrity of the process, I cannot engage further in it. I have concluded, with great regret and sadness, that I ought not continue to hold the office of President.'

It turned out that a junior barrister, Ryan Haddrick, who was close to both Carmody and the Attorney General (having been his chief of staff) had expressed displeasure at the Bar Council's view on

---

13. *Brisbane Times*, 19 June 2014 reporting the broadcasted remarks of Tim Carmody on Fairfax Radio 4BC on 13 June 2014 at < http://www.brisbanetimes.com.au/queensland/queensland-court-of-appeal-judge-calls-on-tim-carmody-to-decline-promotion-20140619-zse1p.html>. Accessed 3 December 2014.

who should or should not be appointed as Chief Justice. Haddrick thought the Bar needed to accept the *fait accompli* that Carmody would be appointed, and arrogantly and high-handedly wrote to Mark Plunkett, a member of the Bar Council saying, 'Common sense needs to prevail. There are two more Supreme Court appointments, three District appointments and about five Magistrates to go this term. I want some of them to be barristers!! and not solicitors!!!'.[14]

The president of the Law Society wrote to all the solicitors saying, 'The matters raised by Peter Davis QC are of singular concern as they go to the process of judicial appointment which, if tainted, runs the very great risk of undermining the confidence of the profession and the community in individual appointments which then flows onto the larger institution of the courts. Such an outcome cannot be contemplated. The issues raised must be addressed if we are to preserve confidence in our system of justice.'[15]

Queensland is in for a very hard time with the community's confidence in the courts being tested while politicians beat the 'law and order' drum. New South Wales Chief Justice Bathurst in October 2013 observed:

> Because the judiciary has neither 'the might of the sword or of the purse', as the old saying goes, the institutional strength of the courts necessary for judicial independence itself largely relies on community confidence. It is, at least in part, the community's confidence and support for the judiciary that serves to protect the courts from incursions by other arms of government. In other words, community confidence in the judiciary is both a goal, and an important element in maintaining, the separation of powers.[16]

14. *Courier Mail,* 14 June 2014.
15. Ian Brown, President, A Statement to the members of the Queensland Law Society, 14 June 2014, at < http://www.justinian.com.au/storage/pdf/QLS_CJ_statement_June%2014_2014.pdf>. Accessed 3 December 2014.
16. Chief Justice Tom Bathurst, 'Separation of Powers: Reality or Desirable Fiction?', Judicial Conference of Australia Colloquium, 11 October 2013 at <http://www.austlii.edu.au/au/journals/NSWJSchol/2013/39.pdf>. Accessed 3 December 2014.

Campbell Newman and his Attorney have trashed this community confidence for dubious short-term political gain.

Once the governor in council appointed Tim Carmody, Paul de Jersey, the Chief Justice soon to be governor said, 'It became incumbent on all of us who are involved in the legal process to support its current expression. The stability of the legal system is integral to our democratic system and must be maintained.'[17] This injunction would have carried greater weight if the Chief Justice had not agreed to the Executive takeover of the Supreme Court building to conduct what government media outlets described as the launch of the Chief Justice. It would have carried greater weight if the serving Chief Justice had abided by precedent and not joined members of the Executive when announcing the new Chief Justice. It would have carried greater weight if the new Chief Justice were to present himself in his new court for a public swearing in and official welcome by the profession, the government and the people of Queensland. The statement would have carried greater weight if it had made mention of the integrity of the legal system as well as its stability. When opening the new Supreme Court building in Brisbane in 2012, Chief Justice de Jersey rightly praised the splendid architecture of the building which reflected the transparency and openness of the judicial process. Sadly, his vision turned to ashes as he departed for Government House.

In Queensland, the Carmody court has its work cut out for it given the present 'law and order' mindset in the Executive government and the perennial curial challenge to maintain the separation of powers, the subservience of all branches of government to the law, and the independence of the legal profession. Those of you who are barristers should cherish Pat Keane's reminder: 'Barristers tend to be the natural enemies of those with power; and sometimes the power we are obliged to oppose is the power of the State. No-one who has power likes to be thwarted in the exercise of power for what seems to him or her to be the public good.'[18]

---

17. *The Australian*, 20 June 2014.
18. Justice Patrick Keane, Speech on the occasion of life membership of the Queensland Bar, 27 February 2014.

I wish Chief Justice Carmody well now that he has been sworn in as Chief Justice of the State of Queensland. For the sake of stability and integrity of the legal system, it is now time for all of us to drop the public questioning of his suitability for high office and to subject his judgments to the same scrutiny and to treat them with the same respect as we would accord any other judgments from the Supreme Court of Queensland. It is time for the Newman government to return to appropriate modes of consultation with the legal profession about judicial appointments and to the more traditional modes of announcing such appointments. We must avoid the public perception of a fudging of the separation of powers, with the Executive appropriating to itself the mantle of judicial independence expressed by the last Chief Justice de Jersey having to stand silent in his own court building while politicians used the state's most senior judicial appointment to further a crass law and order campaign, heaping humiliation upon a judiciary and a legal profession committed to according all persons justice according to law. At his farewell as Chief Justice, Paul de Jersey paid tribute to the legal profession's 'efficiency, ethical commitment and established independence'.[19] Long may those attributes inform the character and focus of the Queensland Council for Civil Liberties. Thank you for the opportunity to return to my home state and to offer these reflections on an historic day in the Sunshine State.

---

19. ABC News, 26 June 2014.

9

Respecting Religious Freedom and Freedom of Conscience

While conducting the National Human Rights Consultation in 2009, I was invited to address an international conference on values and public policy in Melbourne. The Victorian parliament had just legislated to take the away the right to freedom of conscience for any nurse or medical practitioner opposed to abortion. The keynote speaker was the American intellectual Martha Nussbaum who had just published her book Liberty of Conscience. *I spoke on 'The Place of the Religious Viewpoint in Shaping Law and Policy in a Pluralistic Democratic Society: a case study on rights and conscience'. The objectionable Victorian law is still on the statute books.*

I concluded my book *Acting on Conscience* with a recollection of a mass celebrated in the Dili Cathedral in 2001 by Nobel Peace Prize Winner Bishop Belo. As Director of the Jesuit Refugee Service, I was working in East Timor at the time and I accompanied Bishop Belo at the mass that was offered in thanks for the contribution by the departing Australian INTERFET forces. At the end of the mass, Major General Peter Cosgrove (now Sir Peter Cosgrove, Governor General of Australia) spoke. The burly Australian commander was accompanied by a translator who was a petite Timorese religious sister in her pure white habit, replete with veil. Before them was the usual international media scrum which accompanies such events in countries overrun by the UN and international NGOs. Cosgrove recalled his first visit to the cathedral three months earlier when he was so moved by the singing that he realised two things: the people of East Timor had not abandoned their God, and God had not abandoned the people of East Timor. His words surprised me, and I knew that this speech would not be reported back in Australia. We don't do religion in public this way. It was unimaginable that an Australian military leader would give such a speech back in Australia. I am sure that our honoured guest Martha Nussbaum would concede that if Cosgrove were a US General, we would expect it. As I said in *Acting on Conscience*:

> Here in Australia, the public silence about things religious does not mean that religion does not animate and inspire many of us. It just has a less acknowledged place in the public forum. It marks its presence by the reverence of the silence. That is why we Australians need to be so attentive to keeping politics and religion in place. Each has its place and each must be kept in place for the good of us all, and for the good of our Commonwealth.[1]

Many citizens wanting to contribute to the shaping of law, public policy, and conversation in the public square come to the task with their own comprehensive worldview. For some, that view is shaped not just by their culture and intellectual peers but also by their religious tradition and beliefs. Just because they do not often talk about such tradition and beliefs outside their own circle of family and friends does not mean that these tradition and beliefs are left at home once the individual steps into the public square. Launching his new foundation on 'Faith and Globalisation', the retired British Prime Minister Tony Blair observed that his former press secretary, Alastair Campbell, was fond of saying, 'We don't do God'. Blair clarified that Campbell 'didn't mean that politicians shouldn't have faith, just that it was always a packet of trouble to talk about it'. In the British culture, as here in Australia, Blair notes that 'to admit to having faith leads to a whole series of suppositions, none of which are very helpful to the practising politician'. He listed five suppositions:

---

1. Frank Brennan, *Acting on Conscience* (Brisbane: University of Queensland Press, 2007), 231.

First, you may be considered weird. Normal people aren't supposed to 'do God'.

Second, there is an assumption that before you take a decision, you engage in some slightly cultish interaction with your religion–'So, God, tell me what you think of City Academies or Health Service Reform or nuclear power' i.e. people assume that your religion makes you act, as a leader, at the promptings of an inscrutable deity, free from reason rather than in accordance with it.

Third, you want to impose your religious faith on others.

Fourth, you are pretending to be better than the next person.

And finally and worst of all, that you are somehow messianically trying to co-opt God to bestow a divine legitimacy on your politics.[2]

Whether or not our comprehensive worldview is shaped by religious influences, it informs the development of values which the individual expresses and lives out in their own specific cultural context. From those values, one is able to articulate principles which underpin informed and considered decision making about laws, public policies and public deliberation on contested social questions.

We can practise politics, that art of compromise in the public square where laws and policies are determined in relation to the allocation of scarce resources or in relation to conflicts where there is no clear resolution either in principle or by the exercise of legitimate authority. Public policy can include the allocation of preferences by the state extended to individuals who can avail themselves of state benefits while avoiding state burdens. Laws can include the dictates of the State enforceable against individuals who fail to comply voluntarily.

The retired Archbishop of Canterbury Rowan Williams has pointed out that rights and utility are the two concepts that resonate most readily in the public square today. But we need concepts to

---

2. Tony Blair, 'Faith and Globalisation', The Cardinal's Lectures 2008, Westminster Cathedral, 3 April 2008 at <http://www.tonyblairoffice.org/speeches/entry/tony-blair-faith-and-globalisation-lecture/>. Accessed 3 December 2014.

set limits on rights when they interfere with the common good or the public interest, or dare I say it, public morality—the concepts used by the UN when first formulating and limiting human rights sixty years ago. These concepts are no longer in vogue, at least under these titles.

We also need concepts to set limits on utility when it interferes with the dignity of the most vulnerable and the liberty of the most despised in our community. Addressing the UN General Assembly to mark the anniversary of the UN Declaration of Human Rights (UNDHR), Pope Benedict XVI said, 'This document was the outcome of a convergence of different religious and cultural traditions, all of them motivated by the common desire to place the human person at the heart of institutions, laws and the workings of society, and to consider the human person essential for the world of culture, religion and science . . . (T)he universality, indivisibility and interdependence of human rights all serve as guarantees safeguarding human dignity.'[3] It would be a serious mistake to view the UNDHR stipulation and limitation of rights as a western Judaeo-Christian construct.

Mary Ann Glendon's *A World Made New* traces the remarkable contribution to that document by Eleanor Roosevelt and an international bevy of diplomats and academics whose backgrounds give the lie to the claim that any listing of human rights is a Western culturally biased catalogue of capitalist political aspirations. The Frenchman Rene Cassin, the Chilean Hernan Santa Cruz, the Christian Lebanese Adam Malik and the Chinese Confucian Peng-chun Chang were great contributors to this truly international undertaking. They consulted religious and philosophical greats such as Teilhard de Chardin and Mahatma Gandhi. Even Aldous Huxley made a contribution. It was the Jesuit palaeontologist Teilhard who counselled that the drafters should focus on 'man in society' rather than the person as an individual.[4]

---

3. Benedict XVI, Meeting with the Members of the General Assembly of the United Nations Organisation, 18 April 2008 at
   <http://www.vatican.va/holy_father/benedict_xvi/speeches/2008/april/documents/hf_ben-xvi_spe_20080418_un-visit_en.html>. Accessed 3 December 2014.

The drafters knew that any catalogue of rights would need to include words of limitation. The Canadian John Humphrey who was the Director of the UN secretariat servicing the drafting committee prepared a first draft of forty-eight articles. The Australian member of the drafting committee Colonel Hodgson wanted to know the draft's underlying philosophy. Humphrey refused to answer, replying 'that the draft was not based on any particular philosophy; it included rights recognised by various national constitutions and also a number of suggestions that had been made for an international bill of rights'. In his memoirs, Humphrey recounts: 'I wasn't going to tell him that insofar as it reflected the views of its author—who had in any event to remain anonymous—the draft attempted to combine humanitarian liberalism with social democracy.'[5]

It is fascinating to track the different ways in which the committee dealt with the delimitation of rights. Humphrey proposed that an individual's rights be limited 'by the rights of others and by the just requirements of the State and of the United Nations'.[6] Cassin proposed only one limitation on a person's rights: 'The rights of all persons are limited by the rights of others.'[7] The 1947 Human Rights Commission draft stayed with Cassin's one stated limitation on rights: 'In the exercise of his rights, everyone is limited by the rights of others.'[8]

By the time the draft reached Geneva for the third meeting of the Human Rights Commission in May 1948, there was a much broader panoply of limitation on individual rights introduced, taking into account the person's social character and re-introducing Humphrey's notion of just requirements of the state: 'In the exercise of his rights every one is limited by the rights of others and by the just requirements of the democratic state. The individual owes

---

4. Mary Ann Glendon, *A World Made New* (New York: Random House, 2001), 76.
5. John P Humphrey, *Human Rights and the United Nations: A Great Adventure*, (New York: Transnational Publishers, 1984), 40.
6. Article 2, Humphrey draft at Glendon, *A World Made New*, 271.
7. Article 4, Cassin draft at Glendon, *A World Made New*, 276.
8. Article 4, Human Rights Commission Draft, June 1947, at Glendon, *A World Made New*, 281.

duties to society through which he is enabled to develop his spirit, mind and body in wider freedom.'[9]

The Commission then reconvened for its last session at Lake Success in June 1948. They approved the draft declaration 12–0. Glendon notes: 'Pavlov, the Ukraine's Klekovkin, and Byelorussia's Stepanenko, in line with instructions issued before the meeting had begun, abstained and filed a minority report.'[10] The Commission moved the words of limitation to the end of the draft and married the limitation to a statement about duties. Article 27 (which ultimately became Article 29) provided:

> Everyone has duties to the community which enables him freely to develop his personality.
> In the exercise of his rights, everyone shall be subject only to such limitations as are necessary to secure due recognition and respect for the rights of others and the requirements of morality, public order and general welfare in a democratic society.

So here in the heart of the modern world's most espoused declaration of human rights came an acknowledgment that we all have duties and not just rights, duties to the community, which, perhaps counter-intuitively, enable us to develop our personalities. I doubt Eleanor Roosevelt coined that phrase. At the Commission, it was said that 'morality' and 'public order' were 'particularly necessary for the French text, since in English, 'general welfare' included both morality and public order.'[11] At one stage it was suggested that the term 'public order' was too broad, permitting the grossest breach of human rights by those committing arbitrary acts and crimes in the name of maintaining public order.

The commission considered the substitution of 'security for all' for 'public order', similar to the 28th article of the American Declaration

---

9.   Article 4, Geneva Draft, at Glendon, *A World Made New,* 289.

10. Glendon, *A World Made New,* 120.

11. Erica-Irene A Daes, *The Individual's Duties to the Community and the Limitations on Human Rights and Freedoms Under Article 29 of the Universal Declaration of Human Rights,* UN Doc. E/CN.4/Sub.2/432/Rev.2, 1983, 72.

of the Rights and Duties of Man, but decided to stay with the more jurisprudentially certain European term 'public order'.[12] But also we have the acknowledgment that individual rights might be limited not just for the preservation of public order and for the general welfare of persons in a democratic society, but also for morality—presumably to maintain, support, enhance or develop morality in a democratic society. Sixty years later, these words of limitation might not sit with us so readily.

The draft then went from the Human Rights Commission to the Third Committee of the UN General Assembly. The Committee convened more than 80 meetings to debate the declaration which it renamed the Universal Declaration of Human Rights rather than International Declaration of Human Rights. The limitation clause was considered during three of those meetings. The limitation clause was further amended:

> Everyone has duties to the community in which alone the free and full development of his personality is possible.
> In the exercise of his rights and freedoms, everyone shall be subject only to such limitations as are determined by law solely for the purpose of securing due recognition and respect for the rights and freedoms of others and of meeting the just requirements of morality, public order and the general welfare in a democratic society.
> These rights and freedoms can in no case be exercised contrary to the purposes and principles of the United Nations.

Though there was much discussion of amendments to omit references to 'morality' and 'public order', the Third Committee decided to retain these terms as to delete the mention of them 'would be to base all limitations of the rights granted in the declaration on the requirements of general welfare in a democratic society and consequently to make them subject to the interpretation of

---

12. Daes, *The Individual's Duties*, 72.

the concept of democracy, on which there was the widest possible divergence of views'.[13] As amended, this article was carried by forty-one votes to none, with one abstention.[14] The General Assembly then voted to adopt the universal declaration with forty-eight in favour, eight abstentions and none opposed.

In recent times, the Australian government led by Prime Minister Kevin Rudd sought to follow the UK, Ireland and New Zealand with a commitment to social inclusion giving all Australians the opportunity to: secure a job; access services; connect with family, friends, work and their local community; deal with crises; and have their voices heard. It may be in this grey area between rights and utility that social inclusion has work to do—work that was previously distributed among concepts such as human dignity, the common good, the public interest and public morality. Regardless of religious affiliation, individuals and community groups living under law in the State are entitled equally to connect with their local community, to deal with crises in religiously and culturally appropriate ways, and to have their voices heard unfiltered by those media outlets that transmit only the secular.

In the legal academy there is presently a great evangelical fervour for bills of rights. This fervour manifests itself in florid espousals of the virtues of weak statutory bills of rights together with the assurance that one need not be afraid because such bills do not really change anything. It has been a pleasant change for me this past year to be cast in the role of the sceptical agnostic insisting that the promised parousia of enhanced human rights protection be backed by hard evidence of tangibly different outcomes.

As a confirmed fence sitter, I chaired the national consultation on human rights. Those of us with a pragmatic, evidentiary approach to the question are now well positioned given that two of Australia's nine jurisdictions (Victoria and the ACT) have enacted such bills of rights with the double assurance that nothing has really changed and that things can now only get better. It will be interesting to hear

---

13. Daes, *The Individual's Duties*, 74–5.
14. Daes, *The Individual's Duties*, 75.

an assessment of the socially inclusionary benefits of a bill of rights that provides lawyers and judges with greater access to the realm of policy and service delivery.

Once we investigate much of the contemporary discussion about human rights, we find that often the intended recipients of rights do not include all human beings but only those with certain capacities or those who share sufficient common attributes with the decision makers. It is always at the edges that there is real work for human rights discourse to do. In Cambodia in 2008, I met a woman concerned for the well being of a handful of children who had both cerebral palsy and profound autism. There are more than enough needy children in Cambodia. It is not surprising that religious persons often have a keen eye for the neediest, not only espousing their rights but taking action for their well being and human flourishing.

Once we abandon any religious sense that the human person is created in the image and likeness of God and that God has commissioned even the powerful to act justly, love tenderly and walk humbly with their God, it may be very difficult to maintain a human rights commitment to the weakest and most despised in society. It may come down to the vote, moral sentiment or tribal affiliations. And that will not be enough to extend human rights universally. In the name of utility, the society spared religious influence will have one less impediment to limiting social inclusion to those like us, 'us' being the decision makers who determine which common characteristics render embodied persons eligible for human rights protection.

Liberty of Conscience

In his 1789 Letter to the Quakers, George Washington said, 'I assure you very explicitly, that in my opinion the conscientious scruples of all men should be treated with great delicacy and tenderness: and it is my wish and desire, that the laws may always be as extensively accommodated to them, as a due regard for the protection and essential interests of the nation may justify and permit'.[15]

Professor Martha Nussbaum's book *Liberty of Conscience* provides a richly textured treatment of the place of religion in the public square. In her characteristic writing mode, she shares personal anecdotes—this time her conversion from Christianity to Judaism on the occasion of marriage; she treats deftly the classics, and then delves into philosophical reflection on US jurisprudence not all of which travels well across the Pacific. In this book she reflects on the agonising dilemma of Sophocles' Antigone when the State in the person of her uncle Creon has announced that she may not bury her brother, killed attacking the city. Her religion dictates that she must bury her brother. Nussabaum speaks of Creon's alarming rigidity:

> He has defined public policy in a way that favours the interests of most people in the city. In the process, however, he has imposed a tragic burden on one person. The great Athenian statesman Pericles boasted that fifth century democratic Athens did things better, refusing on principle to put people in such dreadful predicaments. Athens, he said, pursues the good of the city, but not by requiring its citizens to violate the 'unwritten laws' of their religions.[16]

She nicely posits the Lockean position of state neutrality whereby 'the state is free to regulate matters concerning property or health or safety even when they bear on religious organisations—so long as it does so impartially'[17] against the more subtle treatment of the seventeenth century American Roger Williams, founder of Rhode Island, who espoused religious accommodation with the declaration, 'It is the will and command of God that (since the coming of his Sonne the Lord Jesus) a permission of the most paganish, Jewish,

---

15. Quoted by Martha Nussbaum, *Liberty of Conscience* (New York: Basic Books, 2008), 115.
16. Nussbaum, *Liberty of Conscience*, 116.
18. Nussbaum, *Liberty of Conscience*, 60.

Turkish, or antichristian consciences and worships, bee granted to all men in all nations and countries'.[18]

Nussbaum sets down six normative principles which I find useful in scrutinising laws and policies that impact on the free exercise of religion and on the broader freedom of conscience. I will take as a case study section 8(1)(b) of the recently enacted Victorian *Abortion law Reform Act*. The issue is not the legality or desirability of abortion on demand. The issue is whether the law ought provide for compulsory referral by a conscientious objector. Section 8(1)(b) provides:

> If a woman requests a registered health practitioner to advise on a proposed abortion, or to perform, direct, authorise or supervise an abortion for that woman, and the practitioner has a conscientious objection to abortion, the practitioner must refer the woman to another registered health practitioner in the same regulated health profession who the practitioner knows does not have a conscientious objection to abortion.

Justice Scalia has pursued the Lockean position on the US Supreme Court, as have groups such as Liberty Victoria in pursuing the enactment of the recent Victorian abortion law including this novel clause stipulating compulsory referral by a conscientious objector. The Williams approach finds expression in the judgments of Justice O'Connor on the United States Supreme Court and in the criticisms offered by some of the faith based groups critical of section 8(1)(b) of the Victorian abortion law. The supporters of section 8 are *ad idem* with Justice Scalia who has said, 'we have never held that an individual's religious beliefs excuse him from compliance with an otherwise valid law prohibiting conduct that the state is free to regulate.'[19]

The Lockean position is the minimal protection provided by the Australian Constitution for freedom of religion. In *The Church*

---

19. Quoted by Nussbaum, *Liberty of Conscience*, 34.

of the New Faith v The Commissioner of Pay-roll Tax (Victoria),
Acting Chief Justice Mason and Justice Brennan wrote that 'canons
of conduct which offend against the ordinary laws are outside the
area of any immunity, privilege or right conferred on the grounds
of religion.' [20]

Australia is a signatory to the *International Covenant on Civil and
Political Rights.* The terms of that Covenant provide a convenient
benchmark for most individuals and groups who espouse human
rights. The freedom of conscience and religion is one of the few non-
derogable rights in the Covenant. This means that a signatory may
not interfere with the exercise of the right even during a national
emergency—whereas other rights in the Covenant can be cut back
during times of public emergency which threatens the life of the
nation—but only to the extent strictly required by the exigencies
of the situation and provided that that cut back applies in a non-
discriminatory way to all persons.   Furthermore the freedom
or thought, conscience and religion is one of the few rights, which
can be confined only if it be necessary 'to protect public safety,
order, health, or morals or the fundamental rights and freedoms of
others'.[21]

Let's first consider Nussbaum's principles:

1. The equality principle: all citizens have equal rights and
   deserve equal respect from the government under which
   they live
2. The respect conscience principle: provide a protected space
   within which citizens may act as their conscience dictates.
   All citizens enter the public square on equal conditions
3. The liberty principle: respect for people's conscientious
   commitments requires ample liberty, and not just a regime
   of equal constraint in which nobody has much religious
   freedom

---

19. *Employment Division v Smith,* 494 US 872 (1990), 878-9
20. (1983) 154 CLR 120 at 136
21. Article 18(3), *International Covenant on Civil and Political Rights*

4. The accommodation principle: sometimes some people (usually members of religious minorities) should be exempted from generally applicable laws for reasons of conscience.
5. The non-establishment principle: the state may make no endorsements in religious matters that would signify any orthodoxy, creating an in-group and an out-group
6. The separation principle: a certain degree of separation should be created between church and state: on the whole, church and state have separate spheres of jurisdiction.[22]

Nussbaum concedes that there may be a need for religion to bear some burdens 'if the peace and safety of the state are really at stake, or if there is some other extremely strong state interest. But it seems deeply wrong for the state to put citizens in such a tragic position needlessly, or in matters of less weight. And often matters lying behind laws of general applicability are not so weighty; sometimes they come down to a mere desire for homogeneity and an unexamined reluctance to delve into the details of a little known or unpopular religion.'[23]

When Lord Joffe's *Assisted Dying for the Terminally Ill Bill* was first drafted in the United Kingdom it contained two clauses similar to section 8 of the Victorian *Abortion Law Reform Act 2008*. Clauses 7(2) and (3) of the original Joffe Bill imposed a duty on physicians who invoked their right to conscientiously object, to 'take appropriate steps to ensure that the patient is referred without delay to a physician who does not have such a conscientious objection'. The Westminster Parliament's Joint Committee on Human Rights remarked:

> We consider that imposing such a duty on a physician who invokes the right to conscientiously object is an interference with that physician's right to freedom of conscience under the first sentence of Article 9(1), because it requires the physician to participate in a process to which he or she has a conscientious

---

22. Nussbaum, *Liberty of Conscience*, 22–5.
23. Nussbaum, *Liberty of Conscience*, 117.

objection. That right is absolute: interferences with it are not capable of justification under Article 9(2).

We consider that this problem with the Bill could be remedied, for example by recasting it in terms of a right vested in the patient to have access to a physician who does not have a conscientious objection, or an obligation on the relevant public authority to make such a physician available. What must be avoided, in our view, is the imposition of any duty on an individual physician with a conscientious objection, requiring him or her to facilitate the actions contemplated by the Act to which they have such an objection.

In the absence of such a provision, however, we draw to the attention of each House the fact that clauses 7(2) and (3) give rise in our view to a significant risk of a violation of Article 9(1) ECHR.[24]

The UK bill was accordingly amended to provide that 'No person shall be under any duty to refer a patient to any other source for obtaining information or advice pertaining to assistance to die, or to refer a patient to any other person for assistance to die under the provisions of this Act' (cl. 7(3)). Under the revised UK provision, the doctor with a conscientious objection would have no additional legal duty other than 'immediately, on receipt of a request to do so, transfer the patient's medical records to the new physician' (cl. 7(6)).

When confronted with clause 8 of the *Abortion Law Reform Bill*, it was not surprising that the Victorian Scrutiny of Acts and Regulations Committee drew attention to the equivalent attempted provision in the UK, the response by the UK Committee, and the amendment proposed in the UK Parliament. The Victorian committee noted:

> The Committee notes that clause 8 sets out the obligations of health practitioners who hold a conscientious objection to abortion, including (in

---

24. UK Parliament, Joint Committee on Human Rights, Twelfth Report, 12 May 2004, ##3.14-3.16 at <http://www.parliament.the-stationery-office.co.uk/pa/jt200304/jtselect/jtrights/93/9307.htm>. Accessed 3 December 2014.

clause 8(1)(a)) an obligation to refer women who request an abortion to another practitioner who has no conscientious objection. The Committee observes that some practitioners may hold a belief that abortion is murder and may regard a referral to a doctor who will perform an abortion as complicity in murder. The Committee therefore considers that clause 8(1)(a) may engage the Charter right of such practitioners to freedom of belief.[25]

The Committee rightly observed that the compatibility of this clause with the Charter 'depends on its satisfaction of the test in Charter s. 7(2), including whether or not there are less restrictive means available to achieve the purpose of the clause'. The Committee then very properly referred two questions to Parliament for its consideration:

1. Whether or not clause 8(1)(a), by requiring practitioners to refer patients to doctors who hold no conscientious objection to abortion, limits those practitioners' freedom to believe that abortion is murder?

2. If so, whether or not clause 8(1)(a) is a reasonable limit on freedom of belief according to the test set out in Charter s. 7(2) and, in particular, whether or not there are any less restrictive means available to ensure that women receive appropriate health care?

No credible answers were provided by parliament. The questions could only have been answered, Yes to the first and No to the second. Victoria is the first Australian state to have legislated a *Charter of Human Rights and Responsibilities Act*. It reproduces many of the rights in the ICCPR including the freedom of thought, conscience,

---

25. Scrutiny of Acts and Regulations Committee, Alert Digest No 11 of 2008, 6 at <http://www.parliament.vic.gov.au/archive/sarc/Alert_Digests_08/08alt11body.htm#Abortion_Law_Reform_Bill_2008>. Accessed 3 December 2014.

religion and belief (s.14). Unlike the ICCPR, the Victorian Charter does not specify that any rights are non-derogable. And all rights can be restricted for reasons other than the need 'to protect public safety, order, health, or morals or the fundamental rights and freedoms of others'.[26] Section 7(2) specifies the justified limits on rights:

> A human right may be subject under law only to such reasonable limits as can be demonstrably justified in a free and democratic society based on human dignity, equality and freedom, and taking into account all relevant factors including—
>
> (a) the nature of the right; and
> (b) the importance of the purpose of the limitation; and
> (c) the nature and extent of the limitation; and
> (d) the relationship between the limitation and its purpose; and
> (e) any less restrictive means reasonably available to achieve the purpose that the limitation seeks to achieve.

Helen Szoke, Chief Conciliator/CEO, Victorian Equal Opportunity and Human Rights Commission purported to answer the questions posed by the Scrutiny of Bills committee when she wrote to *The Australian* on 1 October 2008 stating:

> The purpose of the charter is to provide a framework to help us balance competing rights and responsibilities. Freedom of conscience is not the only issue at stake here, and to suggest so is to simplify an extremely complex issue. In this case, a doctor's right to freedom of conscience needs to be balanced with competing considerations such as a patient's right to make a free and informed choice. Sometimes limits on human rights are necessary in a democratic society that respects the human dignity of each individual.

---

26. Article 18(3), ICCPR.

Suffice to say that this simple solution is in stark contrast to the reasoning and conclusion reached by the UK Parliament in its consideration of a similar clause.

The various codes of ethics for obstetricians and gynaecologists have now for some years emphasised the patient's right to receipt of service over and above the conscientious objection of the health practitioner. This has not been the case for the general code of ethics for the medical profession generally. The AMA Code of Ethics provides:

> When a personal moral judgement or religious belief alone prevents you from recommending some form of therapy, inform your patient so that they may seek care elsewhere.
>
> Recognise that you may decline to enter into a therapeutic relationship where an alternative health care provider is available, and the situation is not an emergency one.
>
> Recognise that you may decline to continue a therapeutic relationship. Under such circumstances, you can discontinue the relationship only if an alternative health care provider is available and the situation is not an emergency one. You must inform your patient so that they may seek care elsewhere.[27]

The AMA thought clause 8(1)(b) unwarranted because it departed from the existing AMA Code of Ethics. AMA Victoria advised its members in these terms:

> Last week, AMA Victoria met with Minister Andrews' adviser and Department of Human Services legal counsel to seek their understanding of the clause, and we have also sought independent legal advice. The government and the advice confirmed that clause 8 changes the existing law. The existing common law and

---

27. AMA Code of Ethics, under the heading 'The Doctor and the Patient: Patient Care', Para (p) – (r), 2.

existing codes of practice require that a doctor with a conscientious objection to a particular service inform the patient of that conscientious objection and ensure that the service is available elsewhere. The existing law and practice also provide that doctors have a duty to assist in an emergency. AMA Victoria supports the existing law and ethical obligation to properly inform patients and ensure that services are elsewhere available.

The Victorian Law Reform Commission took a similar view, noting that the AMA Code of Ethics 'provides an appropriate balance between the needs of the practitioner and the patient'.[28] Dr Doug Travers, President, AMA Victoria, had written to the Premier on 1 September 2008, stating:

The Bill infringes the rights of doctors with a conscientious objection by inserting an active compulsion for a doctor to refer to another doctor who they know does not have a conscientious objection. Respect for a conscientious objection is a fundamental principle in our democratic country, and doctors expect that their rights in this regard will be respected, as for any other citizen.

The AMA asked the Premier to consider removing clause 8 and rely on the existing law, or amend the section to reflect the existing law. In the week prior to the introduction of the bill into the upper house, the AMA once again stated:

We are still concerned about the conscientious objection clause, and would like to see it amended. The Victorian Law Reform Commission stated that the AMA Code of Ethics provided a sensible balance between the needs of practitioners and patients, and we have asked the Parliament to amend the legislation to reflect the existing law.

---

28. Victorian Law Reform Commission, *Law of Abortion: Final Report*, tabled in the Victorian Parliament on 28 May 2008, 115.

That remained the AMA's position right through the debate in both houses of parliament. It is still the AMA's position.

By requiring a compulsory referral, section 8 works interference on the right to freedom of thought, conscience and belief of a medical practitioner with a conscientious objection to abortion. The minister introducing the bill provided no assessment of this clause in light of the *Charter of Rights and Responsibilities*. No fair-minded assessment of the clause could render a decision that the interference with the right to freedom of thought, conscience and belief had been worked so as to provide the least 'restrictive means reasonably available to achieve the purpose that the limitation seeks to achieve'. Thus the right is not subject under law only 'to such reasonable limits as can be demonstrably justified in a free and democratic society'. Furthermore, the clause is not only more intrusive on the right than need be, it is unworkable.

On 9 September 2008, *Liberty Victoria* issued its only press release on the bill stating, 'The *Abortion Law Reform Bill* should be passed without amendment'. Then writing in *The Age* on 24 September 2008, Anne O'Rourke, the vice president who had the public carriage of the issue for Liberty Victoria claimed that the conscientious objection clause was 'consistent with the Australian Medical Association's code of ethics'. She went on to say, 'To claim the *Abortion Law Reform Bill* breaks new ground or imposes unprecedented obligations on hospitals or medical staff is wrong and misleading. The bill does not do so'.

Liberty Victoria's public position was in stark contrast to the position taken by the AMA. In his letter to the Victorian Premier, Dr Doug Travers, the President of the AMA (Victoria Branch) pointed out that doctors are 'not currently forced to provide a service they believe to be unethical or immoral'. He acknowledged that 'the existing common law and existing codes of conduct require that a doctor with a conscientious objection to a particular service inform the patient of that conscientious objection and . . . ensure that the service is available elsewhere'. But he pointed out that the proposed legislation goes beyond this: it 'infringes the rights of doctors with a conscientious objection by *inserting an active compulsion* for a doctor to refer to another doctor who they know does not have a conscientious objection. Respect for a conscientious objection is a fundamental principle in our democratic country, and doctors expect that their rights in this regard will be respected, as for any other citizen'.

Julian Burnside QC, president of *Liberty Victoria*, wrote to members of parliament on 8 October 2008 purporting to resolve the conflict of rights between the patient desirous of an abortion and the conscientiously objecting doctor. Burnside told the politicians, 'The tension can be resolved either by requiring the objecting doctor to refer the patient in a manner which facilitates her right, or by permitting the doctor to frustrate or delay her right by refusing to refer her to a doctor who does not object on grounds of conscience.' But no referral is required for an abortion in Victoria. Could not the tension be resolved by simply requiring the doctor to comply with the existing AMA code of ethics?

According to Burnside, there was 'a real risk that the patient's right will be defeated: some patients may not have the sophistication or the resources to find a doctor who does not object on grounds of conscience, and this is more likely to be the case, where the patient is young or lives in a remote or regional area with limited medical facilities'. Burnside did concede, 'There is no doubt that the wording is awkward. But the intention is clear'. He said, 'In my view the Clause may be complied with if a doctor with a conscientious objection simply refers his or her patient to a public hospital or to a recognised independent pregnancy advice service'. He insisted that it 'is not a requirement that the practitioner name another doctor with whom they know they have a conscientious disagreement'. And yet this is precisely what the clause requires.

Neil Young QC concluded that the drafting of clause 8(1)(b) 'appears to go beyond' the AMA code of ethics. He pointed out that though under the AMA code of ethics, 'the conscientious objector is required to provide information', 'the objector is required to ascertain or know the views of other practitioners or to refer the woman to a speciifc practitioner who does not have a consceintious objection to abortion.'[29] Young expressed the view that 'clause 8(1)(b) cannot be interpreted or applied consistently with the human right set forth in section 14 of the Charter' (the right to freedom of thought, conscience, religion and belief).[30] Further Young must be right when he states that clause 8(1)(b) cannot be justified by recourse to section 7(2) of the Charter.

Was a less restrictive means available? Yes. As Young says, 'clause 8(1)(b) could have adopted the language used in the AMA Code of Ethics, which provides a satisfactory and reasonably available alternative. Other less coercive means can be postulated, such as the maintenance of a public register of practitioners who hold no conscientious objection to abortion.'[31]

None of this analysis was done by the Parliament, nor by the advocacy groups like *Liberty Victoria*, nor by the statutory bodies such as the Equal Opportunity Commission. Candy Broad who had introduced an earlier measure for abortion law reform highlighted the confusion over what was required by way of referral. She told parliament:

> Mr Hall raised, at clause 8(1)(b), which states: refer the woman to another registered health practitioner . . . I am advised and I fully expect the minister who has carriage of the bill in this house, Minister Jennings, will confirm that 'refer' is to be taken to have its plain English meaning; therefore it means 'advice' and does not have a more technical meaning in this context. [32]

Then Mr Jennings, Minister who had the carriage of the bill in the upper house when asked to define 'referral' said:

> The effective referral that is being required is to an equivalent medical practitioner, which is very consistent with what has been discussed in connection with this

29. Neil Young QC and Peter Willis, *Joint Opinion, In the Matter of the Abortion Law Reform Bill 2008*, 3 October 2008, #57.
30. Young and Willis, *Joint Opinion*, #59.
31. Young and Willis, *Joint Opinion*, #62.

bill and is consistent with the college and the Australian Medical Association's guidelines and ethical framework that covers this field, and so those concepts are not new. The difference is between the recommendation, which is clear and unequivocal in terms of the code of ethics that says you should do something, and this legislation which says you must do something.[33]

Why impose a legal requirement that the doctor with a conscientious objection to abortion provide a referral when the service can be, and usually is, provided without a referral?

Burnside QC concedes that clause 8 is awkwardly worded and not clear. But it is clear on one point. The conscientiously objecting medical practitioner is legally obliged to 'refer the woman to another registered health practitioner in the same regulated health profession who the practitioner knows does not have a conscientious objection to abortion.' It is not enough simply to give information about the existence of a hospital or a service. The doctor must REFER the patient to another health practitioner known (and not just suspected) not to have a conscientious objection.

Is there a less restrictive means reasonably available to achieve the purpose that the limitation seeks to achieve? Julian Burnside implies that clause 8 does nothing more than implement the AMA Code of Ethics. The AMA thinks clause 8 goes well beyond the Code. Why not stick with the AMA Code of Ethics, while ensuring better information in country towns about the working of the internet, and the existing availability of abortion services provided with maximum encouragement and minimal red tape? Does clause 8 limit the right only to such limits as can be demonstrably justified in a free and democratic society? No. It limits the right with a completely unworkable regime which overreaches the more practical alternative. It is also unworkable because it does require all Victorian medical practitioners to know their colleagues' view on when they would perform an abortion.

---

32. Victoria Parliament, Legislative Council, *Hansard,* 7 October 2008, 3919
33. Victoria Parliament, Legislative Council, *Hansard,* 10 October 2008, 4253

In my opinion, this was the first real test of the Victorian *Charter of Human Rights and Responsibilities Act* and it failed spectacularly to protect a core non-derogable ICCPR human right which fell hostage to a broader social and political agenda for abortion law reform and a prevailing fad in bioethics which asserts that doctors should leave their consciences at the door.

Groups such as *Liberty Victoria* provided no coherent answers. Academic experts on the Charter largely remained silent. The Equal Opportunity and Human Rights Commission simplistically dismissed freedom of conscience. Given that the referral clause was both unnecessary, unworkable, and more intrusive than state notification of available abortion providers, one can only conclude as did Justice Kennedy in the leading US gay rights decision *Romer v Evans*: the clause 'seems inexplicable by anything but animus toward the class it affects; it lacks a rational relationship to legitimate state interests.'[34]

I daresay most civil libertarians and Charter advocates are little worried by this first test of the Victorian Charter because they share the view of Julian Savulescu that doctors' consciences should be left at the door in the name of patient autonomy. Doctors are simply there to provide a service as if they are automatons. In his article 'Conscientious objection in medicine', Savulescu commences with a literary reference—not to Sophocles' Antigone but to Shakespeare's Richard III. When Richard III roused from his dream he made his declaration:

> Let not our babbling dreams affright our souls: conscience is but a word that cowards use, devised at first to keep the strong in awe: Our strong arms be our conscience; swords our law. [35]

Savulescu quotes only the sentence: 'conscience is but a word that cowards use, devised at first to keep the strong in awe'.[36] Here is the context. During Richard's dream the night before going into battle, he confronted the eleven ghosts of those he had callously murdered

34. *Romer v Evans* 517 US 620 (1996) at 633.

including the Ghost of Prince Edward, son to King Henry VI who proclaimed 'Let me sit heavy on thy soul to-morrow! Think, how thou stab'dst me in my prime of youth. At Tewksbury: despair, therefore, and die!'[37]

And the Ghost of King Henry VI who proclaimed 'When I was mortal, my anointed body by thee was punched full of deadly holes. Think on the Tower and me: despair, and die! Harry the Sixth bids thee despair, and die!'[38]

Hardly the model for the discerning medical practitioner, hardly the literary quote likely to evince sympathy for the primacy of conscience, a non-derogable human right. For those who want swords to be their law, there is every reason to view conscience as a word used only by cowards. It is those sorts of people who demand that conscience be left at the door. It is only by discarding conscience at the door that one can argue: 'Doctors who compromise the delivery of medical services to patients on conscience grounds must be punished through removal of licence to practise and other legal mechanisms'.[39]

Martha Nussbaum's concluding chapter in *Liberty of Conscience* is titled with a question: 'Toward an Overlapping Consensus?' She makes the point that laws do matter as 'good laws and institutions set limits on people's ability to act on their intolerant and inegalitarian views'. She describes Roger Williams' challenge to the new colonies: 'that they find, and learn to inhabit, a shared moral space, without turning that space into a sectarian space that privileges some views over others'.[40]

That challenge was not met when the Victorian Parliament, academy and civil society endorsed an unworkable, unprincipled, and useless compulsory referral clause trampling the conscientious beliefs of some medical practitioners with no workable benefit being

---

35. William Shakespeare, *Richard III*, V.iv.
36. Julian Savulescu, 'Conscientious objection in medicine' in *British Medical Journal*, 332 (2006): 294.
37. William Shakespeare, *Richard III*, V.iii.
38. William Shakespeare, *Richard III*, V.iii.
39. Savulescu, *Conscientious objection*, 296.
40. Nussbaum, *Liberty of Conscience*, 360.

accorded their patients. We need to do better if faith communities and minorities are to be assured that a Victorian style charter of rights is anything but a piece of legislative window dressing which rarely changes legislative or policy outcomes, being perceived as a device for the delivery of a soft left sectarian agenda—a device which will be discarded or misconstrued whenever the rights articulated do not comply with that agenda.

Nussbaum finds hope in John Rawls' notion of overlapping consensus whereby those holding different religious and secular comprehensive doctrines can live together on terms of equal respect 'agreeing to share a "freestanding" ethical conception in the political realm, and agreeing, at the same time, to forgo the search for the dominance of any one comprehensive doctrine over the others'. Those who think that conscience is but a word that cowards use are unlikely 'to forgo the search for dominance of their comprehensive doctrine over others'.[41]

We still have much more work to do in Australia if we are to take seriously in law and policy Nussbaum's 'respect conscience principle' and her 'accommodation principle'. Our protection of human rights for all will be much enhanced if we are better able to provide 'protected space within which citizens may act as their conscience dictates'[42] and if we can acknowledge that 'sometimes some people (usually members of religious minorities) should be exempted from generally applicable laws for reasons of conscience'.[43]

---

41. Nussbaum, *Liberty of Conscience,* 361.
42. Nussbaum, *Liberty of Conscience,* 22.
43. Nussbaum, *Liberty of Conscience,* 24.

10

Recognising Aboriginal Rights

In 2005, I delivered one of the annual Amnesty International Lectures in Oxford. The theme for that year's lectures was indigenous land rights. I entitled my address: 'Standing in Deep Time; Standing in the Law: A Non-Indigenous Australian Perspective on Land Rights, Land Wrongs and Self-Determination'.

Mr Rhodes, *Terra Nullius* and Contemporary Values

There is something passing strange about an Australian Catholic priest, descended from Irish immigrants, standing at the podium in the Sheldonian Theatre here at Oxford in 2005 daring to offer an opinion on indigenous land rights and self determination. What right do I have to speak? What could I usefully say?

I take heart from Amnesty International's conviction that the ordinary person can make a difference by having a commitment to public advocacy and private communication with both the prisoner and the jailer, acting in solidarity with the prisoner and putting pressure on the jailer. As a non-indigenous advocate for indigenous rights, I am committed to dialogue with all parties and to public advocacy that keeps hope alive—the hope of finding common ground, sharing country and reconciling differences in societies whose indigenous members have survived the adverse effects of colonisation.

Being a priest speaking about land rights on the cusp of old Europe, I am haunted by the words of Chief Justice Marshall in the 1823 decision of the US Supreme Court *Johnson v McIntosh*:

> On the discovery of this immense continent, the great
> nations of Europe were eager to appropriate to themselves
> so much of it as they could respectively acquire. Its
> vast extent offered an ample field to the ambition and
> enterprise of all; and the character and religion of its
> inhabitants afforded an apology for considering them
> as a people over whom the superior genius of Europe
> might claim an ascendancy. The potentates of the old
> world found no difficulty in convincing themselves,
> that they made ample compensation to the inhabitants
> of the new, by bestowing on them civilization and
> Christianity, in exchange for unlimited independence.[1]

I have agreed to participate in this Amnesty lecture series knowing
that indigenous speakers have preceded me. In my home country I
have been a long time advocate of Aboriginal land rights and self-
determination. That has not spared me some spirited disagreement
with Aboriginal representatives. And of course, government
apologists see me as an incurable romantic dreaming of the noble
savage's renaissance. Having been privileged over many years to
participate in the indigenous struggle for land rights in my home
country, I still believe in that struggle and the primacy of Aboriginal
aspirations for self-determination while Aboriginal leaders seek
to accommodate themselves to the realities of their traditional
communities, the demands of government and the expectations of
the descendants of their colonisers.

Without land rights and self-determination, indigenous peoples
in previously colonised societies are treated as the members of one
polity without a voice and as people without distinctive rights. With
land rights and self-determination they are members of two polities
with their own conflicting voices (realist, liberal and idealist), living
under two laws that require reconciliation when the indigenous
law and the coloniser's law collide or when the indigenous person
asserts individual rights against the collective rights of the clan or

---

1.   21 US (1823) 240, 253.

community. Land rights and self-determination provide the space and the time for these indigenous peoples to live in their two worlds.

Indigenous people without land rights and without a modicum of self-determination are individuals and societies denied the place and opportunity to maintain themselves with their distinctive cultural identity in a post-colonial, globalised world. Indigenous people with land rights and a modicum of self-determination are individuals and societies with an enhanced choice about how to participate in the life of the nation state and of the global economy while being guaranteed the place and opportunity to maintain their cultural and religious identity with some protection from State interference and from involuntary assimilation into the predominant post-colonial society.

I argue four propositions about previously colonised societies with indigenous minorities:

- Law and policy should recognise that even today indigenous minorities in these societies have to live in two worlds, and the common good of these societies (as well as respect for the rights of the indigenous citizens) requires some recognition of land rights and self-determination.

- Indigenous leaders are like politicians dealing in international affairs. They have to deal with their domestic constituencies and treat with the leaders of other governments that happen to be the elected governments of all the people in the post-colonial society. As in the field of international relations, there will be indigenous leaders and theorists who are realists or idealists and others, seeking reconciliation in the centre, who are liberals. All must be heard.

- Indigenous people should be free to opt for their individual rights as citizens regardless of the arrangements between government and the indigenous leadership.

- Only by tolerating the uncertainty and complexity of land rights and self-determination can non-

indigenous people own their history and their
responsibility for the continuing plight of their
indigenous citizens.

It is appropriate in Oxford to commence discussion about land
rights with reference to the Privy Council's 1919 decision *In re
Southern Rhodesia* in which Mr Rhodes' British South Africa
Company was a party. This decision related to land transactions
between Cecil Rhodes and the natives of Zimbabwe that may in part
have contributed to some of you being able to study here at Oxford,
while the indigenous people suffered dispossession and deprivation.
The other parties to the proceedings were the Legislative Council of
Southern Rhodesia, the Crown and the natives. Lord Sumner in his
report of the Privy Council wrote:

> By the disinterested liberality of persons in this country
> their Lordships had the advantage of hearing the case
> for the natives who were themselves incapable of urging,
> and perhaps unconscious of possessing, any case at all.
> Undoubtedly this inquiry has thereby been rendered
> more complete.[2]

Leslie Scott KC and Stuart Bevan are described as appearing 'for
the natives', perhaps the shortest and most generic description of a
party ever to appear in the authorised law reports. On the next page
of his Report, Lord Sumner writes:

> The estimation of the rights of aboriginal tribes is always
> inherently difficult. Some tribes are so low in the scale
> of social organization that their usages and conceptions
> of rights and duties are not to be reconciled with the
> institutions or the legal ideas of civilized society. Such
> a gulf cannot be bridged. It would be idle to impute
> to such people some shadow of the rights known to
> our law and then to transmute it into the substance of
> transferable rights of property as we know them.[3]

---

2. *In re Southern Rhodesia* [1919] AC 211, 232.
3. *In re Southern Rhodesia*, 233–4.

Lord Sumner observed that there was 'a wide tract of much ethnological interest' between these tribes and other indigenous peoples 'whose legal conceptions, though differently developed, are hardly less precise than our own'. He thought the natives in question 'approximate rather to the lower than to the higher limit'.[4] According to the Privy Council, the maintenance of native title rights 'was fatally inconsistent with white settlement of the country' which 'was the object of the whole forward movement', pioneered by the Company and controlled by the Crown 'with the result that the aboriginal system gave place to another prescribed by the Order in Council'. The Privy Council concluded its consideration of the native title claim, 'Whoever now owns the unalienated lands, the natives do not'.[5] The natives were the people of one new polity without a voice, under one new law without rights.

Turning to the dispute between the company and the Crown, the Privy Council decided that the British South Africa Company was entitled to dispose of any unalienated lands using the proceeds to offset the costs of administration. Should the crown terminate the Company's administration of Southern Rhodesia, the company was entitled to reimbursement from the Crown for previous costs— either from the proceeds of further land sales or from public funds.

At the height of colonial expansion by European empires, those indigenous groups who bore some resemblance to their colonial masters were to enjoy some recognition and protection. Those differing from their new masters who could barely comprehend their social reality were to be denied any semblance of land rights and self-determination. Such Eurocentric notions put blinkers on the law's horizons of justice.

Seventy-four years after the Privy Council's decision about the fortunes of the British South Africa Company, the High Court of Australia had, for the first time in the *Mabo* case, to consider the rights of the Australian 'natives' to the 'unalienated lands'. In 1992, that

---

4. *In re Southern Rhodesia*, 234.
5. *In re Southern Rhodesia*, 235.

court decided to discard the distinction between inhabited colonies that were deemed to be *terra nullius* and those which were not:

> If it were permissible in past centuries to keep the common law in step with international law, it is imperative in today's world that the common law should neither be nor be seen to be frozen in an age of racial discrimination. The fiction by which the rights and interests of indigenous inhabitants in land were treated as non-existent was justified by a policy which has no place in the contemporary law of this country.[6]

With the removal of the blinkers used by Lord Sumner and most Europeans of his time, indigenous people are not guaranteed a better life, but they can be assured the legal and political preconditions for better participation in the life of the nation state, while maintaining and adapting their traditional places and lifestyle. The contemporary Australian court went on to say:[7]

> Whatever the justification advanced in earlier days for refusing to recognize the rights and interests in land of the indigenous inhabitants of settled colonies, an unjust and discriminatory doctrine of that kind can no longer be accepted. The expectations of the international community accord in this respect with the contemporary values of the Australian people.[8]

Does this reference to contemporary values imply that the judges thought the majority of Australians, if asked in an opinion poll, 'Do you support aboriginal land rights?', would have answered unequivocally 'Yes'. I do not think it can mean that. I am prepared to accept that the majority of Australians if asked that question in 1992 would have answered 'No'. The values that underpin the

---

6. Justice Brennan (Mason CJ and McHugh J concurring) in *Mabo v Queensland (No. 2)* (1992) 175 CLR 1, 41–2.

7. *Mabo*, 42.

8. *Mabo*, 42.

Mabo decision are respect for property, the desire for certainty in the conduct of relations relating to land, predictability in the application of the law by courts for the resolution of conflict, and non-discrimination in the sense that governments should not treat persons differently unless there is a coherent rationale for such different treatment. In particular, governments should not treat more adversely people's property rights simply because they are members of a particular race. These are the enduring values of contemporary Australians.

After the *Mabo* decision, I met with the senior partners of one of Australia's largest legal firms. They were agnostic about the decision's effect, doubting that it had really changed anything. I pointed out that my line of work had not changed but that prior to *Mabo* it was called politics; post *Mabo* it was called law. It was unimaginable prior to *Mabo* that a Jesuit working for Aboriginal rights would have been invited to the annual retreat of a leading law firm. Something had changed.

At the end of the session, one of the lawyers, a Mr Murphy pointing out that his ancestors were Irish, asked: 'If there are special rights for the Aborigines, why don't you have special rights for the Irish?' Being a Brennan and my mother an O'Hara, I have some sympathy for the rights of the Irish in Ireland. I take some consolation and pride in the fact that there is somewhere on earth that the Irish can be as Irish as they like, with minimal interference by other persons. The more relevant comparison is not with the rights of the Irish in Australia but with the rights of the Irish in the Republic of Ireland.

There is only one place on earth where Australian Aborigines have any prospect of living out the fullness of community lives as Aborigines. That is on the Australian continent, though as part of a nation state where as an indigenous minority, they will be far more circumscribed in their distinctive cultural choices. But there are possibilities for them, and those possibilities are enhanced by recognition of their land rights and their ongoing entitlement to self-determination within the life of the nation.

The Symbolism and Utility of Land Rights

Indigenous groups with some recognition of their land rights face the dilemma: how to live within the nation state participating in its economy while maintaining distinctive culture and heritage. That ought be their decision, and no one else's, even if that someone else be a government with a fresh political mandate. Those of us who are non-indigenous members of such nation states need to guarantee the minimum requirements for these indigenous groups to make a realistic choice. Doing so, we have the opportunity, at some considerable cost, to ground our national identity and project in the depth and complexity of the history of our land and all its peoples.

In 1995, I made my first trip to the United States. I headed directly to Alaska. On arrival at the St Marys Yup'ik Eskimo community on the Andreafski River, a small tributary of the mighty Yukon, a local community member offered to show me around the community. Despite my jetlag, I readily agreed. I was keen to meet members of an indigenous community who were assured a significant degree of self-determination and land rights as far as the eye could see. This woman took me first to the local cemetery. I was perplexed. She told me the story of the lives and deaths of the three young men who had been most recently buried in the cemetery. She told me the story of the community without breaching the confidences or imposing on the privacy of any of the living. There were tales of violence, alcoholism, and dreadful accidents. The similarities with so many tales that I had heard on Aboriginal communities over the years were stark - and far more immediate than the legal and political differences that distinguished the land rights and self-determination of Alaskan and Australian communities.[9]

---

9. A 2003 editorial of the *British Medical Journal* reported: 'The gap in life expectancy between indigenous and non-indigenous populations is estimated to be 19-21 years in Australia, 8 years in New Zealand, 5-7 years in Canada, and 4-5 years in the United States. These continuing disparities in health are a matter of major concern, but it is none the less important to recognise the substantial narrowing of the gap in health between indigenous and non-indigenous people in the United States, Canada, and New Zealand. In Australia the gap in median age at death seems to have widened.' (Vol 327:404 (23 August 2003)).

That night I was devastated as I reflected on what I had heard at the cemetery. One of the local Jesuits showed me a series of newspaper articles highlighting the dreadful social problems confronted by indigenous communities living close to the Yukon. But how could this be? These people had not only secure land title over their community lands but also other economic benefits flowing from the *Alaska Native Claims Settlement Act of 1971*. They had self-determination. They not only had their own law-making councils. They had their own courts and their own police; their own schools and a secure land base together with the economic security of a fishing resource that was seemingly boundless in that part of the world—all we could have dreamt of in Australia. And they lived in such a remote place that very few outsiders had an interest in living there or disturbing them. They had known Russian and American governments and prided themselves on maintaining their traditions and identity no matter which flag flew at the post office.

No matter which country you survey, no matter what that government's policy, no matter what the present strategy of indigenous leaders, and no matter what the public understanding or sympathy about the position of indigenous minorities, land rights for indigenous people are an essential component in providing indigenous citizens with the choice and the potential to live an authentic indigenous life within the realistic confines of nationality and economy. Land rights are also the cornerstone for the settlement of historic post-colonial grievances in:

- Providing a land base for some indigenous persons and communities
- Providing some indigenous communities with economic and political bargaining power, assuring them a place at the table
- Recognising the entitlement of indigenous communities to maintain and sustain their religious beliefs and practices, without threatening the public order of the society after colonisation

- Correcting some historic injustices which can be put right without occasioning injustice to other persons
- Validating the post-colonial legal system, providing a greater coincidence between law and justice
- Providing a necessary forum for the resolution of conflicting claims
- Assisting all citizens of the nation state to appreciate the place and entitlements of indigenous people
- Assisting all citizens of the nation state reach a better understanding of their history and their place in the world.

Australia is distinctive because our history of land rights is so brief, our approach so pragmatic and belated, and our commitment to land rights so refreshingly new, fragile and wavering. While no one seriously suggests substantive change to the system of land holding for indigenous communities in New Zealand, Canada or the United States, some Australians now entertain the hope or thought that Aboriginal problems could be solved if community land titles were transformed into alienable individual titles, encouraging indigenous communities to leave behind their traditional ways and enter the contemporary market place with an initial bonus of transferable land title.

Captain Arthur Phillip arrived at Sydney Cove on 26 January 1788 and established a penal colony for undesirable persons from this part of the world, given the future unavailability of the American colonies that had revolted. The six Australian colonies were the only British colonies in which there was no recognition of land rights. Only in the last thirty-five years in Australia, land rights have been recognised for the first time, accepted as part of the just settlement, and now questioned as symbolic, wasteful and misdirected policy. Land rights and self-determination are the stuff of 'culture wars' in Australia.

While everyone is in favour of reconciliation between indigenous and other Australians, protagonists distinguish practical reconciliation and symbolic reconciliation.[10] Conceding the legitimacy of past grievances, some now see land rights as a symbolic issue providing little practical assistance to Aborigines wanting to live contemporary lives, or even worse, as providing a dead end panacea for life separated from the mainstream in the backwater of community life without economic prospects or relief from the entrapment of the past. While land rights is seen by some supporters as an honouring of the Aboriginal spiritual relationship with land, others view land rights as a simple matter of setting right an historic injustice, or as a matter of economic empowerment. I was once asked by a publisher, 'Is land rights about power or culture?' I answered, 'Both', and still do.

Sir David Lange, ex-Prime Minister of New Zealand and renowned Oxford debater once gave the after-dinner speech at an Australian conference on indigenous and environmental issues. Lange was bemused by his trans-Tasman audience and told us: 'You Australians are always looking for the final answer to the Aboriginal question. There is no final answer. There are only durable solutions which can last a generation or two when once again you will have to sit down and negotiate an agreement for the future.' That is one reason why the more conservative Australian politicians have always opposed the idea of a modern treaty. It never gets to the stage that you can draw the line and put the past behind you. There will always be indigenous dissatisfaction because of the historic injustices and because of the ongoing marginalisation that comes from being a minority in the post-colonisation society. There is no definitive answer for those living in two polities under two laws.

---

10. Professor Fiona Stanley, Australian of the Year in 2003, wrote in the *British Medical Journal*: 'In Australia, there is currently a debate about symbolic versus practical reconciliation—the latter approach suggesting that it is best not to acknowledge the history and its influence on current outcomes, and that to move forward to improve living conditions and other activities that enhance wellbeing is in effect ignoring the root causes. However, evidence shows that the most effective programmes are those which acknowledge the devastating impact of removing people from their land, removing children from their families and from their culture, and marginalising people so that they cannot access any of the advantages of the dominant culture, such as education and employment, which would have enabled them to participate and control their own lives.' (Vol 327: 404 (23 August 2003)).

Indigenous Claims to Land Rights in the *Terra Nullius* of Australia

At Yirrkala, Arnhem Land in the Northern Territory, no penal colony had ever been established. The people there had traded regularly with the Macassans from Indonesia. A few Englishmen had come there attempting to run pastoral properties in the nineteenth century but they failed and moved on. In 1935, the first white men settled there. They were a couple of Methodist missionaries and their families. Some Aborigines from Arnhem Land had visited Darwin and seen the conditions in which the Larrakeah people were living as fringe dwellers on the outskirts of town. They did not much like what they saw of white urban society and its treatment of their Larrakeah kinsmen. In 1963, the Commonwealth government excised 300 square kilometres from the Aboriginal reserve in Arnhem Land in preparation for the proposed granting of a forty-two year lease to a Swiss consortium Nabalco for the mining of bauxite.

Some forms of mining are not very intrusive. Bauxite mining requires the stripping away of the entire land surface. Regeneration of the land takes many decades. Aborigines who had a long undisturbed and spiritual relationship with the land, celebrating ceremonies at sacred sites for which they cared, were very troubled to learn that a government in Canberra thousands of miles away could give permission to a foreign corporation to destroy their land, invade their community and upset their sacred sites. With the help of the Methodist missionaries, they sent bark petitions in their own language and in English to the parliament in Canberra respectfully requesting that they be consulted about any measures impacting on their community or on their lands. The first petition concluded:

- That the people of this area fear that their needs and interests will be completely ignored as they have been ignored in the past, and they fear that the fate which has overtaken the Larrakeah tribe will overtake them.

- And they humbly pray that the Honourable the House of Representatives will appoint a Committee, accompanied by competent interpreters, to hear the views of the people of Yirrkala before permitting the excision of this land.
- They humbly pray that no arrangements be entered into with any company which will destroy the livelihood and independence of the Yirrkala people.
- And your petitioners as in duty bound will ever pray God to help you and us.

Then in 1966, the Gurindji people living at Watti Creek in the Northern Territory walked off Lord Vestey's cattle station demanding better wages and title to their traditional land. They were also concerned about the sexual exploitation of their women by white workers on the Vestey property. This 'walk-off' became one of the great emblematic events in Australian land rights. The leader of the walk-off Vincent Lingiari became the father figure of land rights. Nine years after the walk-off, Prime Minister Gough Whitlam went to Watti Creek, now known by its traditional name 'Dagaragu', to hand over a lease of the land to the traditional owners. Pouring a handful of earth into the hands of Vincent Lingiari, Whitlam spoke for the nation when he declared:

> Vincent Lingiari I solemnly hand to you these deeds as proof, in Australian law, that these lands belong to the Gurindji people and I put into your hands this piece of the earth itself as a sign that we restore them to you and your children forever.[11]

Lingiari replied, 'We are all mates now'. The leaders of two polities had met and the voice of each was heard. This was a novel development in the *terra nullius* of Australia. Each leader spoke with authority for

---

11. Gough Whitlam, Thirty Year Celebration of Walkoff from Wave Hill at Daguragu, Northern Territory, 23 August 1996, Whitlam Institute.

the land: two polities, two laws. Two song writers (Kevin Carmody, an Aboriginal, and Paul Kelly, a white Australian) wrote a song 'From Little Things Big Things Grow':

> That was the story of Vincent Lingiari But this is the story of something much more
> How power and privilege can not move a people Who know where they stand and stand in the law

They sang the song in Sydney Town Hall at Gough Whitlam's funeral in November 2014.

Four years before the ceremony at Dagaragu, I had commenced my university studies. A student of politics and law, I was interested to hear Aboriginal protesters who came on campus demonstrating against the policies of the Queensland government on Aboriginal reserves. Like many white Australians, I had not previously heard Aborigines speak. I found it difficult to believe that there were places where Aborigines lived, managed by white public servants who controlled many aspects of Aboriginal life. I heard stories about the need for Aborigines to receive government approval to marry. Public servants could even dictate the style of swimming costume that could be worn. These communities had no right to their traditional lands and they were still paid minimal wages. Aboriginal voices were heard on the national airwaves. Aborigines were pleading their case with the people, with the parliaments, and finally in the courts.

Having received no satisfaction from the politicians after the lodging of their 1963 petitions, the Yirrkala Aborigines turned to the courts in 1968. Thus began one of the long games of legal and political ping pong in which the cause of land rights went backwards and forwards between the courts and the parliaments, over the net of public opinion. Milirrpum and Mungurrawuy were the leaders of the two clan owning groups, the Rirratjingu and the Gumatj clans. They were joined by Daymbalipu, the leader of the Djapu clan who had access to the Rirratjingu and Gumatj lands for hunting and foraging. Expert anthropologists, including W E H Stanner, joined traditional Aboriginal owners in explaining the system of traditional Aboriginal law and the Aboriginal connections with land. The judge, Sir Richard Blackburn was impressed but troubled. After considerable delay, he handed down his decision in 1971, which happened to be my first year of law studies. Justice Blackburn observed:

> The evidence shows a subtle and elaborate system highly adapted to the country in which the people led their lives, which provided a stable order of society and was remarkably free from the vagaries of personal whim or influence. If ever a system could be called 'a government of laws, and not of men', it is that shown in the evidence before me.[12]

However he felt compelled to rule that the British common law did not recognise communal interests in land as described in the evidence in court. Even if it did, he ruled that all such interests would have been extinguished by the assertion of sovereignty by the British crown. The lawyers for the traditional owners saw little point in appealing the case even though these were disputed propositions of law because the judge had also ruled against the Aborigines on the facts. He said, 'I am not satisfied, on the balance of probabilities, that the plaintiffs' predecessors had in 1788 the same links to the same areas of land as those which the plaintiffs now claim'.[13]

With no further recourse in the courts, the Aborigines looked again to the politicians. Change was in the air with the election of the Whitlam Labor government in 1972. That government was elected with a commitment to legislate for the recognition of Aboriginal land rights in the Northern Territory. After a royal commission, legislation was proposed and it was passed in amended form by the Australian Parliament at the instigation of the Liberal Country Party Government led by Malcolm Fraser after the then Governor-General, Sir John Kerr, dismissed the Whitlam Labor government.

---

12. *Milirrpum v Nabalco* (1971) 17 FLR 141, at 267.
13. *Milirrpum v Nabalco*, 198.

Aboriginal traditional owners were granted inalienable title to their lands and a right to veto mining on their lands. The veto armed these owners with economic bargaining power. If they had the power to say 'No', they were able to say 'Yes, subject to conditions favourable to us'. The recognition of the Aboriginal spiritual relationship with land carried with it the prospect of economic enhancement.

Meanwhile Eddie Koiki Mabo, a Torres Strait islander, was living on the Australian mainland, having been denied permission to return to his island homeland by Queensland public servants who thought him to be a troublemaker. He decided to organise the Meriam people, a group of Torres Strait Islanders from the Murray Islands, to bring a case in the High Court of Australia to challenge the findings of law made by Sir Richard Blackburn in the 1971 *Milirrpum* decision.

He thought Blackburn got the law wrong. He also argued that even if the High Court agreed with Blackburn, the case of the Torres Strait Islanders was distinguishable from that of mainland Aborigines for two reasons. First, Torres Strait Islanders were not traditionally hunters and gatherers. They cultivated vegetable gardens and lived in huts in settled villages, thereby having individual interests in discrete blocks of land rather than communal interests in vast tracts of country. Second, the Queensland crown as sovereign had continued to recognise Torres Strait interests in land. The Queensland government had even set up courts to determine land disputes between islanders even though no land titles had been granted by the crown.

Mabo had a passion for putting right an ancient wrong, and the imagination and bold vision to see it through to the highest court in the land. It is one of the tragic ironies of the law that Eddie Mabo, like the claimants in the original *Milirrpum* case, did not establish his own native title claim because the trial judge did not accept his evidence. However his co-plaintiffs, including Father David Passi, did succeed. Mabo's action provided the vehicle for a declaration of native title by the nation's highest court.

The Queensland government's response to Mabo's claim was one of the last ditch stands by governments still blinkered by the *terra nullius* mindset. The government introduced to the Queensland parliament the *Queensland Coastal Islands Declaratory Bill* of 1985. The bill was promptly passed. It was only 14 lines long. It deemed that Torres Strait Islanders did not have any rights to their traditional lands prior to the assertion of the Crown's sovereignty over the islands in 1879 or that alternatively all rights were extinguished retrospectively to 1879 with no compensation being payable. The government explained that this bill would avoid the need for limitless research work on mere matters of history being agitated in the courts.

As the legislation was inconsistent with the Commonwealth Parliament's *Racial Discrimination Act*, the High Court struck down the Queensland provision in 1988, giving Eddie Mabo and his co-plaintiffs the much needed encouragement and opportunity to proceed with the substance of their case.[14] On 3 June 1992, the High Court of Australia declared that 'the Meriam people are entitled as against the whole world to possession, occupation, use and enjoyment of the lands of the Murray Islands' and that 'the title of the Meriam people is subject to the power of the Parliament of Queensland and the power of the Governor in Council of Queensland to extinguish that title by valid exercise of their respective powers, provided any exercise of those powers is not inconsistent with the laws of the Commonwealth'.[15]

As the sun rose over the tip of Cape York on 12 October 1993, the waters of the Torres Strait were exceedingly calm. As the sun glistened on the water, Father David Passi, the Anglican Pastor of the Island of Mer in the Murray Islands group, stood at the back of the speed boat pointing at a small island close to the shore, declaring, 'That's Possession Island.' David smiled broadly as he explained this was the place where James Cook came ashore after his epic voyage up the Australian eastern coastline in 1770, raising his King's flag and claiming possession in His Majesty's name of all he had sailed passed. David chuckled, 'Cook had his back to the Torres Strait when he claimed possession.'

14. *Mabo v Queensland* (1988) 166 CLR 186.
15. *Mabo v Queensland (No. 2)* (1992) 175 CLR 1, 217.

Next day at Bamaga on the tip of Cape York, David explained the significance of the *Mabo* decision to a meeting of his fellow Anglican clergy. His people believe that in ancient times a figure named Malo set down the law for relations between islanders regarding their lands and waters. All islanders speak of the myth of Malo-Bomai. Malo and his maternal uncle made a long sea journey from West New Guinea across to Mer in the east. These mythical heroes, Malo resembling an octopus, brought the eight peoples or clans into one, 'strengthening them with the qualities of a diversity of sea creatures, so giving the power to match the sea and make long journeys across Malo, the deep seas, for canoes and for battle.' In this part of Australia, the indigenous people define themselves in relation to land, sea, each other and seasonal time or prevailing wind.

Fr Passi, known also as Kebi Bala, explains Malo's law:

> For thousands of years we have owned the land and Malo who was the Meriam centre of it made sure that members of the society were given land. They are our laws. We have Malo ra Gelar. It says that Malo keeps to his own place; Malo does not trespass in another man's property. Malo keeps his hands to himself. He does not touch what is not his. He does not permit his feet to carry him towards other men's property. His hands are not grasping. He holds them back. He does not wander from his path. He walks on tip-toe, silent and careful, leaving no signs to tell that this is the way he took.

Passi explains that since colonisation there have been two laws, 'the white man's law and Malo's law'. Malo's law is respectful of people's history and connection with the land. The white man's law is strong. It believes might is right. Those who believe in Malo's law have to convince those who practise the white man's law that Malo's law is right. Might alone is not right. Speaking about two laws, David Passi was using the discourse of two polities and two religious traditions.

Ian McLachlan who had been president of the National Farmers' Federation was the most trenchant critic of the *Mabo* decision in the

Australian Parliament. After traveling to the Torres Strait he said, 'It is perfectly obvious to me that those people have owned that land forever as history has been recorded. But it is different to say that all over Australia we should have a feast for lawyers'.

The decision was basically a judicious realignment of the common law developed by judges to match the historical reality with the historic land grievance that for the first time had come before the highest court in the land. The decision posed no threat to sovereignty or to the Treasury coffers. The decision was an honest acknowledgement that most Aborigines had been long dispossessed of their lands and any restitution or compensation was a matter for parliaments rather than the courts.

The decision provided an historic opportunity to put right those wrongs of the past that could be put right and to acknowledge those wrongs which forever stained the nation's identity. This could be done without any threat to any other person's land rights or legitimate economic interests. The decision provided a unique opportunity for a negotiated settlement of the nation's longstanding land rights question with Aborigines at the government's negotiating table and holding some of their own trump cards.

Two centuries after European settlement, most Aborigines had been dispossessed of their lands. A just settlement of land grievances required more than the recognition of those rights that had escaped extinguishment by governments which had operated for generations with a *terra nullius* mindset. The Parliament set up a land fund for the purchase of lands on the open market for the benefit of those Aborigines who had lost their traditional lands.[16] There is now a National Native Title Tribunal which has over 400 claims pending. There have been over 300 native title claims determined. There are over 900 registered indigenous land

---

16. That fund is now self-perpetuating, allowing purchases of more than $45 million each year. The Indigenous Land Corporation (ILC) has acquired 5.86 million hectares of land providing employment outcomes for 5,315 indigenous Australians. The 2013-4 Annual Report for the ILC notes: 'The Indigenous estate comprises more than 20% of Australia's landmass and the ILC plays a critical role in assisting its management to achieve social, cultural, environmental and economic benefits for Indigenous people' (15).

use agreements. The government funds Aboriginal representative bodies which have their own advisers. Professor Marcia Langton says, 'What's become clear is that whereas litigation is costly and time consuming, agreement-making costs less and is more timely'.

There have been more High Court cases since *Mabo*.[17] Both the Labor and Liberal-National Party governments have tried their hands at legislative responses to the High Court's native title decisions.

Paul Keating led the nation in espousing the correctness and decency of *Mabo*. John Howard told Parliament that *Mabo* 'now with the passage of time, seems completely unexceptionable to me. It appears to have been based on a good deal of logic and fairness and proper principle'.[18] The dust has settled. The decision is not seen as a revolution but as a belated common sense piece of legal reasoning.

Initially the mining industry was very concerned that the recognition of native title could cause a massive slowdown in mining and exploration. On the tenth anniversary of the decision, Tim Shanahan, CEO, Chamber of Minerals and Energy (WA) said, 'Mining companies in the early days weren't as sanguine or accepting of native title. These days it's seen as part of the normal business of mining'. The belated recognition of native title has helped to put right what two of the High Court justices described as our 'national legacy of unutterable shame'.[19]

The High Court still has its work cut out interpreting the fine print of the excessively amended *Native Title Act* and filling in the detail of

---

17. *Native Title Act Case* (1995) 183 CLR 373, *North Ganalanja Aboriginal Corporation v Queensland* (1996) 185 CLR 595, *Wik Peoples v Queensland* (1996) 187 CLR 1, *Fejo v Northern Territory* (1998) 195 CLR 96, *Yanner v Eaton* (1999) 201 CLR 351, *Commonwealth v Yarmirr* (2001) 208 CLR 1, *Western Australia v Ward* (2002) 213 CLR 1, *Wilson v Anderson* (2002) 213 CLR 401, *Yorta Yorta v Victoria* (2002) 214 CLR 422. The key questions have been about the capacity of native title to co-exist with other interests in land such as pastoral leases, and the relationship between common law native title and the native title rights defined in the *Native Title Act 1994–8*.

18. (1996) CPD (HofR) 345; 6 May 1996. Again on 26 June 1996, John Howard told Parliament: 'I have always regarded the *Mabo* decision itself as being a justified, correct decision. I have stated that on a number of occasions.' (1996) CPD (HofR) 2791.

19 Justices Deane and Gaudron, *Mabo v Queensland* (No) 2 (1992) 175 CLR 1 at 104.

common law native title, providing considerable feasting for lawyers. Indigenous communities still have their problems and we still have a national problem in reconciling ourselves. The denial of land rights and the failure to accord equal protection and respect under the law are no longer part of the Australian solution. That is a better starting point than the *terra nullius* mindset which preceded *Mabo*.

Justice McHugh, one of the now retired judges who decided the *Mabo* case has had cause to look back over the history of native title litigation. Ten years after *Mabo*, he wrote in a judgment:

> The dispossession of the Aboriginal peoples from their lands was a great wrong. Many people believe that those of us who are the beneficiaries of that wrong have a moral responsibility to redress it to the extent that it can be redressed. But it is becoming increasingly clear—to me, at all events—that redress cannot be achieved by a system that depends on evaluating the competing legal rights of landholders and native-title holders. The deck is stacked against the native-title holders whose fragile rights must give way to the superior rights of the landholders whenever the two classes of rights conflict. And it is a system that is costly and time-consuming. At present the chief beneficiaries of the system are the legal representatives of the parties. It may be that the time has come to think of abandoning the present system, a system that simply seeks to declare and enforce the legal rights of the parties, irrespective of their merits. A better system may be an arbitral system that declares what the rights of the parties ought to be according to the justice and circumstances of the individual case.[20]

---

20   *Western Australia v Ward* (2002) 213 CLR 1 at 240–1 (This case deals with the claim by the Miriuwung and Gajerrong People to lands in the East Kimberley region of Western Australia, including part of the Ord River scheme.) During argument in the earlier case *Fejo v Northern Territory* (1998) 195 CLR 96, Justice McHugh said during argument: 'My view was that native title would apply basically to only unalienated Crown land. If, for example, I thought it was going to apply to freehold, to leaseholds, I am by no means convinced that I would have not joined Justice Dawson (the sole dissentient in *Mabo*), and it may well be that that was also the view of other members of the Court.' (Transcript 22 June 1998)

Other High Court judges have voiced similar concerns.[21] The issue now is not the legitimacy of land rights but determining the cut-off point for recognising native title rights when other parties also have rights over the same land, and matching the remaining native title rights with the real, rather than imagined, Aboriginal and Torres Strait Islander aspirations. Aboriginal lawyer, Noel Pearson, says that 'native title is all about what is left over. And land rights have never been about the dispossession of the colonisers and their descendants. Whether it be statutory land rights or common law land rights— these land rights have always been focused on remnant lands'.[22] Sixteen per cent of the Australian continent is now owned or controlled by Aboriginal and Torres Strait Islander people. And yet Graeme Neate, the inaugural President of the Native Title Tribunal, said:

> It is my view that far too great a weight of expectation has been put on native title to deliver what it was not capable of delivering. There are areas of Australia where native title will deliver little or nothing.[23]

A country's system of land law and governance is undoubtedly more complex once indigenous land rights are recognised. The

---

21. In *Wilson v Anderson* (2002) 213 CLR 401 at 454, Justice Kirby said: 'The legal advance that commenced with *Mabo v Queensland* (No 2) or perhaps earlier, has now attracted such difficulties that the benefits intended for Australia's indigenous peoples in relation to native title to land and waters are being channelled into costs of administration and litigation that leave everyone dissatisfied and many disappointed.'
    In *Western Australia v Ward* (2002) 213 CLR 1 at 398-9, Justice Callinan J said: 'I do not disparage the importance to the Aboriginal people of their native title rights, including those that have symbolic significance. I fear, however, that in many cases because of the chasm between the common law and native title rights, the latter, when recognised, will amount to little more than symbols. It might have been better to redress the wrongs of dispossession by a true and unqualified settlement of lands or money than by an ultimately futile or unsatisfactory, in my respectful opinion, attempt to fold native title rights into the common law.'
22. Noel Pearson, 'Where we've come from and where were at with the opportunity that is Koiki Mabo's legacy to Australia', *Mabo lecture*, AIATSIS Native Title Conference 2003, 'Native Title on the Ground', Alice Springs, 3–5 June 2003.
23. Graeme Neate, *The 'Tidal Wave' of Justice and the 'Tide of History'*, Address to 5th World Summit of Nobel Peace Laureates, Rome, 10 November 2004, 27.

cost of this complexity is high when a country like Australia has long delayed the recognition. The benefits to indigenous people are less and patchy when many of the dispossessed have had no option except to live away from their lands for generations. The complexity and patchiness provide no warrant for returning to the *terra nullius* mindset.

Formal Equality Under the law, Land Rights and Self-Determination

Equality does not mean treating everyone the same. If a law is to treat indigenous people differently from other citizens, indigenous people through their representatives should first give their consent and those indigenous citizens who want to receive the same treatment as other citizens should be able to opt out of the special arrangements for their own people and enjoy the usual benefits of citizenship. Sometimes the different treatment will be an undisputed added benefit to make up for past disadvantage or to accelerate access to the benefits of life in the post-colonial society. But there are instances when the treatment is adverse to individuals on the basis of their race or membership of a particular indigenous community. Their individual rights are to be foregone for the common good. The limits of self-determination for a community are now set when an individual claims not only the entitlements of community membership but also the human rights recognised in international instruments. The giving of young women in traditional marriage may be an integral part of traditional land holding arrangements but such practices must yield when a young woman wants the right to choose her husband. Traditional punishments such as spearing may assist elders maintain public order, but the elders must surrender their authority when a young man insists on a trial in court and a punishment in jail.

If there still be a case for traditional marriage or traditional punishment, that case should be put by Aboriginal representatives who are attentive to the concerns of young Aboriginal women who want to choose their own husband and of young Aboriginal men who would prefer jail to spearing. Though these traditional practices may tie all community members to their land, kin and ancestral meanings, they are practices that cannot be imposed on young persons living in two worlds, many of them having watched more television episodes of *LA Law* and *Dallas* than I would ever want.

Fifty years ago, there was controversy about the wage and employment conditions for Aborigines on vast pastoral properties in the north of Australia. Now the issue is access to social welfare payments and alcohol on Aboriginal communities. The denial of equal wages or personal social welfare payments or the denial of access to alcohol is a denial of formal equality under the law. Are there some social ramifications to the granting of formal equality that are so adverse to the common good of indigenous communities and the personal well-being of community members that the indigenous leaders in a self-determining community are not only entitled but also are right to forego the formal equality for their community members so that the community might advance its communal prospects?

In 1965, the Commonwealth Conciliation and Arbitration Commission was asked by the Australian Workers' Union to grant equal pay to Aborigines in the pastoral industry. These workers lived and worked on cattle and sheep properties in the remoter parts of Australia. The union called no evidence but simply enunciated the principle of equal pay. The pastoralists called much evidence to demonstrate the problems and expected social effects of paying equal wages. Many Aborigines had lived on pastoral properties that were their traditional lands, receiving minimal pay for what the pastoralists regarded as minimal work.

No Aborigines were called to give evidence about the effects. Sir James Gobbo who was counsel for the Commonwealth government revealed thirty years later that, when he 'sought some such evidence, I was instructed that there was no stockman suitable for the somewhat daunting task of giving evidence and being cross-examined'. Gobbo was deeply troubled but unable to do anything.

He was receiving instructions from two government departments. The Department of Labour and Industry was adamant that all workers should be paid the same wage regardless of their race. The Department of Territories 'was very concerned about the impact of equal pay because of the risk to the existing arrangements on the stations. It would result in the abrupt end to the provision of steady employment and accommodation for Aborigines'.[24] Sir John Kerr was counsel for the pastoralists. He submitted:

> It seems to the pastoralists to be nonsense to say that men are better off, unemployed in thousands, but maintained in settlements in growing degrees of comfort when they could work in the real world with growing degrees of efficiency and growing economic reward.[25]

The Commission acknowledged that massive disemployment was the likely result of granting equal wages. Once a stockman was unemployed, it was likely that he and his extended clan group would be moved off a pastoral lease which was on their traditional country. The effects of disemployment would be catastrophic for these small communities who had never known life in the economic mainstream. In its decision the Commission noted:

> (If) aborigines are to be paid the same as whites, then employers would prefer to employ whites because they could employ far fewer with the same results. We accept the employers' evidence that as at present advised many of them expect to change over to white labour if aborigines are to be paid at award rates. We do not flinch from the results of this decision which we consider is the only proper one to be made at this point in Australia's history. There must be one industrial law, similarly applied to all Australians, aboriginal or not. If

---

24. James Gobbo, 'Citizenship in Australia', Address to Australian Reconciliation Convention 1997

25. John Kerr, 'Reflections on the Northern Territory Cattle Station Industry Award Case of 1965 and the O'Shea case of 1969', Address to HR Nicholls Society, 28 February 1986.

any problems of native welfare whether of employees or their dependants, arise as a result of this decision, the Commonwealth Government has made clear its intention to deal with them.[26]

Employers were given twenty months leeway to arrange for those Aborigines who were union members to be employed under award conditions. As predicted, many Aborigines were turned off pastoral properties, living in fringe camps on the outskirts of country towns and becoming long term recipients of social welfare.

Government initiatives including the purchase of pastoral properties for Aboriginal communities, the purchase of excisions on other pastoral properties, and preferential employment and education programs on remote Aboriginal communities have ameliorated some of the problems. But the payment of sit down money is now judged by government and many indigenous leaders to be no solution at all.

Andrew Robb, previously the Chief Executive of the National Farmers Federation and National Director of the Liberal Party, was elected to the Australian Parliament in 2004. In his maiden speech, he recalled his many visits to pastoral properties in Northern Australia after the granting of award wages and land rights. In his opinion, 'The land rights legislation was a totally inadequate response to the real issue - namely, the collapse of personal dignity and self-esteem among many Aboriginals, particularly the young.'[27] He compared the living circumstances of Aborigines on pastoral properties before and after land rights, before and after equal wages:

> On many occasions, I would be taken to a bend in a river on a cattle station and shown where 100, 200 or 300 Aboriginals had lived for decades, with the men employed on the stations as stockmen and drovers, the older men as gardeners, and the women in the

---

26. *The Northern Territory Cattle Industry Case* (1965) 113 CAR 651 (Cth), followed up elsewhere in Australia in *Australian Workers Union v Graziers Association of New South Wales and Others* (1967) 121 CAR 454 (Cth).

27. 2004 CPD (HofR) 6; 29 November 2004

homestead. In many cases, schools were provided for the children. Aboriginal people were disadvantaged, but they had work and self-esteem, reasonable quality of life, strong mentoring from their elders, schooling and strict controls on alcohol. Of course, all that ceased in the early 1970s following the understandable granting of equal wages in the pastoral industry, along with the misplaced provision of unfettered and generous welfare handouts. The related exodus of these people from their ancestral lands saw them living in settlements and on the fringes of towns. As I was driven around vast cattle stations, I witnessed cattlemen come across an Aboriginal elder known to them. The mutual respect was palpable. On the same day I saw the same cattlemen come across young Aboriginal men seriously affected by years of alcohol and aimlessness, young men stripped of any personal dignity or self-esteem. The cattlemen's contempt was palpable. The chilling fact is that the very fabric of a proud and fascinating culture, many thousands of years in the making, has been brought to its knees in less than thirty years by well-intentioned but seriously misguided policy. For me the lesson is clear. People are very, very responsive to incentives, for good or bad. The wrong incentives, no matter how well meaning, can debilitate a community in no time. In this case, unconditional handouts have provided the seeds of destruction in a breathtakingly short period of time.

Fifty years ago, no indigenous person participated in the decision or was even heard about the inevitable effects of granting equal wages. The members of one polity made decisions about those of the other polity without consulting them. Nowadays there is consultation. Those of us who are not indigenous are able to spare our consciences the moral quandary choosing between conflicting goods—formal equality under the law, and government prescriptions which are race-based and race-targeted—by leaving the matter to discussion between government and indigenous leaders chosen and responsible through self-determining indigenous procedures.

But then we are troubled by the voice in the wilderness of other indigenous leaders who proclaim that their indigenous opponents have no option than to do the government's bidding if they are to breathe the scarce political oxygen available for indigenous leaders in a society which has grown weary and doubtful about even medium term solutions for the plight of marginalised indigenous community members. It is even more troubling when government and/or the media decide which indigenous leaders will be given airplay regardless of their mode of selection as leaders or spokespersons. Indigenous leaders need credibility in both polities—the indigenous community and the mainstream society.

The Contemporary Problems of Indigenous Communities

In 1981, I was junior counsel in an Aboriginal murder trial in Queensland. Alwyn Peter was the fifteenth Aboriginal male in three years to have killed another Aboriginal person on an Aboriginal reserve. In these cases, the victim was usually the accused's woman partner. The senior defence counsel told the court that the homicide rate was the highest recorded among any ghetto group in the western world. In each case, the accused and the victim were shaped by life on a reserve; and each in their own way was destroyed by it. To be a member of such a group, one did not have to be bad or mad; one had only to be Aboriginal. We defence lawyers had a good win in the *Peter* case. Having pleaded a defence of diminished responsibility, Alwyn walked free within weeks of the completion of the court proceedings. A woman anthropologist left me with the chilling observation that our forensic win had removed the one inadequate protection for defenceless women in remote Aboriginal communities—the minimal deterrence of the whitefella legal system. Meanwhile I was privileged to receive the last letter that the anthropologist WEH Stanner ever wrote on 4 October 1981, he having been our key anthropological witness:

> I am fascinated by the question: how do general ideas about human conduct change so quickly? I can recall

about fifty years ago appearing as a witness for the
defence in an Aboriginal murder case in Darwin before
Wells J. He was notably unimpressed by my arguments
but nevertheless reluctantly took them into account in
mitigation, while looking round the court as if expecting
trouble. Or do I mean 'remarkably quickly'?

For the last thirty years, I have been preoccupied with the
interrelatedness of Aboriginal dispossession, disadvantage and
marginalisation and I have sought to articulate a publicly coherent
policy of reconciliation, justice and recognition for indigenous
Australians. I do not come with the answers. Noel Pearson, one of
the most prominent Aboriginal spokesmen in Australia has opined
that it was the 'symptom theory' that underpinned our approach to
the *Alwyn Peter* case. Pearson says:

> All that was achieved by presenting a deeper historical
> understanding of the background to indigenous crimes
> and dysfunction was that the criminal justice system
> became sensitive to this background—and sentences
> became increasingly lenient. After a couple of decades
> we then reached a point where judges and observers—
> not the least Aboriginal people—started to wonder
> whether the loss of Aboriginal life was less serious than
> that of non-Aborigines. The criminal justice system may
> have tried to accommodate an understanding of the
> factors which Brennan and those who followed him had
> illuminated in the *Alwyn Peter* case, but it did nothing
> to abate offending and the resultant 'over representation'
> of indigenous people in the criminal justice system. In
> fact I would say that it made this problem worse.[28]

These are troubling conclusions for any lawyer committed to justice
according to law for all persons, including indigenous Australians
who are more likely than any other group to be appearing in court

---

28. Noel Pearson, 'A Fair Place In Our Own Country: Indigenous Australians, Land
Rights And The Australian Economy', Castan Public Lecture, Castan Centre For
Human Rights Law, Monash University, June 2004.

for a custodial sentence. Once again, the proper application of law, including formal equality under the law, and the criminal law's attention to all relevant factors in the mitigation of punishment, may have unintended and negative consequences for the public order or common good of indigenous communities while displaying an admirable commitment to the human rights of the individual.

Life for the contemporary indigenous person is a life of choice and diverse possibilities. Law and social policy should provide the possibility of a realistic choice on a spectrum of possibilities from the pursuit of a traditional lifestyle on traditional lands to fully integrated participation in the social, economic and political life of the nation state while maintaining cultural traditions and perspectives. In Australia, the resurgent opponents of land rights and self-determination think the former is not an option; thus this is an unreal choice, or at least a very cost ineffective choice. They argue for laws and policies which provide no option but accelerated access to the benefits of mainstream society or to the modern lifestyle which is not contingent on traditional cultural trappings.

Indigenous Australians may hold a secure title to sixteen per cent of the land mass but their living conditions are still terrible. Thirty years ago, conservative politicians such as Sir Joh Bjelke-Petersen were expressing concern that the granting or recognition of land rights would result in Aborigines being more removed from and less responsive to the health and education services of the mainstream community.

At first, Sir Joh refused to discuss the possibility of land rights with the Commonwealth government.[29] He thought the Commonwealth's legislation in the Northern Territory in 1977

---

29. On 20 October 1974, Prime Minister Gough Whitlam wrote to Sir Joh Bjelke-Petersen recalling their discussion in March 1974 about land rights. The Australian government 'did not wish to push the matter ahead of the Aboriginal Land Rights Commission Report'. Now that the report had been received, every indication from the Queensland government was that the premier 'believed the whole question of Aboriginal land rights need no longer be discussed'. Stalling the matter, Sir Joh replied on 1 November 1974: 'It is a matter for you and your government to decide what action you propose to take. However, in the circumstances, it may be thought desirable to delay any possible action until further consultation has taken place between our respective ministers.'

was 'carelessly introduced' and he was concerned that the granting of land rights and self-management to Aboriginal communities in remote parts of Northern Australia could contribute to social isolation. In Queensland he was particularly critical of the Uniting Church which had encouraged Aborigines in their aspirations to return to traditional country setting up outstations 'many miles from conventional facilities such as hospital, schools, etc, where reversion to the '"tribal" pattern of life was encouraged':

> School attendances dropped forty per cent and we cannot accept or tolerate a situation in this State where the young people of a community are thrust into an isolated situation, where by denial of fundamental education and health care services, and by an ideological indoctrination of Aboriginal separation and separate development, they would, by contrast with all other Queenslanders, be seriously impaired in choosing to pursue broader horizons of life in the future should they wish to do so. That Aborigines may be socially and educationally equipped to make such a choice in life is the fundamental aim of our Aboriginal advancement policy.[30]

These concerns are now being voiced by many indigenous leaders, not to decry land rights but to plead for government intervention aimed at improving the health, education and employment prospects for Aborigines and Torres Strait Islanders living on their remote communities or seeking a life for their children in the urban areas of Australia. The children and grandchildren of Milirrpum, Mungurrawuy, Eddie Mabo, David Passi, and Alwyn Peter want to live in the best of all possible worlds, being Aboriginal but open to all the world has to offer, not being swamped by it, being able to stay afloat, able to make sense of it, able to embrace the mystery of it, even able to shape it, and to hand on to their children the uniqueness of their cultures and the universal possibilities of life in the modern world.

---

30. Letter by Sir Joh Bjelke-Petersen to Bishop William Murray, 8 February 1979.

Land rights secure the place for this to happen. The option of self-determination expands the possibilities within the limitations of the sovereign nation state. In Australia, life in the mainstream with some limited preferential access to a secured land base may turn out to be the preferred option for most Aborigines as well as for government. This will be an improvement on life in the mainstream with no secured land base addressing the historic dispossession. It will be different from living the life of a sovereign indigenous people, but with colonisation that was never an option. It may also be very different from life on a self-determining community choosing the best of both lifestyles. This has appeal and possibility only for a minority of contemporary indigenous Australians. It must remain an option. Bridging the gap between life in two polities, under two laws, is the contemporary indigenous reality. It ought be recognised and respected by the state.

The Challenges of the Future

Once a land base is secure, how do government and indigenous leaders find the balance between the individual rights of the indigenous community member and the collective entitlement of the community to order its affairs for the common good and cultural survival? Man does not live on bread alone. Man does not live on land alone. Aboriginal identity is tied to land, family, and the ancestral world of 'the Dreaming'. Unemployment, underemployment, alcohol and substance abuse are enormous problems on indigenous communities. Years ago I was riding in a four wheel drive truck in the Pitjantjatjra lands of South Australia after a big land rights meeting. On the back of the truck sat some Aboriginal youths huddled in blankets sniffing petrol. I wanted to stop the truck and do something. But what? One of the white community advisers told me that petrol sniffing was a legitimate expression of self-determination for a marginalised people without job prospects. These kids were addling their brains as we drove home. When parents do not take action, what role is there for indigenous leaders in co-operation with government to stop the truck and take action? John Howard, when Prime Minister in 2004, said:

> I think for the first time we are starting to see a recognition that the emphasis that's been placed on the rights and symbolic agenda over the last twenty or thirty years to the detriment of a greater sense of community responsibility and personal responsibility has been an error, and when you listen to the remarks of people like Noel Pearson and you hear their solutions in areas such as the Cape, you begin to understand that if communities are given a power to run their own affairs and to impose their own internal disciplines you will, over time, see an enormous improvement.[31]

Howard thought 'we ought to be listening a lot more to those who believe that self-responsibility and personal empowerment in Aboriginal communities and the end of the welfare mentality is essential before we bring about a profound change for the better'. But how is this to be done in the modern democratic state?

The Australian government and some of the more willing indigenous leaders have seized upon the idea of 'mutual obligation'. Under the first and most publicised mutual obligation agreement, the Mulan community in Western Australia agreed with government that parents and community leaders would attend to child hygiene and government would pay the cost of installing new petrol pumps. Aboriginal leader, Patrick Dodson saw resonance between a conservative government's notion of mutual obligation and the traditional Aboriginal notion of reciprocity. But Dodson warned:

> We don't want to see mutual obligation as a principle, or as a concept, trivialised by some of the stupidity that is associated with those contracts—like telling people to wash their kids' faces twice a day.[32]

Many advocates for indigenous rights bemoan the fact that indigenous leaders are not more united in their stand for land rights and self-determination. But a leader of an indigenous minority in

---

31. John Howard, *Lateline*, ABC Television, Australia 28 September 2004.
32. *The Weekend Australian*, 4 December 2004.

a previously colonised society needs to act like an international statesman attentive to the domestic and international constituencies. In the politics of international relations, it has long been accepted that there are realists, liberals and idealists. The realist is pessimistic about human nature and believes that the struggle for and exercise of power is central. The realist plays the government at their own game. The liberal 'contends that realism has a stunted vision that cannot account for progress', and the idealist 'illuminates the changing norms of sovereignty, human rights and international justice'. An indigenous leader like Noel Pearson has a strong realist strand in his thinking, action and advocacy. He deals with the government of the day. He uses their rhetoric and meets them on their ideological ground, seeking political leverage and real outcomes for his people. In 1993, he eye-balled Paul Keating on native title. Then he met John Howard on mutual obligation saying:

> There is no argument with the principle of mutual obligation if we are going to get things fixed. The mistake we made in the past was to think indigenous salvation came from legal and political acts. This is part of it. But we must assume responsibility and recognise these things are achieved through social and economic progress.[33]

With a more liberal strand, an indigenous leader like Patrick Dodson will work within the limits set by government but insists that there is a broader agenda that is incomplete. Dodson says:

> In Australia, the direction and emphasis of the reconciliation process and the position of Aboriginal people's unresolved issues with the nation are known points of difference between the Howard Government and Aboriginal people. We have agreed to work on what we have in common rather than what we may still disagree about, in search of a common good. The Aboriginal people must come to terms with the Howard

---

33. *The Weekend Australian*, 4 December 2004.

Government's social reform agenda in Aboriginal affairs. These are policies that stress mutual obligation and personal responsibility. This should never be interpreted as a rejection by the Aboriginal leadership in the struggle to have Aboriginal people in this country recognised as the first Australians and their rights to practise and enjoy their language, law and culture as the indigenous peoples of the nation. These are matters for future engagement and resolution, not matters to be discarded as irrelevant leftovers of another time and political reality.[34]

Idealists demand that government play their game. An idealist like Michael Mansell insists that Aboriginal sovereignty is non-negotiable. Mansell says:

Pearson's ideas are that any blame for Aboriginal disadvantage has more to do with Aboriginal recalcitrance than loss of land, or the extraordinary degree to which Aborigines have been dominated for so long. The aim is to hurry up assimilation—push more Aboriginal kids into private schools, make people work or have the dole cut off, and participate within Australian society as a minority group. A significant portion of the Aboriginal population believes the political foundation for an Aboriginal future is sovereignty. That base enables Aborigines to negotiate suitable political structures that promote Aboriginal identity, culturally sensitive education, a substantial land and economic base and political representation independent of white politicians. This view has significant support within the Aboriginal population but little from white Australia.[35]

As in international relations, the realist, liberal and idealist perspectives all have their contribution to make 'providing the

---

34. Patrick Dodson, 'Why I've Changed My Mind', *The Australian*, 7 December 2004.
35. Letter to the Editor, *The Australian*, 18 January 2005.

vocabulary and conceptual framework to ask hard questions of those who think changing the world is easy'.[36]

While Australia's indigenous leaders are seeking a way forward for their people in the short and long terms, the academic historians have been at war interpreting and re-interpreting the conflict and meeting between Aborigines and the colonisers. Following the publication of Keith Windschuttle's *The Fabrication of Aboriginal History*,[37] Stuart McIntyre published *The History Wars*[38] and then edited a collection entitled *The Historian's Conscience: Australian Historians on the Ethics of History*.[39]

Greg Dening wrote an essay in the latest collection entitled 'Living With And In Deep Time'. He recalls the celebration at the National Library in Canberra when two items of Australian heritage were placed on the Memory of the World Register. Those items, joining documents from other countries such as the Magna Carta and the US Declaration of Independence, were not the Australian Constitution or even the batting records of Donald Bradman, but rather Captain James Cook's journal from the Endeavour voyage of 1768–1771 culminating in his hoisting the flag on Possession Island, and the papers relating to Eddie Mabo's case in the High Court. Dening described the reverence with which he donned the cotton gloves to peruse these documents in the Manuscript Reading Room of the library. He takes up Eddie Mabo's drawings of his land and his people. This file 'needs a slow, slow read'. Dening says this file is Mabo's 'expression of how deep time has left its mark on the present'. Here is Dening's evocative description of his reading of these papers:

> He (Eddie Mabo) taps a truth the way we all tap truths from living, but in ways which need to be tolerated by those whose notion of law and evidence is blinkered

---

36. Jack Snyder, 'One World, Rival Theories', in Foreign Policy (November/December 2004): 53 at 62.
37. Keith Windschuttle, *The Fabrication of Aboriginal History*, volume one, *Van Dieman's Land 1803–1847* (Sydney: Macleay Press, 2002).
38. Stuart McIntyre, *The History Wars* (Melbourne: Melbourne University Press, 2003).
39. Stuart McIntyre (ed.), *The Historian's Conscience: Australian Historians on the Ethics of History*, (Melbourne: Melbourne University Press, 2004)

by legal tradition and constitution and who need to find some entry into Eddie Mabo's otherness. The other papers in the Mabo Papers—of judges, lawyers, anthropologists, historians, witnesses of first people telling their stories—belong to the Memory of the World because the whole world faces the issue of how it lives with the Deep Time of all its first peoples, overrun and dispossessed as they are. It belongs to World Memory because the papers are we, the Australian people, struggling to do justice and to live with the Deep Time all around us. And we are in this instance the world.[40]

Though land rights and self-determination provide no utopia for the contemporary indigenous Australian community, they have belatedly put right an ancient wrong. The cost and inconvenience are unavoidable. *Terra nullius* is no longer an option. The Australian novelist Tim Winton reminds us, 'The past is in us, and not behind us. Things are never over'.[41] The words of Chief Justice Marshall in *Johnson* v *McIntosh* still ring out today:

[H]umanity demands, and a wise policy requires, that the rights of the conquered to property should remain unimpaired; that the new subjects should be governed as equitably as the old, and that confidence in their security should gradually banish the painful sense of being separated from their ancient connections, and united by force to strangers.[42]

We Australians belatedly have come to the right starting point on an endless search for justice between indigenous and non-indigenous

---

40. Greg Dening 'Living With And In Deep Time', in *The Historian's Conscience: Australian Historians on the Ethics of History*, edited by Stuart Macintrye (Melbourne: Melbourne University Press, 2004), 43.

41. Tim Winton, 'Aquifer', in *The Turning* (Sydney: Picador, 2004), 37 at 53.

42. 21 US (1823) 240 at 260. Marshall goes on to say: 'When the conquest is complete, and the conquered inhabitants can be blended with the conquerors, or safely governed as a distinct people, public opinion, which not even the conqueror can disregard, imposes these restraints upon him; and he cannot neglect them, without injury to his fame, and hazard to his power.'

citizens. Though it is no longer fashionable or politically correct in Australia, there is no getting away from Prime Minister Keating's insight that we white Australians must start with an act of recognition:

> Recognition that it was we who did the dispossessing. We took the traditional lands and smashed the traditional way of life. We brought the disasters. The alcohol. We committed the murders. We took the children from their mothers. We practised discrimination and exclusion. It was our ignorance and our prejudice. And our failure to imagine these things being done to us. With some noble exceptions, we failed to make the most basic human response and enter into their hearts and minds. We failed to ask - how would I feel if this were done to me? As a consequence, we failed to see that what we were doing degraded all of us.[43]

These sentiments should rightly continue to haunt all citizens of post-colonial societies where indigenous people 'united by force to strangers', still live on the fringes. With a confident identity and secure sense of belonging in both worlds, indigenous people might 'gradually banish the painful sense of being separated from their ancient connections'. Those citizens who are recent migrants are joined with the descendants of the colonisers, accepting the national responsibility of correcting past wrongs so that the descendants of the land's traditional owners might belong to their land, their kin and their Dreaming in the society built upon their dispossession.

While we continue to blame the victims, we are haunted by Andrew Robb's observation from the opposite side of the parliamentary chamber echoing the Keating declaration. In his maiden speech to the Australian parliament, Robb said, 'We have basically poisoned recent generations; poisoned their bodies with alcohol and other substances and poisoned their spirit and self-belief with handouts and welfare dependency.'[44] Land rights and self-determination

---

43 Paul Keating, Australian Launch of the International Year for the World's Indigenous People, Redfern, 10 December 1992.
44 2004 CPD (HofR) 6; 29 November 2004.

11

Dealing with Asylum Claims

In 2003 and 2007, I published two editions of my book Tampering with Asylum. *I was delighted in 2007 that the then newly elected Rudd government loosened the policy towards asylum seekers arriving by boat providing a more humane response to those arriving on our shores. I was later a strong critic of Julia Gillard's Timor and Malaysia solutions. I was troubled by the radical increase in boat arrivals in 2013, and very critical of Kevin Rudd's proposal to re-institute asylum processing and resettlement on Nauru and Manus Island, but in even more punitive form than first proposed by John Howard.*

I thought there was a need to get back to basics, wondering how Australia might decently deal with the issue. Commencing in June 2013, I gave a number of speeches critical of Australia's inhumane post-arrivals procedures for boat people, but suggesting it was time to think about the pre-conditions for being able to stop the boats decently. This upset many refugee advocates who were adamant that we could never stop the boats and some very reputable international lawyers who argued that all asylum seekers now had a right to enter Australia. I had the opportunity to spell out my views in a public lecture delivered at University College Dublin in September 2014.

Arriving by Boat

My great great grandmother Annie Doyle came from Muckalee down in Kilkenny. Widowed she probably had no option but to leave the farm she had shared with her husband. She and her five children including my great grandfather arrived at Hervey Bay in the British colony of Queensland on the *David McIver* in July 1863. I am one of those many Australians who is a descendant from Irish migrants who came to Australia in search of a better life. In early July 2013, I was sitting alone on the shoreline at Urangan at the entrance to the vast Hervey Bay, 150 years to the day since the *David McIver* entered Hervey Bay carrying 404 immigrants, there having been only one death but also 9 births on the 107 day voyage from Liverpool.

Hervey Bay is a very expansive but shallow bay sheltered from the Pacific Ocean by the majestic Fraser Island. On 6 July 1863, the crew of the *David McIver* spent the day searching for a channel until it was anchored in four fathoms of water. Some of the crew then got into a small boat and made for the shore at Urangan close to where I was sitting 150 years later. They came ashore and found two Aborigines. I presume they were males. Those two Aboriginal men then without protest accompanied the crew in the boat and showed the crew the way to Captain Jeffrey's Admiralty Survey Camp. The *David McIver* was only the second migrant ship ever to come into Hervey Bay and here were two Aborigines happy to extend a helping hand to complete strangers who must have looked very strange indeed. One Aboriginal was then commissioned to send word to Maryborough forty kilometres away.

That Aboriginal walked and ran all through the night to bring word of these new arrivals. A pilot was then dispatched. Within two days, a steamer named *Queensland* arrived, towed the *David McIver* to White Cliff on Fraser Island, and then received the disembarking passengers to transport them up the Mary River to the port of Maryborough where they arrived on 9 July 1863. I know nothing more about those Aborigines who played their part in the safe arrival and settlement of my forebears. I happily acknowledge my family's debt to them even 151 years later.

If my family were to arrive by boat in Australia today uninvited, they would be sent to Papua New Guinea or to a remote Pacific island Nauru, or sent back to where they came from. The debate and policy in Australia about modern day boat people is toxic. 151

years ago, the traditional owners helped my ancestors and their fellow passengers to find safe anchorage so that they might settle permanently calling Australia home. They extended the hand of peace and welcomed the stranger. Many on the *David McIver* were eligible for land grants from the newly established Queensland Government. That was the lure for their coming to the other side of the world. At an earlier time, they would have headed for the United States but I presume the civil war made that a less attractive option for a widow with five children. It's a matter of some pride for me that one of Annie Brennan's great grandchildren, my father, was one of the judges who just twenty-two years ago in the *Mabo* Case decided by the Australian High Court said that Aborigines had always owned the land which had been subject to those gratuitous land grants.

Stopping the Boats

It was Kevin Rudd who as Prime Minister decided in July 2013 that in future any asylum seekers arriving in Australia by boat would be sent to off-shore islands and never be permitted to settle in Australia. John Howard had been the first prime minister to enunciate this sort of policy in 2001 when he instituted the so-called Pacific Solution in response to the situation when 433 asylum seekers in distress had been rescued by the Norwegian ship *MV Tampa*.

The Australian government refused the captain permission to land the asylum seekers on Australian soil. The Australian navy transported them from the Indian Ocean to the Pacific Ocean. New Zealand agreed to take 150 of them. The rest were taken to Nauru for processing. John Howard later bluffed that none of these people would ever be allowed to settle in Australia. But his initial announcement contained an escape clause. He said that 'those assessed as having valid claims from Nauru would have access to Australia and other countries willing to share in the settlement of those with valid claims'. Most of those on *MV Tampa* who were proved to be refugees ended up winning permanent protection in Australia or New Zealand.

When prime minister for the first time, Kevin Rudd did away with the Pacific solution. Then the boats started coming again. When prime minister for the second time, Rudd resurrected the Pacific solution but without the Howard escape clause. He was adamant that those asylum seekers removed to Nauru and Papua New Guinea would never be permitted to resettle in Australia. Before the 2013 election, he challenged all of us do gooders when he said on national television:

> I think you heard a people smuggler interviewed by a media outlet the other day say that this was a fundamental assault on their business model. Well, that's a pretty gruesome way for him to put that, but the bottom line is this, I challenge anyone else looking at this policy challenge for Australia to deliver a credible alternative policy.
>
> The challenge that I put out to anyone who asks that we should consider a different approach is this: what would you do to stop thousands of people, including children, drowning offshore, other than undertake a policy direction like this? What is the alternative answer?[1]

He lost the election, handing the Abbott government his blueprint for stopping the boats. Tony Abbott adopted the Rudd solution without the Howard escape clause, and added his own suite of measures, including the promise to turn back boats to Indonesia when it was safe to do so. Rudd's challenge is still the ethical challenge confronting Australia. I look forward to hearing some Irish wisdom in response to the challenge.

While preparing this address in Boston, I thought back to my visit recently to the Martin Luther King memorial in Washington DC. That splendid memorial etches in stone many of King's great sayings, including: 'We shall overcome because the arc of the moral universe is long, but it bends towards justice.' At his swearing in to the Australian High Court last year, Justice Patrick Keane took some

---

1.   Lisa Wilkinson on the *Today* program, 25 July 2013.

comfort that the Australian judiciary were not a social elite as in some other countries, being drawn from the egalitarian democracy shaped by those Australians of the Depression and War eras who provided selflessly and generously for the education of their children. He invoked King's remark about the arc of the moral universe and, with a touch of nationalistic pride, opined that it bends more sharply in that direction in our part of the southern hemisphere because of the egalitarianism of our forebears. Reflecting on the history of the ethical demands of migration and national border security in our island nation continent, I fear we may be losing some of that edge down under.

Do We Have The Right To Stop The Boats?

The issue which presently confounds us is working out what is ethical and what works when confronting an escalating flow of asylum seekers coming to our shores by boat without visas and risking their lives on perilous voyages. First world countries with maritime borders have been wrestling with this issue now for over thirty years. According to the United Nations High Commissioner for Refugees (UNHCR) there were 45.2 million forcibly displaced people worldwide at the end of 2012. This was the highest number since 1994. Of these, 28.8 million were internally displaced persons, 15.4 million were refugees and 937,000 were asylum seekers.[2] On the latest estimate, there are now 51 million displaced people in the world.

There is much confusion about the ethical and legal considerations that apply when asylum seekers present at the borders of first world countries. For example, in what, if any, circumstances does or ought an asylum seeker have the right to enter a country not her own in order to seek protection? To be blunt, no asylum seeker should be refouled or sent back to the country where they claim to face persecution unless their claim has been assessed and found wanting; while waiting, no asylum seeker has a right to enter any

---

2.   See http://www.immi.gov.au/media/fact-sheets/60refugee.htm

particular country. Should an asylum seeker unlawfully gain access to a country they should not be penalised for such an unlawful entry or presence provided only that they came in direct flight from the alleged persecution.

All lawyers would agree with these blunt propositions. Some, especially those schooled in international law, would go further. They would point not just to a country's ratification of the *Refugee Convention*. But they would claim that those countries that have ratified the *Convention against Torture* and the *International Covenant on Civil and Political Rights* cannot refoule any person until there has been a determination of their claim that they face torture or 'cruel, inhuman or degrading treatment or punishment'.

Some of these lawyers would then take the next leap in human rights protection to assert that all persons have a right to enter any state of their choice provided only they claim to face the risk of persecution, torture, cruel, inhuman or degrading treatment or punishment back home. They translate the right not to be refouled into a right of entry to any state unless and until the state determines that there is no real risk of any of these adverse outcomes. Either the state is able to determine all such claims at the border or else the state must grant entry at least for the purpose of human rights assessment.

At a 1938 conference in Switzerland, TW White, the Australian delegate, misjudged his present and future audience when he simplistically said that it would 'no doubt be appreciated that as we have no racial problem we are not desirous of importing one'.[3] When the *Universal Declaration of Human Rights* (UNDHR) was being drafted after World War II, Australia was one of the countries that was very testy about recognising any general 'right of asylum' for refugees. Australia conceded that a person had the right to live in their country; they had a right to leave their country; they had a right not to be returned to their country if they were in another country and if they feared persecution on return to their own country.

---

3.   Martin Gilbert, *The Holocaust* (London: Collins, 1986), 64.

But Australia believed people did not have the right to enter another country without invitation, having exercised the right to leave their own country, even if they feared persecution. In 1948 the drafters of the universal declaration proposed that a person have the right to be 'granted asylum'. Australia was one of the strong opponents, being prepared to acknowledge only the individual's right 'to seek and enjoy asylum', because such a right would not include the right to enter another country and it would not create a duty for a country to permit entry by the asylum seeker.

During the preparations for the 1948 discussions, Tasman Heyes, Secretary of the Australian Department of Immigration wrote:

> If it is intended to mean that any person or body of persons who may suffer persecution in a particular country shall have the right to enter another country irrespective of their suitability as settlers in the second country this would not be acceptable to Australia as it would be tantamount to the abandonment of the right which every sovereign state possesses to determine the composition of its own population, and who shall be admitted to its territories. [4]

John Howard was not the first Australian to proclaim that the Australian government would decide who came to Australia. Australia was on the winning side of the pre-Convention argument and was able to live with Article 14 of the UNDHR—that 'Everyone has the right to seek and to enjoy in other countries asylum from persecution'. You could ask for asylum. You were not guaranteed a favourable answer, but if you received an invitation to enter, you then had the right to enjoy your asylum.

Professor Guy Goodwin-Gill has observed that Article 14 does not create any binding obligations for states and it suggests 'a considerable margin of appreciation with respect to who is granted

---

4.   Annemarie Devereux, *Australia and the Birth of the International Bill of Rights 1946–1966*, (Sydney: Federation Press, 2005), 70.

asylum and what exactly this means'.[5] The matter returned to the United Nations' agenda with the drafting of the *International Covenant on Civil and Political Rights*. The Australian government's 1955 Brief in preparation for the General Assembly pointed out that the Department of Immigration thought 'any limitation of the right to exclude undesirable immigrants or visitors unacceptable'. In 1960 the Russians proposed a general right of asylum. Australia maintained its resistance. No right of asylum was included in the covenant.

Now let's consider the letter and spirit of the *Refugee Convention*. The 1951 *Convention Relating to the Status of Refugees* does not confer a right on asylum seekers to enter the country of their choice or to choose the country which is to process their refugee claim. In fact it does not confer a right to enter any country. The primary obligations in the Convention when considering proposals for border protection and orderly migration are contained in Articles 31 and 33.

> Article 31(1)
>
> The Contracting States shall not impose penalties, on account of their illegal entry or presence, on refugees who, coming directly from a territory where their life or freedom was threatened in the sense of article 1, enter or are present in their territory without authorization, provided they present themselves without delay to the authorities and show good cause for their illegal entry or presence.
>
> Article 33(1)
>
> No Contracting State shall expel or return ('refouler') a refugee in any manner whatsoever to the frontiers of territories where his life or freedom would be threatened

---

5.   Guy Goodwin-Gill, 'The International Law of Refugee Protection', in *The Oxford Handbook of Refugees and Forced Migration Studies*, 2014, 36 at 42.

on account of his race, religion, nationality, membership of a particular social group or political opinion.

So a refugee or asylum seeker may be illegally present or may have entered a country illegally. The issue is whether the government may impose any penalty for the illegal entry or presence for which the refugee or asylum seeker is required to show good cause.

Much to the consternation of some refugee advocates, the Australian Government continues to claim: 'International law recognises that people at risk of persecution have a legal right to flee their country and seek refuge elsewhere, but does not give them a right to enter a country of which they are not a national. Nor do people at risk of persecution have a right to choose their preferred country of protection.'[6]

Australian governments (of both political persuasions, Labor and Liberal) have long held the defensible view:

> The condition that refugees must be 'coming directly' from a territory where they are threatened with persecution constitutes a real limit on the obligation of States to exempt illegal entrants from penalty. In the Australian Government's view, a person in respect of whom Australia owes protection will fall outside the scope of Article 31(1) if he or she spent more than a short period of time in a third country whilst travelling between the country of persecution and Australia, and settled there in safety or was otherwise accorded

---

6.   See http://www.immi.gov.au/media/fact-sheets/61protection.htm. Guy Goodwin Gill says in 'The Right to Seek Asylum: Interception at Sea and the Principle of Non-Refoulement', *International Journal of Refugee Law* 23 (2011): 443 at 444: 'It is not yet unlawful to move or to migrate, or to seek asylum, even if the criminalisation of 'irregular emigration' by sending states seems to be desired by the developed world. Even so, the range of permissible restrictions on freedom of movement and the absence of any immediately correlative duty of admission, other than towards nationals, make the claim somewhat illusory. Perhaps Article 13(2) of the 1948 Universal Declaration of Human Rights was just a political gesture; perhaps the world today has in fact moved closer to what was then the Soviet position, that the right to freedom of movement should be recognized as *only* exercisable in accordance with the laws of the state.'

protection, or there was no good reason why they could not have sought and obtained protection there.[7]

The right to 'seek and enjoy asylum' in the international instruments must be understood as purely permissive. As noted by Justice Gummow of the Australian High Court:

> [The] right 'to seek' asylum [in the UDHR] was not accompanied by any assurance that the quest would be successful. A deliberate choice was made not to make a significant innovation in international law which would have amounted to a limitation upon the absolute right of member States to regulate immigration by conferring privileges upon individuals ... Nor was the matter taken any further by the International Covenant on Civil and Political Rights . . . Article 12 of the ICCPR stipulates freedom to leave any country and forbids arbitrary deprivation of the right to enter one's own country; but the ICCPR does not provide for any right of entry to seek asylum and the omission was deliberate.[8]

Nation states that are signatories to these international instruments are rightly obliged not to expel peremptorily those persons arriving on their shores, legally or illegally, in direct flight from persecution. That is the limit of the legal obligation. So there may in the future be circumstances in which Australia would be entitled to return safely to Indonesia persons who, when departing Indonesia for Australia, were no longer in direct flight but rather were engaged in secondary

---

7. *Interpreting the Refugees Convention – an Australian Contribution*, Department of Immigration and Multicultural Affairs, Canberra, 2002, 172.

8. *MIMA v Ibrahim* [2000] HCA 55 at 137–38. Justice Gummow adds, '[I]t has long been recognised that, according to customary international law, the right of asylum is a right of States, not of the individual; no individual, including those seeking asylum, may assert a right to enter the territory of a State of which that individual is not a national . . . Over the last 50 years, other provisions of the Declaration have [citing Brownlie] come to 'constitute general principles of law or [to] represent elementary considerations of humanity' and have been invoked by the European Court of Human Rights and the International Court of Justice. But it is not suggested that Art 14 of the UDHR goes beyond its calculated limitation'.

movement seeking a more favourable refugee status outcome or a more benign migration outcome. We Australians could credibly draw this distinction if we co-operated more closely with Indonesia providing basic protection and fair processing for asylum seekers there. Until we do that, I fear there is no way of decently stopping the boats.

Is It Legal To Stop The Boats?

Thirty-three years ago, US President Ronald Reagan frustrated by the flow of asylum seekers across the sea from Haiti signed Executive Order 12324 on the 'Interdiction of Illegal Aliens'. Reagan characterised 'the continuing illegal migration by sea of large numbers of undocumented aliens into the southeastern United States' as 'a serious national problem detrimental to the interests of the United States'.

The Oxford don and guru of the international jurisprudence on refugee issues Guy Goodwin-Gill has opined that this Order became 'the model, perhaps, for all that has followed'.[9] I think he is right. Following the military coup in Haiti in 1991, repatriations were suspended for six weeks. Then in May 1992, 'President (George) Bush decided to continue interdiction and repatriation, but without the possibility of screening-in for those who might qualify as refugees'.[10] When inaugurated as President in January 1993, Bill Clinton maintained the interdiction practice, putting paid to the claim that this was just the initiative of the Republicans. It turned out that both major political parties were committed to stopping the boats, doing whatever it takes. Three decades later, it is the same situation in Australia with both sides of politics being committed to stopping the boats. The US Supreme Court described the matter thus:

---

9.   Guy S Goodwin-Gill, 'The Right to Seek Asylum: Interception at Sea and the Principle of Non-Refoulement', (2011) 23 *International Journal of Refugee Law,* 443

10.   Guy S Goodwin Gill and Jane McAdam, *The Refugee in International Law,* third edition (Oxford: Oxford University Press, 2007), 247

With both the facilities at Guantanamo and available
Coast Guard cutters saturated, and with the number
of Haitian emigrants in unseaworthy craft increasing
(many had drowned as they attempted the trip to
Florida), the Government could no longer both protect
our borders *and* offer the Haitians even a modified
screening process. It had to choose between allowing
Haitians into the United States for the screening
process or repatriating them without giving them any
opportunity to establish their qualifications as refugees.
In the judgment of the President's advisers, the first
choice not only would have defeated the original purpose
of the program (controlling illegal immigration), but
also would have impeded diplomatic efforts to restore
democratic government in Haiti and would have posed
a life-threatening danger to thousands of persons
embarking on long voyages in dangerous craft. The
second choice would have advanced those policies but
deprived the fleeing Haitians of any screening process at
a time when a significant minority of them were being
screened in.[11]

On May 23, 1992, President Bush adopted the second choice. After assuming office, President Clinton decided not to modify that order; it remains in effect today. The wisdom of the policy choices made by Presidents Reagan, Bush, and Clinton is not a matter for our consideration.

It took fifteen months of concerted advocacy from human rights advocates to convince Clinton to institute refugee status determination interviews on board ship. In *Sale* v *Haitian Centers Council, Inc*, the US Supreme Court ruled that these harsh presidential practices were valid. Justice Stevens delivering the opinion of the Court said: 'The President has directed the Coast Guard to intercept vessels illegally transporting passengers from Haiti to the United States and to return those passengers to Haiti without first determining whether they may qualify as refugees. The question presented in this case

---

11.   509 U.S. 155, 163–4 (1993).

is whether such forced repatriation, "authorised to be undertaken only beyond the territorial sea of the United States", violates . . . the Immigration and Nationality Act of 1952. We hold that neither (the Act) nor Article 33 of the United Nations Protocol Relating to the Status of Refugees applies to action taken by the Coast Guard on the high seas.' In relation to Article 33 of the Refugees Convention, the Supreme Court said:

> The drafters of the Convention and the parties to the Protocol may not have contemplated that any nation would gather fleeing refugees and return them to the one country they had desperately sought to escape; such actions may even violate the spirit of Article 33; but a treaty cannot impose uncontemplated extraterritorial obligations on those who ratify it through no more than its general humanitarian intent. Because the text of Article 33 cannot reasonably be read to say anything at all about a nation's actions toward aliens outside its own territory, it does not prohibit such actions.[12]

In an uncharacteristic mode for the usually isolationist US judges, the Supreme Court in footnotes quoted many international law scholars including Guy Goodwin-Gill in support of this proposition. Goodwin-Gill had written: 'A categorical refusal of disembarkation cannot be equated with breach of the principle of *non-refoulement,* even though it may result in serious consequences for asylum-seekers.' They also quoted the respected A. Grahl-Madsen who had worked as an in house lawyer for UNHCR for many years. He had written: '*[Non-refoulement]* may only be invoked in respect of persons who are already present—lawfully or unlawfully—in the territory of a Contracting State. Article 33 only prohibits the expulsion or return *(refoulement)* of refugees to territories where they are likely to suffer persecution; it does not obligate the Contracting State to admit any person who has not already set foot on their respective territories.'

---

12.   509 U.S. 155, 158–9 (1993).

Goodwin-Gill has often pointed out that the *Refugee Convention* has a number of distinct features: as an international text, it must be interpreted in accordance with the general principles of international law; it is 'a 'living instrument' to be interpreted in the light of present day conditions; and it is 'marked by the absence of an in-built monitoring system'.[13] This helps explain why refugee advocates often speak of government policies being contrary to the spirit, if not the letter, of the *Refugee Convention*. That spirit is often enlivened by creative dialogue between UNHCR and the academy. In recent writings Goodwin-Gill has been more critical of those who bluntly espouse that an asylum seeker has no right of entry to a state of his or her choice when in flight from persecution. In his remarks to the 2012 American Society of International Law Conference entitled 'International Norm-Making on Forced Displacement: Challenges and Complexity', he said:

> Although some 148 states are now party to the 1951 Convention and/or the 1967 Protocol, there is no single body with the competence to pronounce with authority on the meaning of words, let alone their application in widely and wildly differentiated and evolving fact situations. In the first instance, it is therefore for each state party to implement its international obligations in good faith and, in its practice and through its courts and tribunals, to determine the meaning and scope of those obligations. [14]

He added:

> Interpreting the 1951 Convention presents the challenge of reconciling a 'living instrument' with consistency with international law. A good-faith interpretation of the treaty is called for, which reflects, if not the unknown intent of the drafters, then its object and purpose and the practice of states and their consent to be bound.[15]

---

13. Guy Goodwin-Gill, 'The Search for the One, True Meaning...', in *The Limits of Transnational Law* edited by Guy Goodwin-Gill and Helene Lambert (Cambridge: Cambridge University Press, 2010), 204 at 206–7.

14. *American Society International Law Proceedings* 106 (2012): 439 at 440.

15. *American Society International Law Proceedings* 106 (2012): 439 at 442–3.

Following upon some Australian controversy about whether boat people had a right to enter Australia seeking protection, Goodwin-Gill published a spirited editorial in the *International Journal of Refugee Law* stating:

> The persistent illusion of an absolute, exclusionary competence is still a matter of concern, however, because it tends to frame and direct national legislation and policies in ways that are inimical to international cooperation and, not infrequently, contemptuous of human rights. This persistence is all the more surprising, given what international law has achieved and what international organization has done to resolve or mitigate humanitarian problems.
>
> .....
>
> The history is important, and no international lawyer can avoid being an historian. This gives us the long view essential to understanding law in the relations of states, and enables us to counter misunderstandings dressed up as advocacy – to point out, for example, that no one in the Commission on Human Rights in 1947–48 ever suggested that a right 'to be granted asylum' (even if it were adopted, which it was not) meant that you could just turn up anywhere by boat and demand and get it. What history tells us, though, is that the French were not without reason to argue that a right to seek asylum would mean little if not linked to a right to be granted asylum. Equally, it shows that other states spoke for their time when responding that this was out of sync with contemporary international law, at least on the narrow, immigration issue of entry and residence. History, then and now, reminds us of the range of legal and practical matters which were left open, and which have since had to be resolved consistently with the general principles of the Declaration at large.

It does not follow, either logically or as a matter of fact, that because states declined to declare a right to be granted asylum in 1948, the individual in flight and at risk of persecution or other relevant harm necessarily has 'no right' to enter state territory at any time. The issue is often one of 'framing', for everything depends on context, and the question for international lawyers (and for governments, legislators, critics and commentators) is when and in the light of what obligations might circumstances requiring entry prevail.

......

Factual scenarios are hugely diverse (which accounts for the difficulty of harmonizing refugee decision making across jurisdictions), but it can never be excluded that the state may well be required, as a matter of obligation, to allow an individual to enter its territory for the purpose of protection. To imagine that this is equivalent to granting asylum, as that is understood in the practice of states, is to miss the whole picture – one which is rich in its complexity, demanding more than the simple intonation of words like 'admission', 'entry', 'right', 'no right', without reference to protection and to context and meaning in international law.[16]

In March 2014, Goodwin-Gill followed up with a very spirited attack on the US Supreme Court's *Sale* decision:

Nor do I think that the judgment of the Supreme Court in *Sale* counts for anything juridically significant, other than within the regrettably non-interactive legal system of the United States. Here, the Court ruled for domestic purposes on the construction of the Immigration and Nationality Act. What it said on the meaning of treaty was merely dictum and the Court was not competent – in at least two senses – to rule on international law.

---

16. Guy Goodwin Gill, 'Editorial: The Dynamic of International Refugee Law', in *International Journal of Refugee Law* 25/4 (2013): 651 at 653–5.

At best, the judgment might constitute an element of State practice, but even here its international relevance can be heavily discounted. The Court failed, among others, to have regard to the binding unilateral statements made by the US when interdiction was first introduced, and the ten years of consistent practice which followed. And as any student of international law will tell you, practice and statements of this nature are highly relevant, particularly when against interest.

UNHCR, moreover, which is responsible for supervising the application of the 1951 Convention/1967 Protocol, protested the judgment at the time and has consistently maintained the position set out in its *amicus* brief to the Supreme Court (and in earlier interventions with the US authorities). Significantly, no other State party to the treaties has objected to UNHCR's position, though the forum and the opportunity are readily available, such as the UNHCR Executive Committee, ECOSOC, or the Third Committee of the UN General Assembly.[17]

Be all this as it may, Goodwin-Gill nonetheless concedes in his most recent writing: 'The 1951 Convention does not deal with the question of admission, and neither does it oblige a state of refuge to accord asylum as such.'[18] Goodwin-Gill's co-author Professor Jane McAdam, when recently explaining the extra-territorial effect of international obligations and the need for Australian personnel on the high seas to be attentive to the protection needs of asylum seekers before refusing them access to Australian territory, claimed:

---

17. Guy Goodwin-Gill, The Globalization of High Seas Interdiction–Sale's Legacy and Beyond, YLS Sale Symposium, at <http://opiniojuris.org/2014/03/16/yale-sale-symposium-globalization-high-seas-interdiction-sales-legacy-beyond/>. Acessed 3 December 2014.

18. Guy Goodwin-Gill, 'The International Law of Refugee Protection', in *The Oxford Handbook of Refugee and Forced Migration Studies* (Oxford: Oxford University Press, 2014), 36 at 45.

Only the United States has said that the *Refugee Convention* does not have that extra-territorial application and that's the basis on which the US justifies its interdiction and expulsion of Haitians and Cubans for instance. The US Supreme Court upheld that view but . . . to borrow Guy Goodwin-Gill's language, the US Supreme Court was not competent in two senses of the word to rule on the international law obligations of the United States; and in any sense, they were really interpreting a domestic statute. UNHCR at the time and subsequently has spoken out very strongly that the US interpretation is wrong as a matter of international law, and not one country has ever contradicted UNHCR. In international law terms, that is a very strong tacit acceptance that UNHCR's position is correct and that the US is out there on a limb.[19]

Whatever of US exceptionalism in international law, its approach has in fact given licence and a paradigm these last two decades to other first world countries worried about an influx of boat people. Australian governments of both political persuasions have adopted the jurisprudence of the US Supreme Court, and to date the Australian High Court has not begged to differ. It has been the domestic courts, as much as the international academy and UNHCR, which has reined in exclusionary states, ever so slightly. In forthcoming litigation in the Australian High Court, the Australian Human Rights Commission has submitted 'that the construction given to Article 33(1) by the majority of the US Supreme Court in *Sale* v *Haitian Centers Council, Inc* is incorrect'.[20]

---

19. Q&A Panel: The High Court and the Asylum Case, Kaldor Centre, University of New South Wales, 22 July 2014, at <http://www.kaldorcentre.unsw.edu.au/node/348#overlay-context=events>. Accessed 3 December 2014.

20. Australian Human Rights Commission, Proposed Submissions, *CPCF* v *Minister for Immigration and Border Protection*, High Court of Australia, 11 September 2014, 8. The AHRC submission provides a novel approach to the historic interpretation of Article 33 when it states at 3: 'According to Goodwin-Gill and McAdam, the first reference in an international agreement to the principle that refugees should not be returned to their country of origin occurred in the 1933 Convention relating to the International

Perhaps in the future, the Australian High Court might be convinced to follow more the jurisprudence of the European Court of Human Rights rather than the US Supreme Court, at least when interpreting Australian statutes which are arguably consistent with the fulfilment of Australia's international treaty obligations. In Europe, the focus has been on boats coming across the Mediterranean Sea. The European Court of Human Rights became apprised of the EU practices in the Mediterranean in the 2012 case of *Hirsi* v *Italy*.

The applicants in that case were eleven Somali nationals and thirteen Eritrean nationals who were part of a group of about two hundred individuals who left Libya aboard three vessels with the aim of reaching the Italian coast. On 6 May 2009, when the vessels were thirty-five nautical miles south of the island of Lampedusa, three ships from the Italian Revenue Police and the Coastguard intercepted them. The occupants of the intercepted vessels were transferred onto Italian military ships and returned to Tripoli. On arrival in the Port of Tripoli, the migrants were handed over to the Libyan authorities.

According to the applicants' version of events, they objected to being handed over to the Libyan authorities but were forced to leave the Italian ships. At a press conference held on 7 May 2009 the Italian Minister of the Interior stated that the operation to intercept the vessels on the high seas and to push the migrants back to Libya was the consequence of the entry into force on 4 February 2009 of bilateral agreements concluded with Libya, and represented an important turning point in the fight against clandestine immigration.

Status of Refugees. Article 3 of that Convention contained an undertaking by States not to remove resident refugees or keep them from their territory 'by application of police measures, such as expulsions or non-admittance at the frontier (refoulement)' unless dictated by national security or public order. The language that ultimately formed the basis for Article 33(1) of the Refugees Convention was the product of an *Ad hoc* Committee on Statelessness and Related Problems appointed by the United Nations Economic and Social Council. A representative of the United States delegation on that Committee provided the following description of the key principle: 'Whether it was a question of closing the frontier to a refugee who asked admittance, or of turning him back after he had crossed the frontier, or even of expelling him after he had been admitted to residence in the territory, the problem was more or less the same . . . Whatever the case may be . . . he must not be turned back to a country where his life or freedom could be threatened.'

The applicants complained that they had been exposed to the risk of torture or inhuman or degrading treatment in Libya and in their respective countries of origin as a result of having been returned. They relied on Article 3 of the European Convention on Human Rights which provides: 'No one shall be subjected to torture or to inhuman or degrading treatment or punishment.'

The Court said:

> The Court has already had occasion to note that the States which form the external borders of the European Union are currently experiencing considerable difficulties in coping with the increasing influx of migrants and asylum seekers. It does not underestimate the burden and pressure this situation places on the States concerned, which are all the greater in the present context of economic crisis. It is particularly aware of the difficulties related to the phenomenon of migration by sea, involving for States additional complications in controlling the borders in southern Europe. However, having regard to the absolute character of the rights secured by Article 3, that cannot absolve a State of its obligations under that provision. The Court reiterates that protection against the treatment prohibited by Article 3 imposes on States the obligation not to remove any person who, in the receiving country, would run the real risk of being subjected to such treatment [21]

The Court ruled unanimously that the applicants were within the jurisdiction of Italy for the purposes of Article 1 of the Convention; that there had been a violation of Article 3 of the Convention on account of the fact that the applicants were exposed to the risk of being subjected to ill-treatment in Libya; and that there had been a violation of Article 3 of the Convention on account of the fact that the applicants were exposed to the risk of being repatriated to Somalia and Eritrea.[22]

---

21. Available at <http://hudoc.echr.coe.int/sites/eng/pages/search.aspx?i=001-109231>, #122. Accessed 3 December 2014.
22. In a separate judgment, Judge Pinto de Albuquerque joined issue with the US

I was interested to note that Lord Neuberger, the Chief Justice of the United Kingdom, was recently in Australia. He took the opportunity to express some forthright views about the European Court of Human Rights. He told the justices of the Victorian Supreme Court:

> I think we may sometimes have been too ready to treat Strasbourg court decisions as if they were determinations by a UK court whose decisions were binding on us. It is a civilian court under enormous pressure, which sits in chambers far more often than in banc, and whose judgments are often initially prepared by staffers, and who have produced a number of inconsistent decisions over the years. I think that we are beginning to see that the traditional common law approach may not be appropriate, at least to the extent that we should be more ready not to follow Strasbourg chamber decisions.[23]

In the end, he came down in favour of the general approach of the European Court, conceding that the UK's ratification of the Convention and the passage of its own Human Rights Act resulted in the courts being 'pitchforked into ruling on the most contentious issues of the day' including asylum seekers' rights. He observed:

Supreme Court. He said: 'It is true that the statement of the Swiss delegate to the conference of plenipotentiaries that the prohibition of *refoulement* did not apply to refugees arriving at the border was supported by other delegates, including the Dutch delegate, who noted that the conference was in agreement with this interpretation. It is also true that Article 33 § 2 of the UN *Refugee Convention* exempts from the prohibition of *refoulement* a refugee who constitutes a danger to the security of a country 'in which he is' and refugees on the high seas are in no country. One might be tempted to construe Article 33 § 1 as containing a similar territorial restriction. If the prohibition of *refoulement* were to apply on the high seas, it would create a special regime for dangerous aliens on the high seas, who would benefit from the prohibition, while dangerous aliens residing in the country would not.

'With all due respect, the United States Supreme Court's interpretation contradicts the literal and ordinary meaning of the language of Article 33 of the UN *Refugee Convention* and departs from the common rules of treaty interpretation.'

23. Lord Neuberger, Address to Conference of the Judges of the Supreme Court of Victoria, 8 August 2014, available at <http://supremecourt.uk/docs/speech-140808.pdf>. Accessed 3 December 2014.

> The fact that 'unelected' judges, especially foreign judges, are perceived to have been given powers which they previously had not enjoyed, coupled with the distaste in some political quarters for all things European, and the media's concentration on prisoners' votes and asylum seekers, has rendered the Convention something of a whipping boy for some politicians and newspapers. This appears to many people to be unfortunate. There are decisions of the Strasbourg court with which one can reasonably disagree, indeed with which I disagree. This is scarcely surprising; indeed, it would be astonishing if it were otherwise. However, to my mind, there are very few of its decisions which can fairly be said to be misconceived.

Australia does not have a *Human Rights Act*, and it is not accountable to any outside judicial body like Strasbourg. This may help to account for Australia's less nuanced approach to 'stopping the boats'. In Australia, the Executive finds itself freer from judicial constraint. Mind you, the Australian High Court flexes its muscle from time to time. Just last week, the court unanimously struck down the government's latest attempt to avoid giving permanent protection visas to asylum seekers proven to be refugees who also pass the requisite health and security checks.[24]

The Law, Politics and Morality of Stopping the Boats

Permit me to be so bold, being a Jesuit and a lawyer, to suggest that domestic judicial review and public moral argument posited

---

24. *Plaintiff S4-2014* v *Minister for Immigration and Border Protection* [2014] HCA 34 (11 September 2014). The plaintiff had no visa permitting him to enter or remain in Australia. On arrival in Australia, at Christmas Island, the plaintiff was lawfully taken into immigration detention where he was held for two years while being assessed for a protection visa. The department determined that the plaintiff was 'grant ready'. 'That is, the department determined that the plaintiff was a refugee and satisfied relevant health and character requirements for the grant of a protection visa.' The Minister then decided not to grant a protection visa but rather another short term visa which would then preclude the grant of a permanent protection visa. The Court ruled that the grant of this visa was invalid as its grant would have undermined the whole legislative purpose of the two year detention, namely assessment for a permanent protection visa.

on religious conviction are two necessary devices for reining in the executive government responding to populist sentiment to secure the borders and stop the boats. It is the judicial method which permits fine consideration of the claims of those who present at our borders, rather than more broad stroke governmental decisions to punish those who present at our borders in order to send a message to other intending asylum seekers and to give a preference to those asylum seekers chosen by government rather than those who self-select by presenting themselves at the border. It is the religiously based moral argument that augments the secular liberal approach within the nation state. The secular liberal finds it hard to formulate an argument for universal care extending beyond the injunction for government to care for their own citizens maintaining the security of their borders. At the very least, the secular liberal should concede the assistance that might be obtained from the religious practitioners who profess the dignity of all human persons, and not just those holding passports for nation states living in peace and with economic security.

Having offered some observations about the effects of the judicial method, I now turn to the effects of religious discourse in the public square, convinced that such discourse can often augment, consolidate and extend the protection of the human rights of those whose interests do not coincide with those of the majority in a nation state. Religious leaders have a capacity to contribute to the amplification of the still, small voice, as of course do international lawyers. The concept of human rights has real work to do whenever those with power justify their solutions to social ills or political conflicts only on the basis of majority support or by claiming the solutions will lead to an improved situation for the mainstream majority. Even if a particular solution is popular or maximises gains for the greatest number of people, it might still be wrong and objectionable. There is a need to have regard to the wellbeing of all members of the human community, and not just those within the preferred purview of government consideration.

Lampedusa continues to be a beacon for asylum seekers fleeing desperate situations in Africa seeking admission into the

EU. Lampedusa is a lightning rod for European concerns about the security of borders in an increasingly globalised world where people as well as capital flow across porous borders. That's why Pope Francis went there on his first official papal visit outside Rome. At Lampedusa on 8 July 2013, Pope Francis said:

> 'Where is your brother?' Who is responsible for this blood? In Spanish literature we have a comedy of Lope de Vega which tells how the people of the town of Fuente Ovejuna kill their governor because he is a tyrant. They do it in such a way that no one knows who the actual killer is. So when the royal judge asks: 'Who killed the governor?', they all reply: 'Fuente Ovejuna, sir'. Everybody and nobody! Today too, the question has to be asked: Who is responsible for the blood of these brothers and sisters of ours? Nobody! That is our answer: It isn't me; I don't have anything to do with it; it must be someone else, but certainly not me. Yet God is asking each of us: 'Where is the blood of your brother which cries out to me?' Today no one in our world feels responsible; we have lost a sense of responsibility for our brothers and sisters. We have fallen into the hypocrisy of the priest and the levite whom Jesus described in the parable of the Good Samaritan: we see our brother half dead on the side of the road, and perhaps we say to ourselves: 'poor soul . . .!', and then go on our way. It's not our responsibility, and with that we feel reassured, assuaged. The culture of comfort, which makes us think only of ourselves, makes us insensitive to the cries of other people, makes us live in soap bubbles which, however lovely, are insubstantial; they offer a fleeting and empty illusion which results in indifference to others; indeed, it even leads to the globalization of indifference. In this globalized world, we have fallen into globalized indifference. We have become used to the suffering of others: it doesn't affect me; it doesn't concern me; it's none of my business!
>
> Here we can think of Manzoni's character—'the Unnamed'. The globalization of indifference makes us all 'unnamed', responsible, yet nameless and faceless.

It is all very well for the pope to say these things. But who is listening? And even if they are listening, who is taking any notice? Should anyone other than Catholics bother taking any notice? Those of us who profess to be Christian living behind secure national borders buttressed by wealth and the rule of law being shared only by the citizenry have been wrestling with the gospel imperatives of justice and compassion expressed in the parables of Jesus such as the parable of the Good Samaritan.

Jeremy Waldron who is now the Chichele Professor of Social and Political Theory at Oxford recently published an article entitled 'Two-way Translation: The Ethics of Engaging with Religious Contributions in Public Deliberation'. He joins issue with John Rawls' assertion that the responsibility falls on the religious speaker rather than the secular listener to translate his propositions and his moral passion into language comprehensible to those who profess nothing more than the tenets of public reason. He quotes the German philosopher Jürgen Habermas who insists that any 'requirement of translation must be conceived as a cooperative task in which the nonreligious citizens must likewise participate.'

Discourse in the public square is a two-way street. Thus there is a place for Pope Francis to be prophetically declaiming the moral turpitude of present state practices at Lampedusa. There is a place for the Australian Catholic bishops to be prophetically declaiming the moral turpitude of present state practices on Christmas Island, Nauru and Manus Island. If only the Abbott government with its disproportionate number of Jesuit alumni Cabinet ministers would listen! There is a place for church leaders drawing on their religious tradition trying to call political leaders and the public back to values, policies and laws which resonate more with the tenets of religious faith. Following Habermas, Waldron states:

> It is not only speakers who bear a burden of civility; the audience does too. The speaker must strain to convey his points in ways that will communicate as much of their content as he can to those who do not share his faith or the biblical or theological resources he is

drawing on. But the listener has a similar responsibility. He must strain to listen and try to understand what is being said, and, if necessary, draw on resources in his own background (even aspects of his background that he has repudiated) or resources in the culture that he has access to, to get a bearing on what is being said, and what is being argued.

Certainly, it is not appropriate—it is not civil—for secular citizens to strain not to understand what is being said to publicly burnish their own credentials as non-believers. It is not appropriate for them to block out or refuse to employ available resources for making sense of what is said, because of their own resolve to purge religion from their lives. Or rather, a person can do that; people do not have the obligation to listen to and grapple with everything that is said in public discourse. But then, if they do turn a deaf ear, for whatever reason, to some of what is being said, they can hardly complain about the incivility of the speaker.[25]

The migration and asylum debate is one debate in which the voice of church leaders needs to be heeded and in which we need to have due regard for political deliberation. It is also a debate that can be properly conducted only with institutional safeguards, those checks and balances ensuring appropriate consideration of the balance between the public interest and the dignity of every person, including the person presenting at the national border in flight from persecution.

This cannot be done without adequate supervision by the domestic courts. It is a debate that requires strong political virtue in national leaders, opinion makers and public advocates. It is a debate that requires a honed ethical inquiry into the ends to be achieved, given the vast numbers of people seeking protection and the heightened need to secure national borders. For example, it is not

---

25. Jeremy Waldron, 'Two-way Translation: The Ethics of Engaging with Religious Contributions in Public Deliberation', in *Mercer Law Review* 63 (2012): 845 at 863–4

an ethical irrelevance that for every person who gains protection at the border in Australia, that is one less place available in the annual immigration intake for a person in great humanitarian need who does not have the resources to get themselves to the border.

In what circumstances are we entitled to be cruel to the person on our doorstep so as to be kind to the person in greater need on the other side of the world? In what circumstances are we entitled to be kind to the person on our doorstep, absolving ourselves from responsibility for the person in greater need in a remote refugee camp where the human rights violations are horrendous? It is facile to suggest that there is some simple mathematical answer to these political and ethical quandaries. In his inaugural lecture at Oxford, Professor Waldron spoke about *political* theory and the need to be 'focusing on issues of institutions as well as the ends, aims, and ideals of politics, like justice'. He observed:

> The deliberative and deliberate processes of a free society slow things down; their articulated and articulate structures stretch things out; they cost money for salaries and furniture and buildings; they provide an irritating place for the raising of inconvenient questions; at their best they respect the dignity of the poorest he or the poorest she that is in England by providing a place for their petitions to be heard. The political institutions of a free society sometimes even require the government to retire from the field defeated, when its victory, in some courtroom or legislative battle, was supposed by political insiders to be a foregone conclusion. I think all of this is to be valued and cherished.[26]

Waldron is adamant that students of politics need to study both institutions and the character of those who inhabit them: 'They should understand something of political virtue and the demands that the requirements of good government make on the character of those

---

26. Jeremy Waldron, '*Political* Political Theory: An Inaugural lecture', in *The Journal of Political Philosophy*, 21/ 1 (2013): 1 at 23.

who take on responsibility for public affairs'. We need to improve both if we are to get better ethical outcomes for laws and policies affecting those who present at our borders seeking protection whether it be from persecution, torture, cruel or inhuman treatment.

Assessing the Australian Measures to Stop the Boats

On 8 September 2014, Zeid Ra'ad Al Hussein, the new UN High Commissioner for Human Rights addressed the opening of the UN Human Rights Council's 27th session. I am well used to this UN body giving more than warranted attention to Western countries and their human rights violations. It is no surprise when they single out the United States for attention. But it is not often that Australia warrants a billing, especially in a high commissioner's first speech to the council. Hussein said:

> I must emphasise that the detention of asylum seekers and migrants should only be applied as a last resort, in exceptional circumstances, for the shortest possible duration and according to procedural safeguards. *Australia's* policy of off-shore processing for asylum seekers arriving by sea, and its interception and turning back of vessels, is leading to a chain of human rights violations, including arbitrary detention and possible torture following return to home countries. It could also lead to the resettlement of migrants in countries that are not adequately equipped.[27]

After surveying recent American abuses he observed:

> The treatment of non-nationals must observe the minimum standards set by international law. Human rights are not reserved for citizens only, or for people with

---

27. Zeid Ra'ad Al Hussein, Opening Remarks at UN Human Rights Council, 8 September 2014, at
    <http://www.ohchr.org/EN/NewsEvents/Pages/DisplayNews.aspx?NewsID=14998>.
    Accessed 3 December 2014.

visas. They are the inalienable rights of every individual, regardless of his or her location and migration status. A tendency to promote law enforcement and security paradigms at the expense of human rights frameworks dehumanises irregular migrants, enabling a climate of violence against them and further depriving them of the full protection of the law.

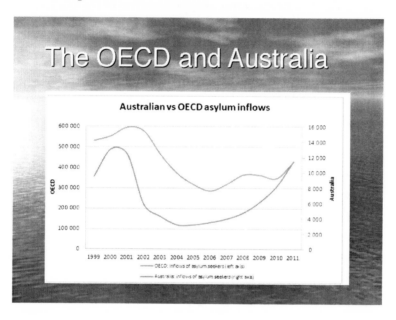

Recently, one of our Australian universities hosted a national asylum summit. Jeff Crisp, the Head of the Policy Division and Evaluation Service of UNHCR in Geneva, delivered the opening keynote address. Jeff provided a graph to show that the ebb and flow of asylum seekers coming to Australia fairly well tracked the ebb and flow internationally. Jeff's graph of 'Australia vs OECD asylum inflows' cut out at 2011.

The rate of boat arrivals had escalated to Australia from 2011 to mid-2013. By then the red line was well off the graph. In the financial year ended 30 June 2013, 25,145 people had arrived on 394 boats—'an average of over seventy people and more than a boat a day' as Scott Morrison, Tony Abbott's then Shadow Minister never tired of telling us. Except for Sri Lankans, most of those arriving by boat came not directly from their country of persecution but via various countries with Indonesia being their penultimate stop.

There was an understandable bipartisan concern in the Australian parliament about the blowout of boat arrivals to 3,300 per month. An arrival rate of that sort (40,000 pa) would put at risk the whole offshore humanitarian program and distort the migration and family reunion program. Thus the need to ensure that those risking the perilous sea voyage were in direct flight from persecution being unable to avail themselves adequate protection or processing *en route* in Indonesia. If they were able to avail themselves such services in Indonesia, the Australian government would be entitled to set up disincentives and to return them safely to Indonesia. If that number were in direct flight from persecution, the Australian government would be justified in setting up measures providing only temporary protection and denying family reunion other than on terms enjoyed by other migrants. But I doubt that it would ever come to that.

I have never understood why the less than honest asylum seeker arriving by plane, having sought a visa not for asylum but for tourism or business, should be given preferential treatment over the honest asylum seeker arriving by boat who says, 'I am here to seek asylum.'

Boat arrivals by calendar year 1979 to 2012 and
financial year 1989-90 to 2012-13

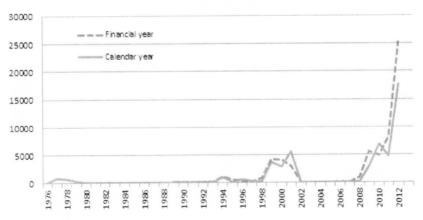

Some people argue that it is immoral for nations now to maintain sovereign borders and that we should permit the free flow of people much as we allow the free flow of capital and produce in an increasingly globalised world. In my own Catholic tradition, Pope John XXIII used to argue for a right to emigrate to the country of one's choice. It is not a right which has been espoused by any subsequent pope.

I accept the moral propriety of nation states maintaining secure borders and insisting on the need for an ordered migration program while playing their part providing protection for people in direct flight from persecution. Australia being a net migration country is well positioned to contribute to the protection mandate. If the rate of boat arrivals in 2012–2013 had continued to escalate at the rate it was, all humanitarian places in the annual allocation would by now have been taken up by the boat arrivals. If the flow was unabated, there was even the possibility down the track that the entire migration program would be filled by boat arrivals.

The current Australian government is almost suggesting that there has been an ethical dividend delivered from the harsh policies. The Australian Minister for Immigration, Scott Morrison, told the National Press Club in Canberra on 10 September 2014: 'In 2012/13 there were just 503 places provided in our special humanitarian program. This year there are 5000. Overall, our refugee and humanitarian program will deliver 4,400 places to those affected by the conflicts in Syria and Iraq this year alone. This is made possible by our border success. No longer are places in this programme being taken by those who have come illegally by boat.' Mind you, these 4,400 places come from the already reduced quota of the special humanitarian program. There has been no increase to the number of humanitarian places on offer in this year's migration intake.

Both sides of Australian politics are now committed to stopping the boats, stopping the drownings, and having additional places available for offshore asylum seekers chosen by the Australian government and not self-selected by those with access to people smugglers. Only the minor parties (Greens, Palmer United and

DLP) express ethical objections to this calculus in the Australian Parliament. The Abbott government was elected with a strong mandate to stop the boats. For the moment, the government is not much interested in public discussion about the ethics of the policy. It is more a matter of 'whatever it takes'. The government needs to engage the community about the ethical bottom line for long term detention and banishment of refugees to countries such as Nauru and PNG. We need to ensure a fair go for all—those on boats, those stranded in remote camps, and those trapped in transit countries.

Is There a More Decent Way of Stopping the Boats?

In the medium term, I think the only way to stop the boats ethically is to negotiate a regional agreement with Indonesia and Malaysia. This would take a considerable period of time, a good cheque book, and a strong commitment to detailed backroom diplomatic work avoiding the megaphone diplomacy which has marked this issue of late. In the short term, the boats can be stopped only with some sort of 'shock and awe' campaign. Can such a campaign be ethically justified? Sadly in Australia at the moment, that is not a question with any political traction. In recent months, there have been two deaths of persons held in detention on Manus Island in Papua New Guinea. The PNG government is showing no indication of delivering on its previous commitment that those asylum seekers taken to Manus Island and proved to be refugees would be resettled in PNG enjoying all rights guaranteed by the *Refugee Convention*. The shock and awe campaign may be truncated not because it is judged unethical but just because it does not work and it is not cost efficient.

I want to outline the contours for a better approach in Australia. Outlining these contours, I want to defend the *Refugee Convention* while urging caution about invoking it as trumps in moral or political discourse or even in legal discourse about decisions of ultimate courts of appeal. I want to urge that Australian political leaders of every ilk maintain a commitment both to the Convention and to onshore processing with minimal detention and adequate rights to work and welfare while awaiting processing in the community.

Hopefully any changes adopted can be worked against a backdrop of our providing at least 20,000 humanitarian places a year in our migration program, at least 12,000 of those being for refugees.

Boats carrying asylum seekers from Indonesia to Australia could legally be interdicted by Australian authorities within our contiguous zone (twenty-four nautical miles offshore from land, including Christmas Island). The passengers could be offloaded and taken to Christmas Island for a prompt assessment to ensure that none of them fit the profile of a person in direct flight from Indonesia fearing persecution by Indonesia. Pursuant to a regional arrangement or bilateral agreement between Australia and Indonesia, Indonesia could guarantee not to refoule any person back to the frontiers of a country where they would face persecution nor to remove any person to a country unwilling to provide that guarantee. Screened asylum seekers from Christmas Island could then be safely flown back to Indonesia for processing.

With adequate resourcing, a real queue could be created for processing and resettlement. Provided there had been an earlier, extensive advertising campaign, Indonesian authorities would then be justified in placing any returned boat people at the end of the queue. Assured safe return by air together with placement at the end of the queue would provide the deterrent to persons no longer in direct flight from persecution risking life and fortune boarding a boat for Australia. In co-operation with UNHCR and IOM (Internationa Organisation for Migration), Australia could provide the financial wherewithal to enhance the security and processing arrangements in Indonesia. Both governments could negotiate with other countries in the region to arrange more equitable burden sharing in the offering of resettlement places for those proved to be refugees. Australian politicians would need to give the leadership to the community explaining why it would be necessary and decent for Australia then to receive more proven refugees from the region, including those who fled to our region fearing persecution in faraway places like Afghanistan.

Indonesia would need to enhance its own border protection regime making it more difficult for asylum seekers in Malaysia who are not in direct flight from persecution in Malaysia to enter Indonesia. The safeguards negotiated in Indonesia and any other country in the region to which unprocessed asylum seekers were to be sent would need to comply with appropriate minimum standards.

In the short term, Australia should escalate its diplomatic efforts with Indonesia to stem the flow of boats and to win agreement to the safe return by air of all asylum seekers interdicted within the contiguous zone or inside Australia's territorial waters once they have been screened out from having any protection claim against Indonesian persecution. Such efforts would need to include commitments to capacity building, countering corruption, and a review of the aid budget. Both governments need to have an incentive to stop the boats. Australia and Indonesia should then join a regional initiative aimed at:

- Setting down a regional principle of non-refoulement
- Setting down regional principles for denying entry and returning asylum seekers no longer in direct flight from persecution to the safe transit country they have just departed
- Setting down regional principles for processing and protection with certification by UNHCR
- Setting quotas for resettlement places for proven refugees who are processed in the region.

Then, and only then, might Australia have some prospect of achieving the policy goal of hermetically sealed borders and ordered migration flows, while honouring the letter and spirit of the *Refugee Convention* in a region where our neighbours are not much interested in signing the *Refugee Convention* but like us are committed to sharing the burden of extending compassion to those in direct flight from persecution. Then, and only then, might we stop the boats once it is known that it is a waste of money to take to the high seas only to be told: 'Please get back to where you already had a realistic opportunity for protection and processing; but if

you are in direct flight from persecution, you are welcome here!'
There would be no need to maintain unprincipled, unworkable
deterrents like offshore processing in Nauru or Manus Island or
offshore dumping in Malaysia or Cambodia. Unless we wrestle with
these complexities, we risk a populist response to all asylum seekers,
including those in direct flight from persecution: 'Get back to where
you once belonged!' The challenge confronting Australia is modest
compared with so many other countries which do not boast the
advantages of which we dare to sing: 'Our home is girt by sea; Our
land abounds in nature's gifts'; 'For those who've come across the
seas we've boundless plains to share.'

Any country is entitled to maintain an ordered migration
program, securing its borders appropriately. A nation like Australia
should maintain a migration program with balance between business
migration, family reunion, and humanitarian needs. All nations
should permit persons in direct flight from persecution to enter
their territory for the purposes of assessment and temporary safe
haven. All nations which are signatories to the *Refugee Convention*
should abide its terms. It should be conceded by legal purists that
strict and complete compliance with the letter and spirit of the
Refugee Convention is possible only when the receiving country is
a developed country with a robust rule of law. Legal purists should
also concede that such compliance renders the *Refugee Convention*
unattractive to a range of countries, especially in South East Asia,
and renders Convention compliant solutions possible only in
a minority of cases. Political pragmatists should concede that a
country's signature on the *Refugee Convention* is not a sufficient
condition for sending refugees for resettlement, especially when the
signature was obtained as part of a UN nation building exercise (eg.
Timor Leste and Cambodia).

Australia could return to a pre-1996 situation, severing the
nexus between successful onshore asylum claims and the quota for
offshore humanitarian places. While the nexus is maintained, the
ethical argument cannot focus only on the plight of those seeking
access onshore to Australia. It must also take into account the plight

of those refugees who have no access to long distance travel to seek asylum. Australia should maintain a special quota for refugees fleeing from countries where Australia has committed troops in war, and the quota should be maintained for twice the period Australians fought there. Australian political parties should adopt the targets set two years ago by the panel set up to review Australia's asylum policies—20,000 humanitarian places per year, with the prospect of an increase to 27,000 by 2017.

Australia needs to work with Indonesia and UNHCR in the first instance, and then with Malaysia to provide the circumstances in Indonesia and Malaysia where asylum seekers can be provided with an acceptable level of protection and processing (approved and supervised by UNHCR), thereby warranting the classification of further movement as secondary movement, permitting interception on the high seas followed by safe and dignified return to the last port of call.

Australia's 'shock and awe' measures instituted by prime ministers Rudd and Abbott since July 2013 have achieved their objective in that the boats have all but stopped and the border with Indonesia is now secure. There is no ongoing justification for the long term detention of asylum seekers (including unaccompanied minors) on Nauru and PNG. There should be an appropriate burden sharing arrangement with Australia accepting ultimate responsibility for those refugees who cannot be resettled elsewhere. If the Australian 'shock and awe' measures are to be maintained, they should be mandated by Parliament either by legislation or by the tabling of designations which are disallowable by either house of parliament. Defending the present scheme in the High Court the Commonwealth in May 2014 said, 'The Minister is politically responsible for the choice that he makes and **the Parliament**—if it disagrees with the choice, either House of the Parliament can stop it from taking effect.' The Commonwealth's lawyer went on later to say 'that it is for the Minister **and for the Parliament** to decide, subject to political accountability, whether or not a designation should occur and be allowed to operate in accordance with the scheme'.[28] The newly constituted Australian Senate should be given the opportunity to scrutinise and debate the scheme. This is a sensible democratic precaution, given that the scheme will be the subject of a royal commission and compensation payments some day.

If the shock and awe measures are to be maintained, the Australian Army (acting much like peacekeepers at the invitation of the host government) rather than an admixture of corporations and NGOs should be responsible for the security and safety of detainees. There is no justification for denying work rights or an adequate level of welfare assistance in the community for those onshore asylum seekers awaiting determination of their claims.

Does the *Refugee Convention* Help us Find the Answer to Stopping the Boats Decently?

In the toxic refugee debate in Australia, I have come to see the *Refugee Convention* as something of a straw man, perhaps even a distraction. Without key countries in the region being signatories, without any reporting mechanism, and without any authoritative curial interpretative body, the Convention to some extent means whatever we want it to mean. Or it means what esteemed international lawyers would want it to mean. We all go off on one of two tracks: the legal purists think it provides a comprehensive code for refugee protection and judgment of the practices and policies of the political pragmatists; and the political pragmatists think it provides a convenient cover for arrangements like off-shore processing, opting out of permanent resettlement, and protracted detention.

We have reached the stage in Australia that government is able to claim that holding 157 asylum seekers (including children) on a navy ship on the high seas for a month is consistent with the *Refugee Convention*. Rather than arguing the toss on the Convention, perhaps

---

28. *Plaintiff S156/2013* v *The Minister for Immigration and Border Protection and Anor*, Transcript, [2014] HCATrans 98 (13 May 2014) at
< http://www.austlii.edu.au/au/other/HCATrans/2014/98.html>. Accessed 3 December 2014.

we are better off in and out of court arguing that such a wanton exercise of extra-territorial executive power without parliamentary warrant is unconstitutional, especially given the absence of any legislative authorisation for the deprivation of liberty for no purpose authorised by statute. Our Australian sense of legal formalism about the *Refugee Convention* has reached the stage that our government proposes sending 1,000 asylum seekers to Cambodia for processing and resettlement, on the basis that Cambodia is a signatory to the *Refugee Convention*. In Cambodia, there is no adequate legal safety net. On 12 September 2014, Vivian Tan, the regional spokesperson for UNHCR told a church news agency:

> UNHCR is not party to this bilateral agreement in any way. We are deeply concerned about the precedent being set by this type of arrangement that in the first instance, transfers asylum-seekers who have sought Australia's protection to Nauru, in conditions that have previously been described as harmful, then relocates refugees recognised in Nauru to Cambodia. Asylum-seekers should ordinarily be processed, and benefit from protection, in the territory of the state where they arrive, or which otherwise has jurisdiction over them.[29]

We are in the realm of morality and politics, not law. The international law is not helping. Rather it is providing the warring parties with their own rationale for their intractability, avoiding the need for moral and political engagement.

We will only return to a decent asylum policy in Australia if we get three things right as Waldron indicated in this inaugural political theory lecture at Oxford: the values of our political leaders, the structures of our political institutions, and the ends of our society including justice and compassion for all including those who present at our borders by boat, without visas, while seeking asylum. We need to work on all three.

Robust judicial review by the domestic courts and moral advocacy

---

29. 'UN refugee agency slams Cambodia-Australia deal', UCANEWS, 15 September 2014

by community leaders including Church leaders are necessary parts of the resolution of the issue. International lawyers also have their place and I applaud their dedication and professionalism, while pleading that international law not be invoked to pre-empt deliberation about either morality or politics. If discussion about the spirit of the *Refugee Convention* is not a distraction, it may simply be a proxy for those who prefer to formulate their moral criteria and political preferences with concepts drawn from international law. Such discussion has its place but it is no substitute for, and neither does it trump, community discussion about right and wrong and domestic court analysis of legality and illegality. Only so much can be achieved by translating discussions of what is morally acceptable or politically achievable into learned deliberations on the spirit, rather than the letter, of unenforceable international human rights instruments, especially one that is as porous, partial in coverage, and lacking in authoritative curial interpretation as the *Refugee Convention.*

Considering again my indebtedness to those two Aborigines who met the *David McIver* 151 years ago, I owe it to all my fellow Australians to agitate these issues of law, morality and politics here in Ireland so that back in Australia, the homeland which, in my religious tradition, was known as the Great South Land of the Holy Spirit, we might continue to sing: 'Our home is girt by sea; Our land abounds in nature's gifts'; 'For those who've come across the seas we've boundless plains to share.'

-o0o-

In December 2014 just before Parliament rose for the Christmas break, Immigration Minister Scott Morrison negotiated an amended Migration and Maritime Powers Legislation Amendment (Resolving the Asylum Legacy Caseload) Bill *through the Senate. In January 2015, the High Court of Australia upheld the legality of the one month detention of 157 Tamil asylum seekers on the high seas.*

It is high time Australia and Indonesia sat down at the table to negotiate the terms for safe and orderly return of unvisaed asylum seekers heading to Australia by boat. Until this is done, we Australians will continue policies both doing untold harm to asylum seekers waiting forever on Nauru and Manus Island, and risking the safety and dignity of those being returned to Indonesia without adequate safeguards. Until this is done, this toxic issue will continue to poison our politics and demean our courts which are unable to deliver justice according to law.

Scott Morrison had a thumping big win in the High Court when it handed down the decision in *CPCF* v *Minister for Immigration and Border Protection* on 28 January 2015.[30] The bench split four to three on a couple of issues. But overall, the Abbott government will be feeling vindicated by its ruthless approach to stopping the boats. All seven High Court judges have made it clear that there is next to nothing that can be done in the courts to question the government's approach. It has got to the stage that it is lawful, acceptable to government, and hardly a matter of concern to the Australian community that 157 asylum seekers, including children, can be kept in windowless detention on an Australian vessel for a month on the high seas in the Indian Ocean.

There is no legal impediment to stopping the boats. Once an asylum vessel enters Australia's contiguous zone (twenty-four nautical miles from landfall, including Christmas Island), Australian maritime officers acting with authority under the *Maritime Powers Act* may detain any persons on the boat without a visa and take them to a place outside Australia. The only requirement is that the maritime officers be satisfied, on reasonable grounds, that it is safe for the persons to be in that place.

In this case, the National Security Committee of Cabinet instructed the maritime officers to take the Tamil asylum seekers back to India where they had come from, having sailed on an Indian vessel. The court ruled that it was irrelevant that the maritime

---

30. [2015] HCA 1

officers were acting on instructions. In fact, it was important that they were following instructions through the chain of command with responsibility ultimately resting with ministers of the crown elected by the people and answerable to parliament. The court also ruled that there was no need for the maritime officers to give asylum seekers an opportunity to be heard before removing them from the Australian contiguous zone.

The three dissenting judges thought the detention of the Tamils unlawful because the detention had commenced before the Australian government had secured authorisation from the Indian government for return of the asylum seekers. The majority judges thought the only result of such a ruling would be that people would be detained on the high seas for even longer, waiting until an appropriate destination could be found. To avoid delay on the high seas, two of the dissenting judges suggested that the only lawful course, in the absence of an agreement with India, would be for the asylum seekers to be brought to Australia (No chance of that!) or immediately taken to Nauru or Manus Island for processing (Thank you, your Honours, but are you the government?). The matter is now somewhat academic. The Parliament when passing the *Migration and Maritime Powers Legislation Amendment (Resolving the Asylum Legacy Caseload) Act* in December legislated that detention would be lawful even if the ultimate destination were undetermined, uncertain or changed. The same case brought under the new law would probably result in a unanimous judgment in favour of the government.

The long term impact of this High Court decision is that academic argument about international law is now even less likely to impact on the interpretation and application of Australian law in relation to asylum seekers. We are used to public disputation in which international lawyers and refugee advocates argue that Australian measures are contrary to the spirit of the *Convention Relating to the Status of Refugees*, with government responding that Australian law complies with the letter of the Convention. The recent laws passed by the Australian Parliament make it clear that Parliament is desirous of stipulating a strict code for dealing with asylum at the frontier. The High Court has made it clear that Parliament is free to do that, and there is nothing the courts can do about it. The matter was neatly summarised by Justice Keane:

> Australian courts are bound to apply Australian statute law 'even if that law should violate a rule of international law'. International law does not form part of Australian law until it has been enacted in legislation. In construing an Australian statute, our courts will read 'general words ... subject to the established rules of international law' unless a contrary intention appears from the statute. In this case, there is no occasion to invoke this principle of statutory construction. The terms of the Act are specific. They leave no doubt as to its operation.

All seven judges of the High Court basically took this approach. The Australian Parliament has been so specific in codifying the law of asylum at the frontier that there is nothing for the judges to do except apply the letter of the law, regardless of the general principles of international law. You may just as well be quoting the *Catechism of the Catholic Church* to them, as be submitting the learned opinions of international lawyers.

Given that both sides of politics are committed to stopping the boats, we need to find a better way than having to maintain the barbaric arrangements on Nauru and Manus Island and allowing government to run undercover turn backs and returns to Indonesia or wherever without adequate safeguards for asylum seekers, even if they no longer be in direct flight from persecution in their home country.

To date, most refugee advocates have ruled out the possibility of working with government to formulate a plan for more decently being able to return asylum seekers to Indonesia which is the country most often transited by those trying to reach Australia for protection and an optimal migration outcome. But unless this is done, Australian governments of both political persuasions will maintain Nauru and Manus Island, and they will return boats to

Indonesia in questionable circumstances without any scrutiny or transparency. We need to engage Indonesia, invoking the principles of international law which our government claims to be reflected in Australian domestic legislation. We need assurances that asylum seekers returned to Indonesia will not be refouled to their home countries or to other places where they might face persecution, torture or other serious harm. We would need similar assurances from India if we were ever to try to send Tamils back there again.

Indonesia is not a signatory to *Refugee Convention,* and it is not likely to be. But it is a signatory to the *International Covenant on Civil and Political Rights (ICCPR)* and the *Convention Against Torture (CAT).* It makes regular reports to the requisite UN bodies. In 2008, the UN Committee Against Torture wanted assurances in Indonesian domestic law that refoulement would never be able to occur. But the UN committee had no evidence of any particular case or alleged violation. In August 2013, the UN Human Rights Committee published its most recent concluding observations on Indonesia. This quite detailed report made no mention of any concerns relating to refoulement—either under *ICCPR* or *CAT.*

Indonesia complies with the reporting provisions of *CAT* and *ICCPR.* There are no confirmed reports of Indonesia wrongly refouling persons returned from Australia. Indonesia is NOT and is not likely to be a signatory to the *Refugee Convention.* Could the conditions ever be fulfilled which would warrant Australia returning asylum seekers to Indonesia provided only that Australia is satisfied that the asylum seekers are not in direct flight from persecution IN Indonesia?

My challenge to my fellow refugee advocates is this. In light of this High Court decision, nothing is to be lost by trying to negotiate transparent agreements with Indonesia and India for the safe and dignified return of asylum seekers who are not in direct flight from persecution in Indonesia or India. Until this is done, we will continue to violate the human rights of asylum seekers on the high seas and then in places like Nauru, Manus Island and Cambodia where our government wants to send them. And there's nothing we can do to change that in the courts, or presently, in our parliament. Parliament is a *cul-de-sac,* and the High Court a dead end.

12

Respecting Autonomy and Protecting the Vulnerability of the Dying

---

With people living longer, with some people spending many years in later life with reduced physical and/or mental capacities, with people fearing pain, suffering, and the loss of autonomy in the closing months of life, there is continued discussion about euthanasia, assisted suicide, and physician assisted death. As with many issues, there is a need to distinguish between the ideal law to be applicable to all persons and the moral teaching to be espoused to one's co-religionists. To date there has been no major change to the law in any Australian jurisdiction but the matter is being constantly discussed. In 2011, I addressed the parishioners at North Sydney.

I should start with two disclaimers. I am not a medical practitioner. And I am not a professional moral theologian. Usually I get asked to talk on issues such as euthanasia when there is a discussion in the public square—whether it be before a parliamentary committee or an IQ2 debate in Angel Place. In those circumstances, we are not usually focussing on personal morality or religious beliefs about euthanasia. Rather we are asking what is the preferable law or social policy on a vexed moral issue in a pluralist democratic society where there are citizens of all religious beliefs and none.

My mother is a medical practitioner. She is very incisive and often blunt about the matter to hand. Now in her eighties, she tends not to waste words in expressing her opinions. When I told her of the topic under discussion, she said to me, 'Well there is not much to say about euthanasia is there? Just don't kill people and look after them while they are dying. What more can you say?' She may be right.

We are talking about euthanasia and physician assisted suicide. If we look at the original Greek meaning of the word euthanasia, it means nothing more or less than a good death: from *eu* 'well' + *thanatos* 'death'. Nowadays euthanasia means the direct causing of death, usually by the administration of a lethal injection by a medical practitioner. There is also the idea of physician assisted suicide or physician assisted death where the doctor prescribes the lethal drugs which the patient then ingests at a later time, perhaps with direct assistance from a loved one or carer.

I wish to commence with a consideration of a recent observation by the Australian Productivity Commission: 'The number of Australians aged eighty-five and over is projected to increase from 0.4 million in 2010 to 1.8 million (5.1 per cent of the population) by 2050'. We are an ageing population.

My second consideration comes from the work done in the UK by Sir Michael Marmot on the social determinants of health. He has found that people living in the poorest, most deprived neighbourhoods will live on average nine years less than those from the wealthiest, best resourced neighbourhoods. And even though they die nine years earlier, they will also spend on average an extra eight years of that shortened life with a significant disability. So we would need to consider a different set of factors if we were looking at providing aged care facilities and palliative care out in the western suburbs of Sydney.

We need to consider three very different questions. (1) How would I want to be treated when approaching death? I am going to presume that we would all like to have a good death. That's implied in our regular prayer to Mary: 'Pray for us sinners, now and at the hour of our death. Amen.' (2) How would I want my loved ones, especially my aged relatives for whom I am responsible to be treated when approaching death? Regardless of the wishes of the dying loved one, and regardless of their own sense of morality, there may be some things they would want us to do which we would not be prepared to do ourselves or which we think treating doctors should not be allowed to do. (3) What should be the social policy and law about euthanasia? Laws and social policies have to be designed for all citizens. The law is not a vehicle for imposing one set of religious or moral beliefs on others. We do not live in a theocracy. I am one of those Catholics who delights and thanks God daily that I am a citizen in a free, democratic, pluralistic society where the laws are not determined by unelected bishops but by elected members of parliament and judges trained in the law.

When considering these sorts of moral quandaries about medical treatment, I like to reflect on the gospel of Luke (6:6–11):

> On the Sabbath Jesus went into the synagogue and taught, and there was a man there whose right hand was withered. The scribes and the Pharisees watched him closely to see if he would cure on the Sabbath so that they might discover a reason to accuse him. But he realised their intentions and said to the man with the withered hand, 'Come up and stand before us.' And he rose and stood there. Then Jesus said to them, 'I ask you, is it lawful to do good on the Sabbath rather than to do evil, to save life rather than to destroy it?' Looking around at them all, he then said to him, 'Stretch out your hand.' He did so and his hand was restored. But they became enraged and discussed together what they might do to Jesus.

I thought Jesus had it easy on one count. The autonomous man with the withered hand wanted Jesus the conscientious healer to do good rather than evil, to save life rather than destroy it. The legalism of the religious authorities could be readily disregarded because the patient's autonomy and the healer's conscience could be honoured by the performance of an agreed healing. But what of the case when the autonomous patient wants the conscientious doctor to perform an action that the doctor thinks wrong and death dealing? And what of the case when the autonomous patient wants the conscientious doctor to desist from doing what the doctor thinks is good and life giving?

The consideration of medico-legal problems in the public square of a pluralistic democratic society keeping pace with profound technological change is often marked by simplistic assertions, precluding considerations of comprehensive world views, whether religious or philosophical. It is now commonplace for doctors to be told to leave their consciences at the door, as their patients are consumers and they are suppliers, and of course the market decides. It is suggested that the doctor has a stark choice: 'What's to come first, the patient or the ethics?' Debates about law and policy are often resolved with simplistic assertions about individual rights and autonomy, with little consideration for the public interest, the common good, and the doctor-patient relationship. Even conscience is said to be a matter for contracting out.

1995 *Evangelium Vitae*–John Paul II

In considering how each of us would want to be treated, I am presuming that Catholic parishioners wish to be informed about Church tradition and teaching on this complex moral issue. This does not mean that I would presume that all Catholics think the same about this issue. But as Catholics we come with open minds expecting that our Church tradition and Church authority have something to teach us or some guidance to offer, if only because it is the result of generations of reflection on experience by believers trying to live their lives in the light of the gospels, trying to follow Jesus more closely in life, suffering and death.

Some Catholics are more fundamentalist than others. They are intellectually content to say, 'What the pope says is right. End of discussion. The fact that the pope says something makes it right'. For most of us, such voluntarism is unattractive. We are more likely to conclude that the pope says something because it is right in the first place. It is not the papal declaration that makes it right.

In 1995, Pope John Paul II issued a papal encyclical entitled *Evangelium Vitae*. He said:

For a correct moral judgment on euthanasia, in the first place a clear definition is required. Euthanasia in the strict sense is understood to be an action or omission which of itself and by intention causes death, with the purpose of eliminating all suffering. 'Euthanasia's terms of reference, therefore, are to be found in the intention of the will and in the methods used'.

Euthanasia must be distinguished from the decision to forego so-called 'aggressive medical treatment', in other words, medical procedures which no longer correspond to the real situation of the patient, either because they are by now disproportionate to any expected results or because they impose an excessive burden on the patient and his family. In such situations, when death is clearly imminent and inevitable, one can in conscience 'refuse forms of treatment that would only secure a precarious and burdensome prolongation of life, so long as the normal care due to the sick person in similar cases is not interrupted'.[1] Certainly there is a moral obligation to care for oneself and to allow oneself to be cared for, but this duty must take account of concrete circumstances. It needs to be determined whether the means of treatment available are objectively proportionate to the prospects for improvement. To forego extraordinary or disproportionate means is not the equivalent of suicide or euthanasia; it rather expresses acceptance of the human condition in the face of death.[2]

Pope John Paul II then went on to make a formal declaration:

Taking into account these distinctions, in harmony with the Magisterium of my Predecessors and in communion with the Bishops of the Catholic Church, I confirm that euthanasia is a grave violation of the law of God, since it is the deliberate and morally unacceptable killing of a

---

1. Quoting the Congregation for the Doctrine of the Faith, Declaration on Euthanasia *Iura et Bona* (5 May 1980), II: *AAS* 72 (1980), 546, 551.
2. Pope John Paul II, *Evangelium Vitae*, #65

human person. This doctrine is based upon the natural law and upon the written word of God, is transmitted by the Church's Tradition and taught by the ordinary and universal Magisterium.

Depending on the circumstances, this practice involves the malice proper to suicide or murder.

Moral theologians and canonists delight in debating how authoritative this papal declaration is when couched in all this high sounding language. I suggest that it is no disrespect to the papacy nor to your Catholicism to assert that very few of you are likely to lie on your deathbeds debating with your relatives just how authoritative this teaching is. In any event you will note that the pope has acknowledged that there is a need to take into account various distinctions and qualifications when declaring the immorality of euthanasia.

A generation ago, many Catholics thought it was wrong to administer large doses of morphine to a dying person if that would shorten their life. They failed to draw a critical distinction. It is wrong to do something intending to shorten the life of a person. It is not wrong to do something intending to relieve someone's pain even if that action would have the unintended side effect of shortening the life of the patient. A generation ago, many Catholics thought you were obliged to avail yourself whatever medical treatment you could afford to lengthen your life. No, we believe death awaits us all on the journey to the Father. We are not obliged to endure therapeutically futile or overly burdensome treatments. The Catholic Health Association has a Code of Ethics that is the moral compass for all Catholic health care providers in Australia. Its provisions are more readable and user friendly than the papal encyclical. So I will set out the key provisions.

CHA Code of Ethics

Palliative care

5.6 Specialist palliative care is oriented to caring for, and accompanying, a dying person and his or her carers in the final phase of life, upholding that person's dignity and respecting his or her spiritual, physical, emotional and social needs. It also encompasses care for bereaved family and others. Though it is integral to all health care, the relief of symptoms has a special place in the care and support offered to people with advanced and inevitably progressive disease.

Withdrawal or withholding of treatment: grounds for the decision

5.9 Decisions about life-sustaining treatments for patients who are terminally ill raise two sorts of challenge: which treatments should be recommended and who should be involved in the decision making process. The fundamental ethical principle in this regard is that treatments may legitimately be forgone (withheld or withdrawn) if they are therapeutically futile, overly burdensome to the patient or not reasonably available without disproportionate hardship to the patient, carers or others.

5.10 Artificial means of life support (including dialysis and ventilation) are often appropriate. Cases do arise, however, in which patients judge that the burdens of using a life support to themselves and/or to others are very grave. If so, a decision to withdraw a complex means of life support may be justified.

5.11 Likewise, the decision not to instigate a form of treatment (e.g. some forms of resuscitation) would be justified if the burden of treatment would be disproportionate to its expected therapeutic benefits or if it would involve an unreasonable burden on the patient (in particular on a frail, elderly or dying patient). Hospitals and aged care facilities should draw up protocols for the use of resuscitation and ensure that these protocols are well known by their staff and patients.

5.12 Continuing to care for a patient is a fundamental way of respecting and remaining in solidarity with that person. When treatments are withheld or withdrawn because they are therapeutically futile or overly-burdensome, other forms of care such as appropriate feeding, hydration and treatment of infection, comfort care and hygiene should be continued. Nutrition and hydration should always be provided to patients unless they cannot be assimilated by a person's body, they do not sustain life, or their only mode of delivery imposes grave burdens on the patient or others. Such burdens to others do not normally arise in developed countries such as Australia.

Withholding or withdrawing of treatment: the decision making process

5.13 Patients and residents in care should be encouraged while they are still competent to discuss their hopes for, and fears of, treatment options with their families, their doctors and other relevant people. They should be informed of their moral right to appoint someone to make decisions about their health care should they become unable to make their own decisions. Because physical or mental illness may impair a person's decision making capacity, it will sometimes be necessary to assess whether a patient or resident is competent to make decisions about life prolonging treatment.

5.15 In the case of a competent patient or resident, a decision to withhold or withdraw a treatment normally requires that the responsible doctor discusses the matter with the patient and establishes that he or she judges on reasonable grounds that the proposed treatment would be therapeutically futile or overly burdensome.

5.16 In the case of an incompetent patient, a decision to withhold or withdraw a treatment should only be made after the responsible doctor has judged that the treatment would be therapeutically futile or overly burdensome. There should be discussion between the responsible doctor, the family, any legal guardian or representative and others relevant to the care of the patient. In particular, proper account should be taken of (a) any information about what the patient would have wanted (if anything is genuinely known about that), (b) any signs as to what the patient in fact wants now, (c) the capacity of the family or others to look after the patient, (d) the views of the family and relevant others regarding the appropriateness of the proposed care, and (e) any relevant authority required by law.

5.17 Treatment decisions should be communicated and explained to nursing and allied staff. The family and relevant others should be given opportunities for discussion and pastoral care. Sensitivity should always be shown towards the religious and cultural background of patients and residents, especially when it is proposed that a treatment be withdrawn or withheld.

5.18 Treatment decisions (including decisions to limit, withdraw or withhold a treatment) should be documented in the patient's record. Documentation should include a brief statement of reasons for the decision, together with a note on the consultation process. These decisions should be reviewed regularly and in response to any significant change in the patient's condition or at the request of the patient, family or relevant others.

Euthanasia

5.20 It is never permissible to end a person's life (whether that decision is made to relieve a patient's suffering by euthanasia, to comply with the wishes of the family, to assist suicide, or to vacate a bed). By euthanasia is meant any action or omission which of itself and by intention causes death with the purpose of eliminating all suffering. Examples of euthanasia include administering deliberate overdoses of otherwise appropriate medications, and the unjustified withholding or withdrawing life sustaining forms of care. Euthanasia must be distinguished from other care decisions which sometimes risk or have the effect of shortening life but which are not intended to hasten death (e.g. the giving of appropriate pain relief, the withdrawal of burdensome treatments). Advances in palliative care are now such that the control of pain should not normally lead to side effects such as loss of lucidity or consciousness or to the shortening of life.

Let's change our focus now from reflecting on our own moral analysis and spiritual reflection on what we would want for our own good death or for the death of an aged loved one, and focus more on what should be the law or social policy regarding palliative care, euthanasia and physician assisted suicide.

It is not simply a matter of saying 'I believe X is wrong, or my Church teaches X is wrong; therefore there should be a law prohibiting X'. Take the simplest case. We all believe that except in some circumstances (such as the Nazis demanding to know whether you are harbouring Jews) it is wrong to lie, even if it be right not to tell the whole truth or acceptable to maintain some moral reservation about telling the whole truth. But that does not mean there should be a law against lying. Yes, it is appropriate to have a law prohibiting lying in some circumstances such as when swearing a statutory declaration or when entering into an insurance contract. But it would be just plain silly to make a law prohibiting lying in all circumstances, or even in all morally clear circumstances. In any event, such a law would be completely unenforceable and capriciously and arbitrarily applied.

At the moment the politics of this issue is difficult because one party, the Greens, tends to have members strongly in support of euthanasia. We have seen a variety of approaches by our bishops in recent elections. I am not one of those priests who think that you should remain silent when bishops are taking a variety of approaches. In the last Federal election, the Australian Catholic Bishops Conference (ACBC) issued a usual sort of bishops' statement for an election saying that electors should scrutinise all candidates and all parties especially on issues such as the right to life, including abortion and euthanasia.

But the Archbishop of Sydney, then Cardinal Pell, urged his listeners and readers 'to examine the policies of the Greens on their website and judge for themselves how thoroughly anti-Christian they are'. He singled out the Greens and described them as 'camouflaged sweet poison'.[3] Strong stuff! At the following Victorian election, the Victorian bishops followed the style of the ACBC and issued a statement *Your Vote, Your Values* in which they said, 'As Bishops we are not advocating any political party. That is not our role. We do however raise some issues and questions which you may wish to address to the candidates for election in helping inform your decision on whom to vote for.'[4]

At the 2011 New South Wales election, most of the New South Wales bishops followed more the path that the then Archbishop of Sydney, Cardinal George Pell, had adopted during the federal election. They focused on the Greens. Though some of the NSW bishops did not sign on, the majority put their name to a statement entitled: 'The Green Agenda'.[5] I would prefer that our bishops subjected all parties and all candidates to equal moral scrutiny. After all a law supporting euthanasia will be passed only if a majority of members of parliament on a conscience vote support it. And there are some Green policies that arguably are more Christian than the policies of the major parties: for example their policies on climate change, refugees, and overseas aid.

In 1995, the Northern Territory Parliament passed Australia's first euthanasia law, *The Rights of the Terminally Ill Act (NT)*. In 1997, the Australian Commonwealth Parliament overrode the Territory

---

3. *Sunday Telegraph*, 8 August 2010.
4. Victorian Catholic Bishops, *Your Vote, Your Values*, 29 October 2010.
5. *The Green Agenda: A Message from Catholic Bishops in NSW*, 17 March 2011

law with its own *Euthanasia Laws Act*. The Commonwealth law did not repeal the Territory law but it rendered it inoperative. I was a strong supporter of the Commonwealth law because I thought the Northern Territory euthanasia law would impact very adversely on the health of Aboriginal Territorians many of whom said they would be scared ever to go to hospital if white doctors were able to kill them.

In 2008, Senator Bob Brown as leader of the Greens took the opportunity, once the Howard government was out of power and no longer in control of the Senate, to introduce his *Rights of the Terminally Ill (Euthanasia Laws Repeal) Bill*. It was a very shoddy piece of legislative drafting and went nowhere. The introduction of the bill was ham-fisted. Even the Northern Territory government opposed the bill. The Chief Minister of the Northern Territory, Paul Henderson, said at the time, 'I find it very high-handed and arrogant of Bob Brown from Tasmania to be introducing legislation in the Federal Parliament that affects the Northern Territory, without any consultation at all with the Territory Government, or the people of the Northern Territory'.[6] If the bill had been passed, it would have had the effect of resuming the operation of the original 1995 Territory law which by then even Dr Philip Nitschke had conceded in an article in *The Lancet* was defective legislation. He and his joint authors observed:

> Our case material shows that the assessment of depression is difficult in the terminally ill, and accurate prediction of prognosis is subject to disagreement. There are clear limitations of the gatekeeping roles of the medical specialist and psychiatrist in the (Northern Territory) legislation.[7]

The Northern Territory law required a psychiatrist to have 'confirmed that the patient is not suffering from a treatable clinical

---

6. ABC News, 5 February 2008
7. David Kissane, Annette Street, Philip Nitschke, 'Seven deaths in Darwin: case studies under the Rights of the Terminally Ill Act, Northern Territory, Australia' in *The Lancet* 352 (1998) 1097 at 1102.

depression in respect of the illness' before a medical practitioner was allowed to administer the lethal injection. Nitschke and his co-authors in *The Lancet* stated: 'Confirmation was not easy since patients perceived such a mandatory assessment as a hurdle to be overcome. PN [Philip Nitschke] understood that every patient held that view. To what extent was the psychiatrist trusted with important data and able to build an appropriate alliance that permitted a genuine understanding of a patient's plight?' Some senators were concerned to learn that Dr Nitschke had personally paid the fee for the psychiatric assessment of one of the patients he euthanased.

In 2011 Australia had a hung federal parliament and the Greens Leader, Bob Brown, wanted to agitate the issue of euthanasia once again. The 1995 Northern Territory law is a bad law even for those who favour euthanasia with appropriate safeguards. So before any other step is taken the Northern Territory parliament should repeal the 1995 law, so we can start with a blank slate.

Since 1997 the legislatures of the Northern Territory, the ACT and Norfolk Island have been precluded by the Commonwealth parliament from passing laws providing for euthanasia. Presumably the Greens will make sure they have the politicians and the people of the territories in the cart before they move next time. But there is no hurry. There is little pressure from the people and legislatures in these places about what is presently an academic issue. To date no State parliament has legislated for euthanasia. Three years ago, I said to the Senate committee:

> [W]hat has changed in 10 years? In terms of what has changed, if you look at the United States, Oregon is still the only state which has euthanasia. Since the Commonwealth exercise, the US Supreme Court has said there is no right to euthanasia. Lord Joffe's United Kingdom legislation has gone down, and we have had very clear statements from the medical authorities in the United Kingdom and a quite eloquent submission here from the AMA. So it would seem to me that on balance nothing has changed or, if anything, the anti-

euthanasia case is probably slightly strengthened if we look at developments in equivalent jurisdictions.

But there is gradual change occurring. There is still no law permitting euthanasia or physician assisted suicide in the UK. But in the US, Montana and Washington State have now gone down the path of Oregon. And here in Australia, there have been recent failed attempts to introduce euthanasia laws in Western Australia, South Australia and Tasmania.

Not all persons agitating these laws are morally insensitive, callous individuals. Some of the advocates are the most humanitarian, caring individuals you could hope to meet. Usually they are concerned to protect the human dignity of that small group of persons whose pain cannot be appropriately managed or who fear the loss of control on approaching death, preferring to have the final say on how they exit this world. Those of us who espouse human dignity must always have a concern for unmanageable pain and for human autonomy. When is the state entitled to place limits on the exercise of individual autonomy?

We would usually answer that question in the same way that we answer questions about the limits on human rights. My right to X is limited by your right to Y. For example, my right of free speech is limited by your right to a good reputation. Also my right to Z is limited by the extent to which the exercise of that right would impact adversely on the public interest or the common good. That's why we have no problem in limiting the freedom of the person to ride a bike without the constraint of a helmet or to ride in a car without a seat belt.

If we were to legislate a right of the dying person to receive a lethal injection on request, we would need to consider the rights of others, the public interest and the common good, and the impact on the person accorded the right. Some of the matters to consider would be: the added pressure on all dying persons to consider whether proactively to seek death rather than letting nature take its course – for example the bed ridden grandmother whose estate could be dedicated to the private school education of the grandchildren; the protection of the most vulnerable in society; the likelihood that budgetary allocation for palliative care and aged care services may be reduced given the cost efficient option of euthanasia; the impact on the doctor-patient relationship.

There may be a tendency to overstate these problems. But caution is always justified. The Oregon experiment in the US is interesting. Oregon's *Death with Dignity Act* (DWDA), enacted in late 1997, allows terminally-ill adult Oregonians to obtain and use prescriptions from their physicians for self-administered, lethal doses of medications. Between 1998-2009, 244 males and 216 females availed themselves of physician-assisted death. In 2010, there were thirty-eight males and twenty-seven females. In that year, there were ninety-six prescriptions of lethal drugs issued but with only fifty-nine deaths occurring and six additional deaths with prescriptions from the previous year.

So there may be another thirty-seven Oregon households with lethal drugs sitting in the bathroom, awaiting use—a not irrelevant consideration in social planning. The median age of those who used the service in 2010 was seventy-two years. 100% of them were white. In Oregon in 2010, 78% of those who opted for physician assisted death had cancer; 97% of them died at home. Despite some of the shock/horror tactics of opponents to physician assisted death, we need to concede that after ten years in Oregon, there are only 20.9 deaths/10,000 deaths resulting from formally recorded physician assisted death.

Those of us schooled in the social justice teaching of the Catholic Church join happily with our fellow citizens who always scrutinise any proposed law for its effect on the most vulnerable members of society. The 2011 Comres Poll in the UK asked 553 disabled persons: 'If there were a change in the law on assisted suicide would you be concerned about any of the following?'

Pressure being placed on you to end your life
prematurely:
Yes: 35%; No: 51%; Don't know: 12%

Pressure being placed on other disabled people to end
their lives prematurely:
Yes: 70%; No: 15%; Don't know: 12%

It being detrimental to the way that disabled people are
viewed by society as a whole:
Yes: 56%

If we do not legislate to permit physician assisted suicide or
euthanasia, there will still be cases where individuals decide that they
have had enough of life, requesting the withdrawal of even hydration
and nutrition. Even if we would regard such withdrawal as wrong,
we need to respect the bodily integrity and moral autonomy of the
mentally competent person who makes such a request whether now
or by means of an advance directive. If I am mentally competent, I
am entitled to lock myself in a room depriving myself of food and
water. And you have no right or obligation to interfere with my
bodily integrity. If you were forcibly to insert a feeding stent in me
without my consent that would be an assault.

If the person not be mentally competent, such withdrawal
could not be justified. There is the difficulty of providing adequate
safeguards for vulnerable individuals in their dying days. In Western
Australia there was a lot of attention to Mr Christian Rossiter's
request for termination of hydration and nutrition. The Western
Australian Supreme Court gave the go ahead. But he decided not
to continue the request. A month after the judgment the media
reported on Mr Rossiter's condition, speculating that he might die
soon from a respiratory infection. *The Sunday Age* reported: 'The sad
irony here, according to Dr Nitschke, "is that [after the court case]
he'd picked up a bit in himself, because people have been paying
him attention".[8] He'd been particularly cheered by the ministrations

---

8.   'Rossiter won right to die, but infection might beat him to it' in *The Sunday Age*, 20
      September 2009

of an outreach carer from Perth Home Care services. The press report continued: '*The Sunday Age* understands the woman, who has been refused permission to speak to the media, had encouraged Mr Rossiter to record his life story, notably about his childhood in South Africa, with the idea of publishing a memoir.' What then was the court case about? He may well have been suffering intense pre-mortem loneliness, as distinct from depression. He died of a chest infection more than a month after the court gave the all clear for his carers to terminate hydration and nutrition should he request it.

There was also the case of Mr JT in the ACT Supreme Court with doctors wanting to terminate treatment. Chief Justice Higgins found that 'the psychotic beliefs JT suffers from are slowly but surely killing him'. He said: 'The patient here lacks both understanding of the proposed conduct and the capacity to give informed consent to it. Thus, those charged with JT's care remain under the common law duty to provide that care to the best of their skill and ability.'[9] The Chief Justice had cause to comment on 'an outrageous approach to ethical standards' disclosed in the case. The judge found that the doctors were engaged in a course of behaviour designed, 'avoiding euphemisms, to allow the patient to starve to death whilst easing the suffering associated therewith'.

The real quandary with assisted suicide through removal of nutrition and hydration is determining when the law will deem a decision to terminate life an act of informed consent, being irrevocable even though the patient has mood swings and moves in and out of consciousness. Not everyone who says, 'I wish to die. Please terminate all nutrition' will remain clearly of that resolve. The law will need to specify the conditions for presuming that a patient has made an irrevocable choice for death even when no one would be adversely affected by the health provider complying with the later revoked wish of the failing patient clutching to life. Presumably, there will be a need to impose an obligation on health

---

9.   *Australian Capital Territory* v *JT* [2009] ACTSC 105 (28 August 2008) at <http://www.austlii.edu.au/au/cases/act/ACTSC/2009/105.html>. Accessed 3 December 2014.

professionals to ensure that the choice to die remains firm until loss of consciousness. If this obligation were always to be faithfully discharged (which it won't be), it would be very onerous.

Euthanasia advocates usually concede that there is a need to set limits on the class of patient entitled to seek euthanasia—usually mentally competent adults who are not depressed and who are terminally ill and enduring unbearable pain. But no advocate has yet come up with a draft bill containing water-tight definitions. For example the recent bill introduced into the South Australian parliament provides in relation to safeguards:

> Each witness who is a medical practitioner must also certify that he or she, having examined the person who made the request for symptoms of depression immediately before the request—
>
> (i) has no reason to suppose that the person is suffering from treatable clinical depression; or
>
> (ii) if the person does exhibit symptoms of depression— is of the opinion that treatment for depression, or further treatment for depression, is unlikely to influence the person's decision to request voluntary euthanasia.

How could any medical practitioner in good conscience certify that a treatment for depression would be unlikely to influence a request for voluntary euthanasia? Another problem is that the most notable cases in the media relate to patients who are not elderly, in the final stages of a terminal illness. They tend to be young rugby players rendered quadriplegic wanting to end life rather than facing decades in a wheelchair, or those like the forty-seven-year-old Debbie Purdy who has been confined to a wheelchair since 2001 in the UK having been diagnosed with MS in 1995. In October 2008 when first going to court to seek the order clarifying that the Director of Public Prosecutions would not prosecute her husband if he were to assist with her suicide once she could no longer control her bodily functions, she said: 'We are not asking for the law to be changed for it to be made compulsory for people at the end of their lives to be dragged off to the knacker's yard. But this should be one of the choices available and for it to be available we need to be clear on the law.' She told the court:

> My dearest wish would be to die with dignity in my own home, with my husband and other loved ones around me. I hate the idea of having to travel to another country when I will be at my weakest and most vulnerable, both emotionally and physically. Going to another country also means that I have to go earlier, because being able to travel such a distance and to make all the arrangements in a foreign country will require me to be physically and mentally capable so that too will mean that my life is further shortened as a result of the lack of a humane law in this country. I hope that one day the law will recognise that this is inhumane and that the law should be changed. My husband has said that he would assist me, and if necessary face a prison sentence, but I am not prepared to put him in this position for a number of reasons. I love him and do not want him to risk ending up in prison. As long as the DPP will not clarify his policy on prosecutions in these circumstances, I worry that as my husband is black and a foreigner, this makes him a more likely target for prosecution.[10]

One could not but be moved by her plea. The Director of Public Prosecutions provided those guidelines including:

A prosecution is less likely to be required if:

1. the victim had reached a voluntary, clear, settled and informed decision to commit suicide;
2. the suspect was wholly motivated by compassion;

---

10. *The Telegraph*, 19 October 2008. Ms Purdy lived another seven years after giving this interview. She died in a hospice where she had been resident for a year on 23 December 2014.

3. the actions of the suspect, although sufficient to come within the definition of the offence, were of only minor encouragement or assistance;

4. the suspect had sought to dissuade the victim from taking the course of action which resulted in his or her suicide;

5. the actions of the suspect may be characterised as reluctant encouragement or assistance in the face of a determined wish on the part of the victim to commit suicide;

6. the suspect reported the victim's suicide to the police and fully assisted them in their enquiries into the circumstances of the suicide or the attempt and his or her part in providing encouragement or assistance.

Chances are that these guidelines would avoid prosecution of those few cases where palliative care is unable to control pain and where the loss of autonomy of the patient occasions extraordinary angst and suffering. Of course, it might be said that it is preferable to change the law to put beyond doubt the legality of the actions of medical practitioners or carers in these fairly rare instances. But once we move from the 'Do no harm' principle, it would be difficult accurately to demarcate what is legal and what is not.[11] I am often reminded of those drivers like me who drive at 105 kph when the speed limit is set at 100 kph. If the limit were lifted to 105 kph, what would drivers like me do? I don't know about you, but I would then drive at 110 kph.

---

11. Edward Pellegrino points out: '[T]he slippery slope is not a myth. Historically it s been a reality in world affairs. Once a moral precept is breached a psychological and logical process is set in motion which follows what I would call the law of infinite regress of moral exceptions. One exception leads logically and psychologically to another. In small increments a moral norm eventually obliterates itself. The process always begins with some putative good reason, like compassion, freedom of choice, or liberty. By small increments it overwhelms its own justifications.' See Edward Pellegrino, 'Physician-Assisted Suicide and Euthanasia: Rebuttals of Rebuttals—The Moral Prohibition Remains', *Journal of Medicine and Philosophy*, 26/1 (2001): 93–100 at 98.

To sum up, I think we do pretty well with a medical profession trained and invoked to 'Do no harm'. I think the moral quandaries are fairly manageable for us when deciding to forego futile or overly burdensome treatments. We should honour the wishes of our mentally competent loved ones who tell us tomorrow or by means of advance directives what they want done or not done, even if that includes the withdrawal of hydration and nutrition. We should have a special care for those who are not mentally competent to make these decisions. And we should always ask how any change to the law or policy will impact on the most vulnerable in society. The Netherlands teaches us that for the most vulnerable in society there is no bright line division between voluntary and involuntary euthanasia.

As we contemplate the increasing demands of our ageing population on scarce health resources, let's not demonise all those who advocate euthanasia or physician assisted suicide. But let's hold them accountable for the unintended but able consequences of their policies. Above all, let's remember: even if there be a euthanasia law passed, there is no compulsion on any of us to avail ourselves of it, and there ought be capacity for all medical practitioners and health care facilities to opt out on the grounds of conscientious objection. In short, as my mother said, 'Don't kill, and look after people when they are dying.' As we recall your parishioner Danielle's maternal plea for her child suffering cystic fibrosis, let's always distinguish the heartfelt cry, 'I don't want to go on living like this' from the anguished cry, 'I don't want to live any more.' The first may be the expression of an impossible desire for a better life rather than a plea for death. Let's kill the pain, not the person. Thank you for the opportunity to share the evening with you reflecting on such an important topic.

-o0o-

The issue continues to be agitated in the courts and parliaments of Canada, the UK and Australia. Once the US Supreme Court has dealt with same sex marriage, it will be sure to revisit requests for acknowledgement of a constitutional right to assistance with death.

Physician assisted suicide and euthanasia are back in the courts of Canada and the United Kingdom, and back in the parliaments of the United Kingdom and Australia. In October 2014, the Supreme Court of Canada finished hearing a case in which the applicants claim that a 1993 Supreme Court decision upholding the criminal ban on euthanasia should be overruled. The House of Lords is still considering Lord Falconer's *Assisted Dying Bill*. Their Lordships will be looking forward to what they think is the appropriate law and policy on assisted suicide, while looking back at a recent decision of the UK Supreme Court which has said there is a need to consider the European Convention on Human Rights' requirement that everyone is entitled to respect for their private life. The Australian Senate recently received a committee report on the Greens' appallingly drafted *Medical Services (Dying with Dignity) Exposure Draft Bill 2014*. The committee recommended:

> that the proponent of the Exposure Draft of the *Medical Services (Dying with Dignity) Bill 2014* might address the technical and other issues raised in evidence to the committee and seek the advice of relevant experts before the Bill is taken further.[12]

A word about each development. No law is ever perfect. Any law can work an injustice in a particular case. That's why we have prosecutors and courts which can exercise discretion. Wherever you draw the line in criminal law, there will always be just and compassionate exceptions you would want to see made on one side of the line, without always moving the line and starting the exercise again. Until fifty years ago, attempted suicide was a criminal offence. Seeing there were better ways to dissuade people from attempting suicide and acknowledging that no purpose was to be served by punishing

---

12. Legal and Constitutional Affairs Legislation Committee, *Medical Services (Dying with Dignity) Exposure Draft Bill 2014, November 2014, 39* at
<http://www.aph.gov.au/Parliamentary_Business/Committees/Senate/Legal_and_Constitutional_Affairs/Dying_with_Dignity/~/media/Committees/legcon_ctte/Dying_with_Dignity/report/report.pdf>. Accessed 3 December 2014.

someone who failed to kill themselves, parliaments abolished the offence of attempted suicide, while retaining the offence of assisting someone else with their own suicide.

With developments in medical technology, patients could avail themselves of life sustaining procedures like respirators. Exercising their autonomy, patients were entitled to ask that the respirator be turned off. If death resulted, the doctor was not liable. In 1993, the Canadian Supreme Court said there was a world of difference between turning off life support at the request of a rational, competent, non-depressed patient and administering a lethal injection to such a patient. The first was allowed; the second was not.

The Canadian Supreme Court has now been asked to rule that the distinction between withdrawing life support and administering a lethal injection is ethically contested and contrary to the *Canadian Charter of Rights and Freedoms* which guarantees everyone the right to life and the right 'not to be deprived thereof except in accordance with the principles of fundamental justice'. The Charter also guarantees equality before the law without discrimination based on mental or physical disability.

The argument runs like this. Since attempted suicide is no longer a criminal offence, everyone has the *right* to commit suicide. A person with a terminal illness and in great pain can decide to commit suicide whenever they wish. But if that person were suffering increasing disability, they would need to commit suicide earlier, while they are still able to perform the death-dealing act. If they were allowed to get assistance with someone else performing the death dealing act, they could decide to live longer, even as long as a person without disability, before then committing suicide with assistance. Unless they have the *right* to assisted suicide, they are being deprived their full right to life contrary to the principles of fundamental justice, and in a discriminatory way. So a law that bans the provision of assistance with suicide is said to be unconstitutional.

The argument against this proposition is that the law banning such assistance can be 'demonstrably justified in a free and democratic society', being necessary to protect the vulnerable in society (whether abled or disabled) who may feel pressured into seeking such assistance or who may be tricked, cajoled or soothed into seeking such assistance in order to satisfy the needs and desires of others, including selfish relatives and overstretched medical personnel. There is no *right* to commit suicide with a correlative duty that the state support the person wanting to commit suicide. There is only a *liberty* to commit suicide with an immunity from state interference. It is likely that the fairly 'liberal' Canadian Supreme Court will recognise a constitutional right to commit suicide and cut back the outright legal prohibition on providing assistance with suicide.[13]

Over in London, Lord Joffe has four times introduced bills to the House of Lords seeking some form of legalised assistance with dying. Each bill has failed. He has passed the baton to Lord Falconer who is now making his second attempt with his *Assisted Dying Bill*. Lords Joffe and Falconer were amongst the forty-two lords who debated the measure in July 2014. The lords are now considering a bill which restricts the assistance by a medical practitioner to preparing medicine for self-administration or preparing a device like one of Philip Nitschke's machines for self-administration of the medicine. The bill specifies that 'the decision to self-administer the medicine and the final act of doing so must be taken by the person for whom the medicine has been prescribed'.

In July 2014, Lord Falconer told the House of Lords, 'I have built on the Oregon model, but with more safeguards. I reject the Belgian and Dutch approach.'[14] He is anxious to avoid arguments about slippery slopes and developments in Belgium and the Netherlands where doctors have performed euthanasia on non-competent patients and on patients who are not suffering terminal illness. To get his bill through, Lord Falconer is even prepared to consider further safeguards. Looking to the UK Supreme Court's recent decision, he has favourably quoted the Chief Justice Lord Neuberger who wrote:

---

13. *Carter* v *Attorney General of Canada*, SCC File No 35591, judgment reserved.
14. House of Lords, *Hansard*, 18 July 2014: Column 776.

> A system whereby a judge or other independent assessor is satisfied in advance that someone has a voluntary, clear, settled, and informed wish to die and for his suicide then to be organised in an open and professional way, would, at least in my current view, provide greater and more satisfactory protection for the weak and vulnerable, than a system which involves a lawyer from the DPP's office inquiring, after the event, whether the person who had killed himself had such a wish, and also to investigate the actions and motives of any assister, who would, by definition, be emotionally involved and scarcely able to take, or even to have taken, an objective view.[15]

Lord Falconer has told the Lords: 'Some say that the courts should be involved as an additional safeguard before an assisted death occurs. We should constructively consider that issue in Committee.'[16]

Meanwhile the Australian Senate is considering a much broader proposal than Lord Falconer's bill. The Greens have formulated the fuzzy notion of a medical practitioner providing 'dying with dignity medical services' including the administration of a lethal substance to a patient at their request. Their bill, unlike the UK bill, would allow Philip Nitschke to administer the fatal injection. Their bill includes the form to be filled in by the patient seeking dying with dignity medical services. The form is so shoddily drafted that it does not even specify a request for any particular services. It is simply a blank cheque given to the doctor stating: 'I am satisfied that there is no medical treatment reasonably available that is acceptable to me in my circumstances.'

The Bill provides: 'No civil, criminal or disciplinary action lies, and proceedings must not be brought, against a person in relation to an act done, or omitted to be done, if the act is done, or omitted to be done' in accordance with the proposed commonwealth law. This is a constitutional nightmare and a federal mess-up of truly Green

---

15. *R (on the application of Nicklinson and another)* v *Ministry of Justice*, [2014]UKSC 38, [108].

16. House of Lords, *Hansard*, 18 July 2014: Column 777

proportions. The criminal law in this area is a matter for the states. If you want certainty in the criminal law, which you do, you change the criminal law in question. You amend the state laws on assisted suicide. You do not have the commonwealth coming in over the top to offer immunity from prosecution for an action which is still a criminal offence in the States.

More problematic is the doubt about the constitutional power of the commonwealth even to make such a law. It would be like the commonwealth legislating a new criminal law in relation to abortion. It is a State issue, not a commonwealth issue. The only time the commonwealth bought into euthanasia was when the commonwealth parliament overrode a law of the Northern Territory. There has never been any suggestion that it would or could override a law of the States. The Greens have not helped anyone with this half-baked exercise.

Lord Sumption stated the issues well in the UK Supreme Court:

> There is no complete solution to the problem of protecting vulnerable people against an over-ready resort to suicide . . . The real question about all of these possibilities is how much risk to the vulnerable are we prepared to accept in this area in order to facilitate suicide for the invulnerable . . . There is an important element of social policy and moral value-judgment involved. The relative importance of the right to commit suicide and the right of the vulnerable to be protected from overt or covert pressure to kill themselves is inevitably sensitive to a state's most fundamental collective moral and social values.[17]

Keeping an eye on developments in Canada and the UK, we Australians need to be clear about the social, philosophical, legal and constitutional issues involved when contemplating our own amendments to the law and practice of assisted suicide.

---

17. *R (on the application of Nicklinson and another)* v *Ministry of Justice*, [2014]UKSC 38, [229].

-oOo-

In November 2014, the House of Lords adopted amendments to Lord Falconer's bill proposing that a court be required to certify a patient's eligibility for physician assisted suicide. In February 2015, the Supreme Court of Canada delivered judgment in the challenge to the criminal law prohibiting assistance with suicide.

In February 2015, the Canadian Supreme Court unanimously ruled that the universal ban on assisting someone to commit suicide was unconstitutional.[18] The Court reversed its previous decision upholding the ban twenty-one years ago, noting there had been changes to the law and end of life care in other places, as well as to the Court's way of interpreting the *Canadian Charter of Rights and Freedoms*. The court has suspended its judgment for a year giving the Parliament time to consider how it will respond.

The court considered the claims of two parties. In 2009, Gloria Taylor was diagnosed with ALS (amyotrophic lateral sclerosis). She knew that she would first lose the ability to use her hands and feet, and that she would progressively lose the capacity to chew, swallow, speak and breathe. She did 'not want to die slowly, piece by piece' or 'wracked with pain'. She wanted to have the option of seeking medical assistance to self-administer a painless, deadly potion at a time of her choosing. She explained:

> There will come a point when I will know that enough is enough. I cannot say precisely when that time will be. It is not a question of 'when I can't walk' or 'when I can't talk'. There is no pre-set trigger moment. I just know that, globally, there will be some point in time when I will be able to say—'this is it, this is the point where life is just not worthwhile'. When that time comes, I want to be able to call my family together, tell them of my decision, say a dignified good-bye and obtain final closure—for me and for them.

---

18. *Carter v Canada (Attorney General)*, 2015 SCC 5

Having commenced the long running litigation, Gloria Taylor passed away in 2012.

In 2008 Kay Carter had been diagnosed with spinal stenosis, a condition that results in the progressive compression of the spinal cord. She told her family that she did not want to end her life 'like an ironing board', having to lie flat in bed all day and all night. In 2010, she convinced her daughter Lee and Lee's husband Hollis to accompany her to Switzerland so she could obtain assistance with dying from *Dignitas*. Lee and Hollis joined the litigation seeking court assurance that they could not be prosecuted for having assisted Kay with her suicide.

The *Canadian Charter of Rights and Freedoms* provides: 'Everyone has the right to life, liberty and security of the person and the right not to be deprived thereof except in accordance with the principles of fundamental justice'. The successful argument put by those seeking approval for assisted suicide ran as follows.

Gloria or Kay is entitled to take her own life at a time of her choosing. If she is denied the capacity to seek assistance with her suicide, she will need to end her life sooner than she otherwise would have chosen because she will need to do it when she is still physically able to arrange her death. If she were permitted to seek assistance she could live longer. The criminal sanction banning assistance with suicide thereby deprives her of some span of life because she needs to choose a premature death.

The court decided that 'the right to life is engaged where the law or state action imposes death or an increased risk of death on a person, either directly or indirectly', regardless of whether death is being chosen by the person claiming the right to life. Considering the right to liberty and security in the context of the personal decision when to commit suicide, the court observed, 'This is a decision that is rooted in their control over their bodily integrity; it represents their deeply personal response to serious pain and suffering. By denying them the opportunity to make that choice, the prohibition impinges on their liberty and security of the person.' So the court ruled that insofar as the criminal law prohibited 'physician–assisted dying for competent adults who seek such assistance as a result of a grievous and irremediable medical condition that causes enduring and intolerable suffering', it 'infringes the rights to liberty and security of the person'.

Under the Canadian Charter, once an infringement of rights is found, it is then necessary to determine whether that infringement is in accordance with 'the principles of fundamental justice'. Twenty-one years ago, the Court had decided that the state's need and desire to protect vulnerable persons from being induced to commit suicide at a time of weakness provided justification for this restriction on liberty and security of the person.

At the trial, the state conceded 'that not every person who wishes to commit suicide is vulnerable, and that there may be people with disabilities who have a considered, rational and persistent wish to end their own lives'. The trial judge observed that Gloria Taylor was one such person: 'competent, fully-informed, and free from coercion or duress'. On appeal the Supreme Court decided, 'The blanket prohibition sweeps conduct into its ambit that is unrelated to the law's objective'.

Having decided that the absolute ban on assisted suicide was a breach of a Charter right, the court needed to consider whether the breach was one which could be 'demonstrably justified in a free and democratic society'. The court usually grants Parliament some deference in making this assessment. But in this case the court observed that the blanket ban on assisted suicide could hardly be viewed as a 'complex regulatory response' to a social ill which would usually garner a high degree of deference.

The court needed to consider whether the absolute ban was the least drastic means of achieving the legislative objective of protecting the vulnerable. The Supreme Court was adamant that a less drastic means was available. The court accepted the trial judge's conclusion that 'it is possible for physicians, with due care and attention to the seriousness of the decision involved, to adequately assess decisional capacity' and that 'the risks associated with physician-assisted death can be limited through a carefully designed and monitored system of safeguards'.

It is disheartening to note the court's unquestioning acceptance of the trial judge's observation that the 'preponderance of the evidence from ethicists is that there is no ethical distinction between physician-assisted death and other end-of-life practices whose outcome is highly likely to be death'. Those other practices are the withholding or withdrawal of lifesaving or life-sustaining medical treatment. The time honoured distinction between act and omission has been erased by judicial *fiat* and the straw vote of ethicists chosen by the parties to a legal dispute. There is now said to be no ethical distinction between turning off the ventilator and administering a lethal injection. The court has moved the debate very rapidly into choppy waters.

The issue is now in the hands of Parliament. If the Canadian Parliament were just to sit on its hands, there would be no ban or regulation whatever of assisted suicide in place in a year's time. Presumably the Parliament will see a need to legislate a complex regulatory response, including the ongoing criminalisation of assistance with suicide other than that considered by the court. The court confined its attention to the case of 'physician-assisted death for a competent adult person who (1) clearly consents to the termination of life; and (2) has a grievous and irremediable medical condition (including an illness, disease or disability) that causes enduring suffering that is intolerable to the individual in the circumstances of his or her condition'. The court stated, 'We make no pronouncement on other situations where physician-assisted dying may be sought.' Who then should decide competence, who should assess how grievous and irremediable a medical condition is, and who should decide whether the suffering is intolerable to the individual, especially if the individual be suffering some form of dementia? What safeguards need to be put in place?

In the UK, the House of Lords has been considering these issues against the backdrop of the decision of the UK Supreme Court delivered in June 2014. Lord Falconer's *Assisted Dying Bill* initially proposed that these issues be resolved just by the patient and their physician. The Bill has now been amended proposing that a court order always be obtained confirming that the adult patient has 'a voluntary, clear, settled and informed wish to end his or her own life' and the capacity to make the decision. Two doctors would need to certify that the patient is terminally ill (being reasonably expected to die within six months) having made the decision voluntarily and on an informed basis without coercion or duress. Terminal illness is defined in the Bill as 'an inevitably progressive condition which cannot be reversed by treatment'. These are the sorts of issues which will now need to be considered by parliaments concerned to protect the vulnerable while providing for those like Gloria Taylor and Kay Carter.

No doubt the US Supreme Court will be called upon to reconsider the issue which was last before that court in 1997. The US court is unlikely to accept a case for hearing until it has first resolved the same sex marriage question. Instead of talking about 'principles of fundamental justice' and what can be 'demonstrably justified in a free and democratic society', the US judges will discuss 'due process' and 'equal protection'. These are the various constitutional devices for determining the judicial morality of vexed social questions. Societies like Canada, the UK and the US are now at the frontier determining whether the administration of a fatal injection is the same as switching off a ventilator and whether state assisted and state authorised suicide should be restricted only to some groups or made available to all self-determining citizens whether or not they are suffering a painful terminal illness.

13

Espousing Marriage and Respecting the Dignity of Same Sex Couples

---

Since 2010, there has been an ongoing debate about same sex marriage. I have been a regular contributor to the debate through my columns in Eureka Street. *Here is a selection of my writings highlighting concerns about how best to espouse the institution of marriage, providing the most secure institution for the bearing, nurturing and education of all children, while respecting and affirming the dignity of same sex couples.*

The Perils of Redefining Marriage

24 November 2010

Last week, the Australian Parliament's 'new paradigm' swung into action with the House of Representatives passing a motion calling 'on all parliamentarians, consistent with their duties as representatives, to gauge their constituents' views on ways to achieve equal treatment for same sex couples including marriage'. If this keeps up, we will have the High Court publishing a judgment calling on all judges to hear argument from counsel for the parties in taxation matters. Even under the old paradigm, it was the job of parliamentarians in a democracy like ours to gauge their constituents' views on matters likely to be debated in parliament, particularly contested moral issues.

Should my local member seek to gauge my views on same sex marriage during the summer recess, I would assure him that paradigms, norms, and symbolism do matter. The distinction between same sex marriage and legal recognition of same sex unions is not just a matter of symbolism. They create different realities regarding children's human rights. Because of that, I support the latter, not the former. 'Marriage' means different things to different people. For me, the paradigm of marriage is an exclusive, indissoluble covenant between a man and a woman entering a partnership for life, ordered to their good and open to the procreation and education of their children.

Not every marriage matches all the features of this paradigm. Some couples are infertile or too old to have children. But such marriages do not overtly breach it, so the paradigm still makes sense. In contrast, same-sex marriage overtly breaches the paradigm that marriage is an institution for the good of the children of the couple. Australian civil law on marriage varies from my paradigm. Under Australian law, marriage is not indissoluble. Either party can terminate a civil marriage on one year's separation. There is no requirement that the parties be open to the bearing and nurturing of each other's children. There are many married couples who choose not to have children.

There are many couples in Australia who choose not to marry. There are many children born out of wedlock. There is an increasing number of children being raised by same sex couples. If same-sex marriage is legalised, because marriage carries the right to found a family, it may not be too long before a significant number of these children share the genetic inheritance of two same sex parents. For the moment, every child has one biological father and one biological mother. In the best of circumstances, the child will know and be nurtured by them.

Especially with an ageing society, the state has an interest in recognising and affirming relationships between persons committed to supporting each other, regardless of their sexual orientation. Discrimination against same sex couples should be removed in the public domain. In the UK, this has been achieved by legislating for civil unions. Archbishop Vincent Nichols, President of their

Catholic Bishops Conference, recently said, 'We were very nuanced. We did not oppose gay civil partnerships. We recognised that in English law there might be a case for those'.[19]

I would tell my local member that it is time Australia went the same way. And I would hope our bishops would see it that way too, though I concede that Pope Benedict did not when he was prefect for the Congregation for the Doctrine of the Faith. Many same sex couples tell us their relationship is identical with marriage. Until the majority of married couples are convinced this is so, politicians would be wise not to consider undoing the distinction between marriage and civil unions. Our parliamentarians could legislate to recognise civil unions, though there is some constitutional doubt whether this would best be done by the commonwealth or state parliaments.

In considering whether to advocate a change to the definition of marriage, citizens need to consider not only the right of same sex couples to equality but even more so the rights of future children. The state has an interest in privileging group units in society which are likely to enhance the prospects that future children will continue to be born with a known biological father and a known biological mother who in the best of circumstances will be able to nurture and educate them. That is why there is a relevant distinction to draw between a commitment between a same sex couple to establish a group unit in society and a commitment of a man and a woman to marry and found a family.

An infertile married couple might expect state assistance in providing them with children who are genetically theirs. In the name of equality of adults, future children should not be deprived the opportunity to be born of a man and of a woman. I rather like having a Mum and a Dad, and I suspect in future that will remain the case for most children. Often, orphans too are consoled to know they have a biological father and a biological mother. And most countries are now legally recognising they have a right to know who they are.

---

19. Archbishop Vincent Nichols being interviewed by Huw Edwards, *BBC*, 24 September 2010

Decisions about adoption and assisted reproduction should always be informed by the best interests of the child. If we go down the track of same sex marriage, we are acknowledging that same sex couples will have an entitlement to utilise technology to produce children with the genetic inheritance of each of them, and that same sex couples will be equally situated with a husband and wife team to adopt children to whom they bear no relationship.

As a matter of social policy, we will be affirming that the state has no interest in privileging a social institution which ensures that children have a genetic inheritance from one biological father and one biological mother, and that, all things being equal, they have the possibility of being adopted by a father and mother. I think we can ensure non-discrimination against same sex couples while at the same time maintaining a commitment to children of future generations being born of and being reared by a father and a mother. To date, international human rights law has appreciated this rational distinction.

Instead of stating 'All persons have the right to marry', the *International Covenant on Civil and Political Rights* provides in Article 23: 'The right of men and women of marriageable age to marry and to found a family shall be recognised.' The Covenant asserts: 'The family is the natural and fundamental group unit of society and is entitled to protection by society and the State.' I believe our parliamentarians should maintain this distinction, for the good of future children, while ensuring equal treatment for same sex couples through the legal recognition of civil unions.

If our parliaments were to legislate, redefining marriage as a relationship centred on the couple regardless of the concerns of children, religious groups should be free to maintain their paradigm of marriage for their own members. After all, we Catholics classify marriage as a sacrament, and even now most civil marriages in Australia are not capable of sacramental recognition in our Church. After the summer recess, I do hope our parliament can get on with its real work for the good of present and future generations of Australians.

In Defence of Same-Sex Unions

9 March 2011

The messy same-sex marriage debate continues in Australia and in the US. I remain of the view that we should not extend the definition of marriage to include same-sex unions; that we should legislate to recognise same-sex unions; and that we should leave questions about the legal availability of new technologies for the creation of children by same-sex couples for determination at a later date.

In Australia, the issue is focused in the parliament; and in the US in the courts. Here the Prime Minister Julia Gillard has committed her party to consulting with the public while deciding how to deal with the Greens on the issue. In the US the president has decided his administration will no longer argue for the constitutionality of the 1996 *Defense of Marriage Act* in court proceedings. For many same-sex marriage advocates, the debate is a matter of equality and non-discrimination. A person should be allowed to marry the person they love whatever the gender of the partner.

The trouble with much human rights discourse is that it is too readily reduced to assertions about individual rights and non-discrimination. Human rights discourse needs to be more subtle when it comes to a conflict of rights situation, or when the law is having to consider the public interest or the common good as well as individual liberties. Historically the state had little interest in recognising and enhancing the place of marriage as a social institution just for the good of the couple. The state interest in marriage is just as focused on the rights of the children and the need to provide support for the social structure most suited to the rearing and nurturing of children.

Though there has never been an ideal time when all children were born into a marriage, we have maintained marriage as the ideal institution for the raising of children by their biological parents. In Australian civil law, we recognise *de facto* relationships as well as marriages. Marriage is covered by commonwealth law, while *de facto* relationships are largely governed by state and territory laws. Marriage should remain a commonwealth matter.

If the commonwealth parliament were to attempt legislatively to expand the common law definition of marriage to include a union between two persons of the same-sex, there would probably be an Australian High Court challenge to determine whether such an attempt was constitutional, given that the commonwealth parliament has a restricted power to make laws 'with respect to marriage'. Under our constitution, the parliament cannot increase its powers just by legislatively redefining the constitutional heads of power. To take a very different example, the commonwealth parliament has power to make laws with respect to 'lighthouses, lightships, beacons and buoys'. It cannot willy-nilly define lighthouses to include tall inner city buildings and then make laws governing those buildings.

Just as the states and territories deal with *de facto* relationships, the best way to proceed is for the states and territories to give recognition to same-sex civil unions. That way we can accord equality to same-sex couples in their relationships without changing the nature of state recognised marriage. While some human rights activists think this approach unprincipled, there are many Catholics who wonder how a Catholic priest can approve even civil recognition of same-sex unions. After all, Pope Benedict, before he became pope, taught constantly the immorality of all homosexual acts. He also spoke against state recognition of same-sex relationships when he headed the Congregation for the Doctrine of the Faith (CDF). Some Catholics agree completely with this teaching. Others find it problematic.

Back in 1986, then Cardinal Ratzinger taught: 'Although the particular inclination of the homosexual person is not a sin, it is a more or less strong tendency ordered toward an intrinsic moral evil; and thus the inclination itself must be seen as an objective disorder.'[20] Though homosexual acts committed by a heterosexual person might be judged immoral, one cannot credibly cast judgment

---

20. Congregation For The Doctrine Of The Faith, *Letter To The Bishops Of The Catholic Church On The Pastoral Care Of Homosexual Persons*, 1986, #3.

on all such acts committed by a homosexual person without first taking into account the personal and relational context of the sexual act. There are homosexual persons who enter into loving, faithful and committed relationships. These persons should be able to live in society free from discrimination, without state interference and with state support and approval. They should enjoy the same state protection as *de facto* couples enjoy under existing state and territory laws.

It is very difficult to characterise such a law giving this non-discriminatory protection to same-sex couples as 'so harmful to the common good as to be gravely immoral' as Benedict has previously done.[21] It is at least contestable whether such a law would be harmful to the common good. Not everyone who opposes same-sex marriage is a religious bigot or enemy of human rights. We need to keep an eye on the rights of all persons, including future generations of children, and on the maintenance of a social institution which is about more than the couple. We should continue to distinguish marriage from other relationships in the law whether they be *de facto* or same-sex.

Gay Marriage Debate Has A Long Way To Go

6 December 2011

On the weekend the Australian Labor Party conference voted to amend the party platform on same sex marriage. The platform now states: 'Labor will amend the *Marriage Act* to ensure equal access to marriage under statute for all adult couples irrespective of sex who have a mutual commitment to a shared life.' Churches and religious organisations will retain the freedom to perform marriage ceremonies only for a man and a woman eligible for marriage under the rules of the church or organisation.

---

21. Congregation For The Doctrine Of The Faith, *Considerations Regarding Proposals to Give Legal Recognition to Unions Between Homosexual Persons, 2003*, #10.

The conference voted by 208 to 184 to allow Labor MPs a conscience vote on the issue. Tony Abbott continues to insist that Liberal MPs will not be granted a conscience vote. This will change. If it does not, several Liberals, including Malcolm Turnbull, will cross the floor. It could even become a leadership issue in the party. Within the life of the present parliament, our elected leaders will probably be voting on the issue, and in all likelihood the members of all major parties will have a conscience vote.

How should the conscientious Catholic member of parliament vote? If I were a member of parliament, I would support a law for the recognition of civil unions similar to the present United Kingdom law, and I would vote against any bill extending the definition of marriage to include the union of two men or two women. I would do so because I think the State should not discriminate against couples who have a mutual commitment to a shared life (whatever their sexual orientation), while affirming that the bearing and nurturing of the children of the union is a constitutive good of marriage (even though not all marriages produce children).

Sadly in Australia, there is not much interest in a national approach for the recognition of civil unions. It is a winner takes all approach: either same sex marriage or no national symbolic, legal recognition of same sex unions. Just as states and territories can legislate with their own variations for *de facto* partnerships, they could also legislate for civil unions—as Queensland has done. Speaking from Rome on the weekend, Cardinal George Pell, Archbishop of Sydney, said: 'Marriage is about man, woman and children, as it has always been. Any Australia-wide political party which repudiates this does not want to govern, and rejects both tradition and the working class.'[22] We need to distinguish between moral teaching and pastoral advice offered our co-religionists, and reasoned advocacy for laws and public policy applicable to all persons.

On the issue of civil recognition of same-sex unions it is not appropriate in the public square simply to agitate about the Catholic view of the sacramentality of marriage. Even the *Catechism of the*

---

22. 'Labor faces pulpit-led backlash on gay marriage', *The Australian*, 5 December 2011.

Catholic Church states: 'The number of men and women who have deep-seated homosexual tendencies is not negligible. This inclination . . . constitutes for most of them a trial. They must be accepted with respect, compassion, and sensitivity. Every sign of unjust discrimination in their regard should be avoided.'[23] How then could the law best express this respect, compassion, sensitivity, and non-discrimination for all persons including same sex attracted persons who commit themselves to loving, faithful relationships?

There is room even in the community of faith for a diversity of views. I have been greatly assisted by the line of Archbishop Vincent Nichols, elected president of the Catholic Bishops Conference of England and Wales by unanimous acclamation in 2009, who last month after their Bishops Conference said, 'We were very nuanced. We did not oppose gay civil partnerships. We recognised that in English law there might be a case for those.'[24]

Archbishop Nichols, Archbishop of Westminster, was also in Rome recently, and speaking about civil unions and same sex marriage. He said: 'Clearly, respect must be shown to those who in the situation in England use a civil partnership to bring stability to a relationship. Equality is very important and there should be no unjust discrimination. (However) commitment plus equality do not equal marriage.'[25] I concede that some Catholic commentators might argue for limits on non-discrimination and compassion on the basis that the very recognition of a same sex relationship is contrary to the natural law. For example, the *Catechism* states:

> The natural law, the Creator's very good work, provides the solid foundation on which man can build the structure of moral rules to guide his choices.

---

23. *Catechism of the Catholic Church*, # 2358.
24. Archbishop Vincent Nichols being interviewed by Huw Edwards, *BBC*, 24 September 2010.
25. 'Archbishop Nichols responds to critics of his civil unions approach' Catholic News Agency, 2 December 2011 at <http://www.catholicnewsagency.com/news/archbishop-nichols-responds-to-critics-of-his-civil-unions-approach/ >. Accessed 3 December 2014.

It also provides the indispensable moral foundation for building the human community. Finally, it provides the necessary basis for the civil law with which it is connected, whether by a reflection that draws conclusions from its principles, or by additions of a positive and juridical nature.[26]

But these commentators would then need to establish that the extension of non-discrimination and compassion to same sex couples would undermine the indispensable moral foundation for building the human community. Even if the Australian Parliament does legislate to expand the definition of marriage beyond its traditional meaning in the *Marriage Act*, there will undoubtedly be a constitutional challenge in the Australian High Court given that the parliament does not have the power to expand its legislative competence beyond the wording of the constitution. Under the constitution, the parliament has power 'to make laws with respect to marriage'.

In 1992, Justice Dawson on the Australian High Court observed that the commonwealth power to legislate with respect to marriage 'is predicated upon the existence of marriage as a recognisable (although not immutable) institution'. He then said, 'Just how far any attempt to define or redefine, in an abstract way, the rights and obligations of the parties to a marriage may involve a departure from that recognisable institution, and hence travel outside constitutional power, is a question of no small dimension.'[27]

So this debate has a long way to go. It would be a pity if those of us trying to contribute the strength of the Catholic tradition to the debate were simply characterised as homophobic naysayers. And it would be helpful if some of the nuances of the experienced UK bishops could get some airplay here from our own bishops who also wrestle with the pastoral and moral dimensions of this question.

---

26. *Catechism of the Catholic Church*, #1959.
27. *The Queen* v *L* (1992) 174 CLR 379, 404.

What Pay Parents Are Worth

6 June 2012

The same sex marriage debate is not going away in Australia or the US. It may be delayed in the UK, and it is concluded in Canada. It is not a debate about what restrictions church communities might continue to impose rightly on church weddings. It is a debate about what recognition the civil law should give to committed monogamous partnerships which may or may not involve the nurturing and education of children.

I remain committed to legal recognition of civil unions while maintaining the distinctive institution of civil marriage as the bond between a man and a woman open to bearing and nurturing each other's children. I am aware that the maintenance of this distinction is causing hurt to some people, while others think it is too compromising. It was a galvanising moment in the same sex marriage debate when audience member Ross Scheepers asked the Hon Joe Hockey on a program on the Australian national broadcaster, *Q&A*, to 'tell us and Senator Wong why you think you and Melissa make better parents than her and Sophie'. Hockey replied: 'I think in this life we've got to aspire to give our children what I believe to be the very best circumstances and that's to have a mother and a father . . . I'm not saying gay parents are any lesser parents but I am being asked to legislate in favour of something that I don't believe to be the best outcome for a child.'[28]

Compere Tony Jones then asked Penny Wong for her opinion. 'It is sad', she replied,

> that some families have to feel that they have to justify who they are because when you say those things, Joe, what you're saying to not just me but people like me is that the most important thing in our lives, which is the people we love, is somehow less good, less valued. And

---

28. ABC, *Q&A*, 14 May 2012 at <http://www.abc.net.au/tv/qanda/txt/s3497231.htm>. Accessed 3 December 2014.

if you believe that then you believe that, but I have a different view.

When asked if it was hurtful Wong replied, 'Of course it is but, you know, I know what my family is worth'. When Wong's partner Sophie Allouache gave birth to daughter Alexandra, many Australians delighted in the front page photograph of the newly founded family. Allouache and Wong are not married but they are committed in love to each other and they have now committed to bringing up their child.

Like all children, Alexandra has a biological father. Unlike the children of Hockey and his wife Melissa, Alexandra will be brought up and nurtured primarily by a couple not including her biological father. In future, couples like Allouache and Wong may have the option of producing a child who does not even have a biological father. The essence of equality is that things which are the same are treated the same and things which are marked by relevant differences are treated differently. If things marked by irrelevant differences are treated differently, there might be a breach of the principle of equality and there might result an unjustified act of adverse discrimination.

It would be wrong for the state not to recognise mixed race marriages. The marriage of a mixed race couple should be treated in the same way as the marriage of a couple of the same race. Race is not a relevant difference when it comes to marriage. On the same reasoning, I've argued that the time has come for the state to recognise the unions of same sex couples who are committed to faithful, supportive, long term exclusive relationships. The state has an interest in seeing such relationships supported even though some citizens for religious or other reasons may have reservations or objections about the sexual relations and sexual acts which might be entailed in such relationships. Basically that is none of the state's business, nor is it the business of religious persons whose views about the good life are not being sought by people living in such relationships.

I have continued to draw the line at civil unions. If a same sex relationship was to be treated exactly the same as a heterosexual marriage, then the couple in a same sex relationship recognised as marriage should have exactly the same entitlements as the couple in a heterosexual marriage.

I have two substantive reservations, which could be held in good faith by people of any religious conviction or none whatever. Couples who are unable to bear their own children can avail themselves of medical and scientific assistance. Naturally couples would like to be able to bear and nurture children who have their genetic imprint, and only theirs.

I am enough of a 'natural lawyer' to think that all persons have a natural right to a known biological mother and a known biological father. The idea that the state would routinely authorise state assistance for the creation of children without a known biological father and a known biological mother concerns me. It will not be long before scientists will be able to create a child from the genetic material of just two men or two women. Such children and their advocates would need to concede that but for such a technological breakthrough they would not exist.

But some of these children will undoubtedly face existential challenges of novel dimensions when they realise that they do not have a known biological father and a known biological mother. I am very wary about the state writing a blank cheque in the name of non-discrimination committing itself to the development and provision of artificial reproductive technology such that children with these challenges will be routinely created.

Though I have no objection to adoption being available to same sex couples when the child for adoption is related to one of the couple (and that is usually the case), I do think that a child who is not related to any prospective adoptive parent should be given in adoption to the available couple most suited to bringing up the child. All things being equal (which inevitably they are not), the state acting in the best interests of the child should be able to show a preference for a family unit including an adult male and an adult female.

Can we have 'marriage equality' while maintaining a ban on reproductive technology using the genetic material of just two men or two women, and while maintaining a state entitlement to choose adoption in the best interests of the child who has no adoptive relations? If not, then we should settle for civil unions which remove all adverse discrimination against a same sex couple by virtue of their relationship while maintaining state preferences for all children having a biological mother and a biological father and for adoption of any unrelated child into a family with an adult male and adult female.

When the matter comes on for debate, all political parties should provide their members with a conscience vote. While some conservative religious groups in Australia support Tony Abbott's denial of a conscience vote, the shoe is on the other foot in the UK where the Liberal Democrats want to force their members to support a vote for same sex marriage. The Catholic Archbishop of Southwark, Archbishop Peter Smith, has said: 'The Government's proposal to change the definition of marriage is a profound legal reform which, if enacted, would have major long term consequences for our society. It is very important in my view that MPs of all parties should be given a free vote on an issue of such major significance. It is an issue of conscience because fundamental moral questions are at stake about the true meaning of marriage and how the common good of society is best served.'[29] This principle should apply whichever foot is shod.

It's Time To Recognise Secular Same Sex Marriage

11 July 2013

The US Supreme Court and Prime Minister Kevin Rudd have put their weight behind legal recognition of same sex marriage. Kevin Rudd before resuming the prime ministership wrote that he had

> come to the conclusion that church and state can have
> different positions and practices on the question of

---

29. 'Archbishop calls for free vote on same-sex marriage', *Catholic Herald*, 1 June 2012.

same sex marriage. I believe the secular Australian state should be able to recognise same sex marriage. I also believe that this change should legally exempt religious institutions from any requirement to change their historic position and practice that marriage is exclusively between a man and a woman.[30]

Change is still some way off here in Australia and the arguments are still a little confused. But change is coming.

On 26 June 2013, the US Supreme Court gave two decisions impacting on same sex marriage under a constitution which vests in the states, and not Congress, the power to make laws with respect to marriage. Here in Australia, the Commonwealth Parliament, and not any state parliament, has the overriding power to make laws with respect to marriage. So Australian states are not assured the constitutional mandate to go it on their own.

One of the US Supreme Court decisions cleared the way for same sex marriage in California, the twelfth state of the union to recognise such marriages, and the other struck down the Congress's *Defense of Marriage Act* which provided that in all federal rules and rulings 'the word "marriage" means only a legal union between one man and one woman as husband and wife'. Writing for the majority in *US* v *Windsor*, Justice Kennedy striking down Congress's attempt to limit marriage to the exclusive union of a man and a woman said:

> It seems fair to conclude that, until recent years, many citizens had not even considered the possibility that two persons of the same sex might aspire to occupy the same status and dignity as that of a man and woman in lawful marriage. For marriage between a man and a woman no doubt had been thought of by most people as essential to the very definition of that term and to its role and function throughout the history of civilisation.[31]

---

30. Kevin Rudd, 'Church and State are able to have different positions on same sex marriage', 20 May 2013 at < http://www.kevinruddmp.com/2013/05/church-and-state-are-able-to-have.html>. Accessed 3 December 2014.
31. *US v Windsor* 570 U.S. ____ (2013), slip opinion, 13.

Cardinal Timothy Dolan, president of the US Conference of Catholic Bishops, described the Supreme Court decisions as a 'tragic day for marriage and our nation', saying, 'The Court got it wrong. The federal government ought to respect the truth that marriage is the union of one man and one woman, even where states fail to do so.' He and his fellow bishops said, 'Marriage is the only institution that brings together a man and a woman for life, providing any child who comes from their union with the secure foundation of a mother and a father.'[32]

Australia's bishops have been fairly quiet on this issue. But in April 2013, Australia's most theologically literate bishop Mark Coleridge appeared on the ABC's program, *Q&A,* opposing not just same sex marriage but any civil recognition of same sex unions, describing homosexuality as 'a warp in the creation' and as an impossibility in God's plan.[33]

It is high time to draw a distinction between a marriage recognised by civil law and a sacramental marriage. In deciding whether to expand civil marriage to the union of two persons of the same gender, legislators should have regard not just for the wellbeing of same sex couples and the children already part of their family units, but also for the wellbeing of all future children who may be affected, as well as the common good of society in setting appropriate contours for legally recognised relationships.

Same sex couples wanting to create their own children may in the foreseeable future be able to use only their own genetic material, precluding the possibility that such children will have a biological father and a biological mother. Whether or not we legislate for same sex marriage, we should restrict artificial reproduction of children such that they will have a biological father and a biological mother, and hopefully being able to be known by them.

---

32. United States Conference of Catholic Bishops, Media Release, 26 June 2013, at <http://www.usccb.org/news/2013/13-126.cfm>. Accessed 3 December 2014.

33. ABC, *Q&A*, Transcript, 1 April 2013 at <http://www.abc.net.au/tv/qanda/txt/s3717805.htm>. Accessed 3 December 2014.

Legislators making laws regarding adoption ought be able to demand that adoption agencies continue to consider the best interests of the child. In the case of a child unrelated to any prospective adopting couple, the adoption agency ought be able to have regard to the desirability of a child being brought up in a family with an adult male and an adult female. If these concerns were met or at least weighed in the balance against the claims of children already in same sex families deserving respect and nurture by the state and society, society could properly move to recognition of civil unions or same sex marriage if and when the overwhelming majority of the population (including those who are presently married civilly) supported such change.

In the US proceedings, the Court was told that there are already 40,000 children in California alone who are being brought up by same sex couples. We need to be mindful of the wellbeing and dignity of these children as well as the handful who will be up for adoption and the unknown number in future who will be created in a test tube. There has been a clear divergence of view within the Catholic Church on civil unions as a means of doing justice and according dignity to gay couples, while leaving unanswered the questions about adopted children and children created with advancing reproductive technology, and maintaining a distinction from marriage even in civil terms.

On 15 June 2012, Coleridge had written to Newman, the Premier of Queensland, urging a repeal of the law recognising civil partnerships. He spoke of

> the evidence that seems to be emerging . . . that there is a slippery slope from registration to civil partnerships to same-sex marriage. I would urge you therefore to honour the promise made before the election—to repeal the civil partnerships legislation in order to safeguard marriage and the family as they have been known through the millennia.[34]

---

34. 'Premier tabled law day after Archbishop visit', *The Australian*, 5 November 2012

On *Q&A* on 1 April 2013 Coleridge then said:

> But what the Church has to do is to remain faithful
> to our understanding of homosexuality and yet, at
> the same time, to work in every way we can to ensure
> justice for homosexual people. Now, clearly this doesn't
> mean to say, for instance, that we support gay marriage.
> The Church's position on that is very well known and
> controversial. But in every other way, to work to defend
> the dignity of homosexual people, just as we work to
> defend the dignity of other people.
> How to do that and to maintain fidelity to our
> understanding of homosexuality, which is grounded
> upon a particular vision of what the human person is
> and what human sexuality is within that context. How to
> hold those two things together is the conundrum that we
> are dealing with. I don't think it is an Achilles' heel but I
> think it is a real conundrum with which the Church has
> to continue to grapple at this time and in this culture.[35]

The Archbishop was right to insist on the need 'to work in every way we can to ensure justice for homosexual people' and 'to
work to defend the dignity of homosexual people, just as we work
to defend the dignity of other people'. It would be just and a service to the common good for the State to give some recognition
and support to committed, faithful, long-term relationships between gay couples deserving dignity, being able to love and support each other in sickness and in health, until death they do part.

Should legislators in our pluralistic democratic society withhold
such just and dignified recognition of civil unions because this
might be a slippery slope to same sex marriage? Pope Benedict XVI
when at the Congregation for the Doctrine of the Faith opposed
even civil unions. However Pope Francis when Archbishop of
Buenos Aires had told gay rights activists that 'homosexuals need to

---

35. ABC, *Q&A*, Transcript, 1 April 2013.

have recognised rights' and that he 'supported civil unions, but not same sex marriage'.[36]

I am with Francis on civil unions but, unlike him, I now accept that we can probably no longer draw a line between civil unions and same sex marriage. That will be the long-term consequence of last month's US Supreme Court decisions which will impact much further west than California.

Show Some Respect When Talking With Homosexuals

18 August 2013

The readings for this Twentieth Sunday in Ordinary Time are very confronting. In the first reading we hear about the prophet Jeremiah who had the misfortune to live and prophesy at a time when Jerusalem was being invaded by foreigners (Jeremiah 38:4–6, 8–10). He advised the people and their king to surrender. They thought he was a traitor, undermining the morale of the troops. It just happened that he was right. They dumped him down a well so that he might die. A few just men came forward and rescued him.

In Luke's Gospel, Jesus is headed for Jerusalem. 'Do you suppose that I am here to bring peace on earth?' Not a bit of it. He promises nothing but fire and division—and not just division and disagreement with our enemies, but division within families and within the church community (Luke 12:49–53).

---

36. 'On Gay Unions, a Pragmatist Before He Was a Pope', The *New York Times*, 19 March 2013. This article reports on the stand taken by Bergoglio in 2010 when Argentina was considering a law recognising same sex marriage: 'Faced with the near certain passage of the gay marriage bill, Cardinal Bergoglio offered the civil union compromise as the "lesser of two evils," said Sergio Rubin, his authorized biographer. He wagered on a position of greater dialogue with society. In the end, though, a majority of the bishops voted to overrule him, his only such loss in his six-year tenure as head of Argentina's bishops' conference. But throughout the contentious political debate, he acted as both the public face of the opposition to the law and as a bridge-builder, sometimes reaching out to his critics. "He listened to my views with a great deal of respect" said Marcelo Márquez, a gay rights leader and theologian who wrote a tough letter to Cardinal Bergoglio and, to his surprise, received a call from him less than an hour after it was delivered. "He told me that homosexuals need to have recognized rights and that he supported civil unions, but not same-sex marriage."'

On my first reflection on these readings, I thought they had no application to us today. But then I thought again. During the week, I had to appear on Australia's Special Broadcasting Service (SBS) program, *Insight*, about same sex marriage.[37] Many bishops were asked but none was available. Same sex marriage is a difficult and complex legal, political and social question in a country like Australia, especially at election time when our political leaders are taking different approaches. So I don't want to preach about that. But I do think it is time from the pulpit to say something about the Catholic Church's attitude to, and language about, people who happen to be homosexual.

The thinking of Joseph Ratzinger before he became Pope Benedict XVI has shaped much of the official Catholic Church teaching on this issue over the last forty years. But even before he became directly responsible for shaping the Vatican's approach in 1981 when he became Prefect of the Congregation for the Doctrine of the Faith, his predecessor in that Vatican office had issued in 1975 a document which distinguished the homosexual orientation from homosexual acts. The latter were described as being deprived of their essential and indispensable finality and as being 'intrinsically disordered'.[38]

Then in 1986 the Congregation, then headed by Cardinal Ratzinger, issued a new document saying that

> an overly benign interpretation was given to the homosexual condition itself, some going so far as to call it neutral, or even good. Although the particular inclination of the homosexual person is not a sin, it is a more or less strong tendency ordered toward an intrinsic moral evil; and thus the inclination itself must be seen as an objective disorder.[39]

---

37. SBS, *Insight*, Gay Marriage, 13 August 2013 at
< http://www.sbs.com.au/news/insight/tvepisode/gay-marriage>. Accessed 3 December 2014.
38. Congregation For The Doctrine Of The Faith, *Persona Humana*, Declaration On Certain Questions Concerning Sexual Ethics, 1975, VIII.
39. Congregation For The Doctrine Of The Faith, *Letter To The Bishops Of The Catholic Church On The Pastoral Care Of Homosexual Persons*, 1986, #3

Many people, including many Catholics and many homosexuals, find such language unhelpful and upsetting; they even contest its truthfulness. Thank God, as Pope, Benedict did not repeat much of this language. But many Church leaders still think it the only Catholic way to speak about homosexuality. Earlier this year, Archbishop Mark Coleridge, probably the most theologically literate bishop in Australia, appeared on the ABC TV program *Q&A* distinguishing between sexual orientation and lifestyle: 'They are not necessarily the same thing. Lifestyle is chosen, sexual orientation is not.' He said the homosexual orientation could be seen as 'a warp in the creation' and that it was 'impossible' from his point of view to be seen as just a part of God's plan.

On the SBS program, *Insight*, Penny Wong, a very eloquent and poised politician who is known to be lesbian, sharing with her partner the parenting of their child, addressed Monsignor John Woods saying, 'I think it's interesting you use words like respect at the same time as having a discussion about whether or not homosexuality is in fact natural or, by implication, you know a result of some form of disorder. I don't think that's particularly respectful.' Much of the two-hour discussion was not put to air by SBS. At one stage of the discussion, I said that I found talk of homosexuality being a disorder unhelpful. Addressing Penny Wong, I said that I thought her homosexuality was as natural, complex and mystical as my heterosexuality.

During the rest of the week, I received a range of emails from some very conservative Catholics who were questioning my moral courage, wondering why I was just going with the prevailing social trend, not being true to church teaching etc. They obviously thought I was being untrue to myself as well as to the Church. There was more than a dose of adverse moral judgment in it all.

Later in the week, as often happens with us priests, someone came to see me for a pastoral conversation. He was an adult Catholic, a good man, and a fine Catholic. He told me that he was gay. He had 'come out' to a number of his friends, but it obviously was not easy. I called to mind the media press conference that Pope Francis gave recently on the plane on the way back from World Youth Day. He was asked about homosexuality and he said, 'If a person is gay and seeks the Lord and has good will, well who am I to judge them?' I think Pope Francis now gives us a better way of engaging in respectful discussion in our Church and in the community about the complex issues relating to homosexuality, including civil recognition of same sex marriage.

Our theological starting point should be that we are all created in the image and likeness of God, whether we be gay or straight; that we are all called along the road to Jerusalem; and that the Lord's purgative fire and promise of division is extended to us all in preparation for the invitation to the banquet where there is neither gay nor straight, and where each of us prays, 'Lord, I am not worthy that you should enter under my roof, but only say the word and my soul shall be healed'.

It's time we dropped the unhelpful, judgmental language of intrinsic and objective disorder when respectfully trying to determine appropriate laws and policies for all people who want to support and nurture each other and their children.

ACT Makes A Dog's Breakfast Of Marriage Equality

28 October 2013

After the June 2013 decisions of the US Supreme Court on same sex marriage, I restated in July 2013 my support for civil unions. Conceding that neither side of the debate was much interested in that outcome, I said, 'We can probably no longer draw a line between civil unions and same sex marriage. That will be the long term consequence of last month's US Supreme Court decisions which will impact much further west than California.'

The caravan has been moving at some pace since then in Australia but it is difficult to assess in what direction or whether it just be around in circles with the advocates for marriage equality digging themselves into a judicial hole from which it might be difficult for either side to emerge.

During the 2013 federal election, Kevin Rudd pulled out all stops to advocate same sex marriage legislation in the commonwealth parliament. Tony Abbott stuck firmly to the line that his party would maintain party policy that marriage is a relationship between one man and one woman to the exclusion of others, and that the party policy would be maintained unless and until the party revised its position, including whether or not to allow a conscience vote. In the Liberal Party, as distinct from the Labor Party, members are always free to cross the floor without the risk of automatic expulsion from the party—though their prospects of promotion tend to take a nosedive.

I remain of the view that any extension of the civil law's definition of marriage should be the preserve of the commonwealth parliament with all members being granted a conscience vote. Presently the 1961 Commonwealth *Marriage Act* as amended states that 'marriage means the union of a man and a woman to the exclusion of all others, voluntarily entered into for life'.

At 11.40 am on 22 October 2013the ACT Legislature voted by nine votes to eight to agree in principle to the passage of its *Marriage Equality Bill*. Thirteen minutes later, they voted by eight votes to seven to agree to twenty-five amendments including a renaming of the bill as the *Marriage Equality (Same Sex) Act 2013*. The purpose of the amendments was to 'clarify that this is a law for same-sex marriage and the ACT is not seeking to legislate in an area of law already governed by the Commonwealth under the *Marriage Act 1961*'. The result is a dog's breakfast. And everyone is now off to the High Court.

Just to give one morsel from the dog's breakfast. The long title of the Act has been amended to read: 'An Act to provide for marriage equality by allowing for marriage between two adults of the same sex, and for other purposes'. But another amendment provides a definition of marriage: 'Marriage means a marriage under the *Marriage Act 1961*.' But the main 'dictionary' definition given in the Act states that 'marriage does not include a marriage within the meaning of the *Marriage Act*'.

So there you have it: under some provisions of the ACT *Marriage Equality (Same Sex) Act*, marriage means a marriage under the Commonwealth *Marriage Act* (which excludes same sex marriage) except presumably when it is a marriage under the ACT *Marriage Equality (Same Sex) Act*, between two adults of the same sex. Under the constitution, the commonwealth parliament has power to make laws with respect to marriage. So too do the states. And since 1978, so too does the ACT Legislative Assembly. But if a commonwealth law covers the field, any state or territory law does not operate to the extent of any inconsistency.

Undoubtedly the commonwealth will argue in the High Court that it has covered the field on marriage since 1961 and it should be left to do so. Advocates for 'marriage equality' frustrated by the slow pace of change at a commonwealth level have decided to pursue state and territory legislation for forms of unequal and inferior marriage recognition in the hope of providing further political pressure for the commonwealth to act.

All this is being done in the name of 'marriage equality'. The sort of marriage being offered same sex couples by the ACT law is so 'equal' as to provide: 'A marriage under this Act ends if either of the parties to the marriage later marries someone else under a Commonwealth law (including a marriage in another jurisdiction that is recognised by the commonwealth as a valid marriage).' No need for a minimum time of separation; no need for a court order; just up and off!

Professor George Williams, one of the legal advisers to the ACT Government on their amended Act, said three years ago: 'It would be better to have a single national law providing for same sex marriage. However, such a law may not be legally possible, and in the short term may be politically unachievable. In these circumstances, we should not discount the possibility of a state leading the way.'[40] Marriage equality advocates are pursuing the issue at a state level in the hope of pressuring the commonwealth. In the process they risk

---

40. George Williams, 'States Could Legalise Same-sex Marriage', *Sydney Morning Herald*, 28 September 2010.

blowing apart the national coherence of marriage laws put in place in 1961.

History provides some salutary lessons about the need for detailed, careful legislative work—other than the thirteen minutes consideration given by the ACT legislature to their amendments last week. History also points to the wisdom of a conscience vote in the national Parliament on this issue. Introducing the Commonwealth *Marriage Bill* on 19 May 1960, Sir Garfield Barwick said he had taken a full year to prepare the legislation and he was prepared to wait many more months to debate the bill 'making with the states the several administrative arrangements which the bill contemplates'. He said: 'the measure will not be treated as a party measure . . . members will be free to adopt their own attitudes and to express them by their vote, freely.'[41]

The original *Marriage Act* contained no definition of marriage. Kim Beazley Snr like other members saw no need for a definition as he thought the marriage customs of Australians were unlikely to be radically changed by legislation. He told parliament, 'The marriage customs of the community are, in fact, customs and they have not been framed around law. Perhaps to a considerable extent they have been framed around religion'.[42] Barwick later wrote:

> 'That the founding fathers of the Commonwealth believed that the fundamental relationship in question should be governed by a national law is evident; for, in a list of subjects, notable neither for its width nor for its length, which were to be conceded to the National Parliament, both marriage and divorce were included.'[43]

Interesting for present purposes, Gough Whitlam, Deputy Leader of the Opposition with the carriage of the matter for the Labor Party, reminded the Parliament on 17 August 1960:

---

41. (1960) CPD (HofR) 2000; 19 May 1960.
42. (1960) CPD 229 (HofR); 18 August 1960.
43. Garfield Barwick, 'The Commonwealth Marriage Act 1961', *Melbourne University Law Review*, 3 (1961-2): 278.

When the Attorney General (Barwick) made his second reading speech on this bill, he announced that while the Government would take full responsibility for having made the proposals contained in the measure and would support them, as a government, the legislation would not be treated as a party measure, and honourable members would be free to adopt their own attitudes to it and express them freely by their votes. The Opposition has resolved to take the same course.[44]

Whitlam went on to say:

This is a field in which the founding fathers themselves, with their very narrow and timid conceptions of the Commonwealth's powers, were agreed that this Parliament should be able to pass laws.

In that respect our Commonwealth is different from the other English-speaking federations, the United States of America and Canada. We have power to pass laws on these subjects. I believe that everyone, whatever he might think of individual features of the bill, would agree that we should pass laws on this subject. As a result of this bill, Australian men and women and their children, wherever they live, will be able more readily and certainly to ascertain and establish their rights to marriage and arising from it.[45]

In what might now be seen as a delightful ambiguity, Barwick, summing up the parliamentary debate, pointed out that there was no definition of marriage in the Bill nor in the Constitution: 'That is because we in this community recognise marriage as monogamous and a voluntary union for life of two people to the exclusion of all others.'[46]

---

44. (1960) CPD 114 (HofR); 17 August 1960.
45. (1960) CPD 117 (HofR); 17 August 1960
46. (1960) CPD 231 (HofR); 18 August 1960

Religion is much less relevant now to the civil definition of marriage because while the crude marriage rate continues to decline (from 7.3 in 1960 to 5.5 in 2008), the proportion of civil marriages continues to increase. A century ago, ninety-five per cent of marriages were church marriages; in 1969, eighty-nine per cent of marriages were still being performed in church. By 2010, sixty-nine per cent of all marriages were performed by civil celebrants.

Some strong advocates of traditional marriage, including the Australian Christian Lobby, have been suggesting that the matter should be resolved by referendum. That is a bad idea. In Australia, we expect our members of parliament to make the statutory law and our judges to shape the common law and interpret the constitution. We the people vote by referendum only to change the constitution. Occasionally there is a case to be made for a plebiscite when we are trying to determine a particular question to put to the people by referendum to change the constitution. This is what we did when we wanted to determine whether we were ready to vote for a particular form of republic.

Groups like the Australian Christian Lobby should be careful what they wish for. If a referendum on same sex marriage, why not a referendum on (say) the death penalty? If the opinion polls are right, there is no doubt the way that one would go. Or a referendum on excluding boat people from Australia? Or a referendum on euthanasia? There are good reasons for avoiding the populist politics of lawmaking by direct popular vote of the people.

A year after the passage of the *Marriage Act 1961*, Barwick observed:

> As I said when introducing the Bill . . . I do not believe that there is any necessary virtue in uniformity; indeed, in many areas of human endeavour, variety may bring strength. 'But' (to quote from Hansard) 'the relationship of husband and wife, parent and child, is common to us all, whether we derive from one State or another'. Also I think it is particularly proper that, as this country increases in international stature, it should have one

uniform law of marriage applicable throughout the Commonwealth.[47]

Writing in an academic journal and reflecting on the passage of the *Marriage Act 1961*, Barwick said:

> To bring unity to the marriage law of Australia was not, however, the main task of the architects of the *Marriage Act*. Their main task was to produce a marriage code suitable to present-day Australian needs, a code which, on the one hand, paid proper regard to the antiquity and foundations of marriage as an institution, but which, on the other, resolved modern problems in a modern way.[48]

This remains our task, and it is best done by the Australian Parliament exercising a conscience vote rather than state and territory legislatures tinkering and then leaving the matter to the High Court. Marriage is too precious a social institution to be put in the mix of a dog's breakfast.

High Court Leaves Same Sex Marriage Door Ajar

15 December 2013

The advocates for 'marriage equality' and their allies in the ACT Legislative Assembly have scored one of the great home goals with the High Court of Australia ruling unanimously in *The Commonwealth* v *The Australian Capital Territory* that 'the whole of the *Marriage Equality (Same Sex) Act* 2013 (ACT) is inconsistent with the *Marriage Act* 1961 (Cth)' and that 'the whole of the *Marriage Equality (Same Sex) Act* 2013 (ACT) is of no effect'.[49]

---

47. Garfield Barwick, 'The Commonwealth Marriage Act 1961', *Melbourne University Law Review*, 3 (1961-2): 277.
48. Garfield Barwick, 'The Commonwealth Marriage Act', *Melbourne University Law Review*, 3 (1961-2): 277.
49. [2013] HCA 55 at <http://www.austlii.edu.au/au/cases/cth/HCA/2013/55.html>. Accessed 3 December 2014.

The advocates for same sex marriage did themselves no favour in terms of public credibility by putting their support behind a dog's breakfast of ACT legislation which even if valid and effective would not have provided marriage equality. The High Court noted that the ACT Act provided 'for the *automatic* dissolution of the marriage if a party marries another under a law of the Commonwealth, or under a law of another jurisdiction that substantially corresponds to the ACT Act.' How could advocates for 'marriage equality' credibly support a 'marriage' terminable without court order, without agreement, without prior notice to the other party—an arrangement able to be dissolved just at the whim of one of the parties walking out the door having found another marriage partner, whether straight or gay? Whatever such an arrangement might be, it is not a marriage. These advocates and the merry band of ACT legislators were happy to legislate for marriage inequality as a stop on the route to Commonwealth marriage equality. This was a stupid political strategy given the unlikelihood that Prime Minister Tony Abbott would be swayed or moved more quickly to action by the referral of such a legal hodge-podge to the High Court. This was not a stop on the route; it was a detour down what could be a *cul-de-sac*. And it was never a close run thing.

The litigation has served one useful purpose. Until now, there was some academic legal doubt whether the Commonwealth Parliament's constitutional power to make laws with respect to marriage would be broad enough to include laws with respect to same sex marriage. In this case, the seventh judge Justice Gageler could not sit because he had previously given legal advice on the matter at hand. The High Court has put this matter beyond doubt with all six sitting judges affirming that 'marriage' for the purposes of defining the constitutional power of the Commonwealth Parliament could not be confined to marriage in the traditional Christian sense. The High Court has said that for constitutional purposes, '"marriage" is to be understood . . . as referring to a consensual union formed between natural persons in accordance with legally prescribed requirements which is not only a union the law recognises as intended to endure and be terminable only in accordance with law but also a union to which the law accords a status affecting and defining mutual rights and obligations'. Under the Australian Constitution, "'marriage" is a term which includes a marriage between persons of the same sex'.

So the court has put beyond doubt two issues. Neither the states nor the territories now have power to go it alone on same sex marriage. New South Wales and Tasmania can put their legislative plans to rest. NSW Premier Barry O'Farrell was right when he said that only the national Parliament could deliver marriage equality and that he did not want 'to see a return to the patchwork quilt of marriage laws that existed in the 1950s'.[50] Second, the Commonwealth Parliament does have power to legislate for same sex marriage. There is no need for a constitutional referendum. From here, the law is simple.

The politics and political morality of change are still not so simple. There is only one way forward. This is a matter for the Commonwealth Parliament. Just as all sides allowed a conscience vote on the original 1961 *Marriage Act*, so too all sides should allow a conscience vote on any amendment of the *Marriage Act* which would permit same sex couples to marry on the same terms as opposite sex couples. Our elected politicians voting according to conscience are those best suited to determine if and when the Australian community is ready to embrace an extension of marriage as a social institution to include same sex couples.

Unlike me, neither side of this debate favours civil unions as a distinct status for same sex couples conferring all the attributes of marriage, while maintaining a commitment to the best interests of children available for adoption, and restricting state authorisation of assisted reproduction so that every child has a biological father and a biological mother. In these circumstances, I accept that ultimately our Parliament will legislate for same sex marriage. I will not lose any sleep when it comes, and I will be happy for those couples who will be helped by such social endorsement to live in a faithful, loving relationship. But in light of this home goal, I cannot see it coming in this parliamentary term. The advocates for marriage equality who

---

50. *The Australian*, 31 October 2013.

were prepared to go via the route of ACT marriage inequality have not done their cause any good this time around.

The Timing Of The Same Sex Marriage Debate

8 December 2014

Another excruciating year in the Australian Parliament ended last week. What a dreadful year it has been for parliamentary democracy. In the House of Representatives, Speaker Bronwyn Bishop has taken pride in the number of members she has ejected, describing the chamber not as 'a polite debating society, not a classroom, but a battlefield and we've given up guns, swords and fists and we fight with words'.[51] The Australian Senate chamber is more fractious than ever. There is nothing unusual in the government not controlling the Senate. Sometimes cross benches can win some concessions from government, improving legislation and gaining special privileges for prized constituencies. The late Brian Harradine whose passing we mourned this year was a past master at it. Tasmania's Jacqui Lambie is still on a rapid learning curve as are Ricky Muir and the other new arrivals on the cross benches. Caught in the cross wires in the refugee debate on the last night of the year's Senate sittings, the motor enthusiast Muir lamented:

> They told the people in detention that they rang the office of the man whose decision it was to decide whether they would be out of detention before Christmas. That man wasn't the minister for immigration; it was me. It should not be like this but it is. The crossbench should not have been put in this position, but it has.[52]

In the next two years, Ricky and his colleagues will be put in this position more often. Liberal Democrat Senator David Leyonhjelm announced in his maiden speech on 9 July 2014: 'I believe we

---

51. 2014 CPD 4 (HofR); 4 December 2014.
52. 2014 CPD 104 (S); 4 December 2014.

are about to begin one of the most exciting periods in the life of the Senate.' Being a little known politician he set out his political philosophy:

> In the service of this mission, at the outset I declare that I am proudly what some call a 'libertarian', although I prefer the term 'classical liberal'. My undeviating political philosophy is grounded in the belief that, as expressed so clearly by John Stuart Mill: 'The only purpose for which power can be rightfully ever exercised over any member of a civilised society against his will is to prevent harm to others.'[53]

He went on to say:

> As William Pitt the Younger observed: 'Necessity is the plea for every infringement of human freedom. It is the argument of tyrants; it is the creed of slaves.' Perhaps some are scratching their heads right now. How can someone support marriage equality, assisted suicide and want to legalise pot but also want to cut taxes a lot? If you are scratching your heads, it is because you have forgotten that classical liberal principles were at the core of the Enlightenment, the period that gifted us humanity's greatest achievements in science, medicine and commerce and also brought about the abolition of slavery.[54]

On 25 November 2014, Leyonhjelm gave notice in the Senate that he would be introducing a bill for the recognition of same sex marriage. He told the Senate that he and his wife of thirty years were not married and that he saw no need for the institution of marriage. But if the institution were to be provided by the state, it should be available to all couples regardless of gender or sexual orientation. In media commentary, he ruled out marriage of close family

---

53. 2014 CPD 4565 (S); 9 July 2014.
54. 2014 CPD 4566 (S); 9 July 2014.

members 'for biological reasons' and he ruled out polygamy for everyone including Muslims who thought it socially and religiously acceptable. So he does see some role for the state in drawing the line. He told the Senate:

> To my libertarian constituency, it barely qualifies as progress. To them, a better option would be to remove the government from marriage entirely by repealing the *Marriage Act* and leaving it to the law of contract— as in civilian countries. I do not disagree, and my own situation reflects that. But that is not as simple to achieve as it sounds. The fact is: the community places a certain significance on the institution of marriage. It accepts that individuals can live together in all kinds of relationships, irrespective of gender and numbers, but marriage is different. We need to respect that.[55]

Next day he introduced to the Senate his *Freedom to Marry Bill 2014*. He told the Senate that the purpose of his bill was to address an injustice: 'When the law says that gay, lesbian, bisexual, trans, and intersex people cannot marry, in an important sense it is diminishing their liberty and their ability to make life plans: a major choice is closed off.'[56]

In the United States, thirty-four states as well as the District of Columbia now permit same sex marriage. In fifteen of those states, the change was made by federal court decisions made and applied in only the last three months. It has been a rapid change, but not driven by state congresses or public referenda. The initiative has come in the federal courts reading the judicial tea leaves in the light of the Supreme Court's 2013 *Windsor* decision which struck down Congress's attempt to limit State laws to marriage between a man and a woman. The Court did not decide whether the States had to legislate for same sex marriage. There are sixteen States where same sex marriage is still not allowed. There are five applications

---

55. 2014 CPD 88 (S); 25 November 2014.
56. 2014 CPD 76 (S) 26 November 2014.

presently before the Supreme Court asking that the court rule in favour of same sex marriage in some of these remaining 16 States. On 16 January 2015, the court decided it was ready to consider the question. As ever, the contested moral political issue will be decided in the United States by the nine Supreme Court judges; here in Australia, the decision will rest with the Commonwealth Parliament. Just as the Supreme Court judges have discretion when to buy into the argument, so too the Coalition party room in Australia has discretion when to decide on a conscience vote for all its members, thereby indicating that the government is ready for the matter to be debated again in the Parliament.

There is very little chance that the Abbott government will want to hand the bouquet for breaking the logjam on same sex marriage to David Leyonhjelm. As I predicted a year ago, the issue is unlikely to come to a head in the Australian Parliament until after the next federal election and after the US Supreme Court has handed down its decision in June 2015.

I continue to support a conscience vote for Australian members of parliament. Given that there is little support on either side of the argument for civil unions, I accept that same sex marriage is the only way ultimately to extend equality and respect to same sex couples wanting state endorsement for their committed relationships, and that the state has an interest in supporting such relationships which enhance the care for such couples especially when they are sick or ageing. But I continue to plead with lawmakers that we not lose sight of cultivating the best possible arrangements for the bearing and nurturing of children.

That is why I continue to favour state adoption agencies being able to consider the desirability of an unrelated child being nurtured in a family unit constituted by an adult male and an adult female. This is still a relevant, though not the only, consideration in determining the best interests of the child. It is also why I favour a review of state administration and supervision of assisted reproductive technology which produces children without one known biological mother and one known biological father. I readily accept that in future there will be many children unharmed by not having such parentage, but I fear there will be some who will find it an unbearable existential burden. Their voices need to be heard amongst the popping of champagne corks in favour of marriage equality. To get this right, we Australians will need our parliament to be a more considered and dignified place than a battlefield, and our politicians will need to use words not just as fighting tools. Those like Ricky Muir on the Senate cross benches will need to brace themselves. And David Leyonhjelm might need to defer to someone in the Coalition joint party room.

Conclusion

Outside the council chamber on Palm Island, Australia's largest Aboriginal community, there is a monument celebrating the seven men who led the 1957 strike against the oppressive reserve conditions of the Queensland Government. The inscription reads:

> In June 1957 seven men were arrested at gunpoint by police, during the night. (They) were herded like cattle onto a boat and sent to Townsville . . . These seven leaders were found guilty of triggering a long planned strike for better wages, food and housing. They also called for the removal of the superintendent. They were deported to other settlements from their home, Palm Island. The media repeated the government's opinion that a riot had been put down. The following inquiry found there had been no damage either to property or persons and the strikers had convincing grievances.

Contemplating this monument, I think back 240 years in legal history to the great judgment of Lord Mansfield in *Somerset's Case*. A public servant Granville Sharp outraged by the treatment of a slave on the streets of London would not rest until he obtained justice. Lord Mansfield declared in 1772, 'The air of England is too pure for any slave to breathe; let the black go free'. It took generations of campaigning by people like Lord Wilberforce and little people of whom we have never heard to agitate for these changes. Ultimately the House of Commons passed the *Slavery Abolition Act* in 1833.

Hal Wootten who was the foundation dean of the University of New South Wales Law School and then a judge and royal commissioner investigating Aboriginal deaths in custody has spoken of what he calls 'the little nudger' view of history. Each of us wonders what contribution we can make to a better world. How can we make a difference? Each of us can be a little nudger like Granville

Sharp. We can nudge things in the right direction—within our profession, within our discipline, in our relationships and within our world. If each of us keeps nudging, every now and again, there will be a Lord Mansfield moment. And every now and again there will be a Lord Mansfield. Twenty-three years ago Australia had its own Lord Mansfield moment when the High Court of Australia recognised the rights of Aborigines and Torres Strait Islanders to their traditional lands in the *Mabo* decision. Wootten says:

> In the end we little nudgers need the Lord Mansfields. We depend on there being people in high places who have the wisdom, the vision and the courage to seize the opportunity and bring the work of the little nudgers to fruition in a form that will command authority and survive.[57]

Wootten says that while all six judges in the majority in *Mabo* joined in the Mansfield role, 'one had to write what would become the leading judgment, find the words and the arguments that could command a majority—the reasons that would survive the scrutiny of future generations of judges and ultimately win the support of the community . . . and that role fell to Justice Brennan'. I dedicate this book of reflections to my father in gratitude for his amplification of the conscientious nudgings of so many and to my mother who has always called us back to that still, small voice.

There is still much for us to do as a nation ensuring justice for all. Think only of our faltering efforts to act justly when dealing with refugees and asylum seekers, wanting to maintain the security of our borders while acting fairly towards all who seek asylum and not just those who can afford to come here by plane or even by leaky boat. We must distinguish that which is workable and that which is ethical or moral.

---

57. Hal Wootten, Response to Sir Gerard Brennan's 2012 Wootten Lecture, University of
     New South Wales at
     <http://www.law.unsw.edu.au/sites/law.unsw.edu.au/files/images/2012_hwl_
     response_final_1.pdf>. Accessed 3 December 2014.

When the going gets tough and the way ahead is not clear, we Church people can take to heart my oft quoted (but now unsourced!) observation by Morris West:

> The pronouncements of religious leaders will carry more weight, will be seen as more relevant if they are delivered in the visible context of a truly pastoral function, which is the mediation of the mystery of creation: the paradox of the silent Godhead and suffering humanity.

That's what Pope Francis has been doing so well of late. At all times in the public domain, whether in dialogue with government about social policy or in giving a public account of church perspectives, we who speak with a Church mantle must speak with the voice of public reason. Therein lies the tension. Without trust between those whose consciences differ, we will not scale the heights of the silence of the Godhead nor plumb the depths of the suffering of humanity; we will have failed to incarnate the mystery of God here among us. This mystery is to be embraced in the inner sanctuary of conscience where God's voice echoes within, to be enfleshed in the relationships we share as the people of God, and to be proclaimed in our calls for justice in the public domain.

Index

A

Abbott, Tony, 13, 276, 282, 330, 336, 345, 351.
Abbott Australian Government, 163, 250, 272, 278, 286, 356.
Aboriginal and Torres Strait Islander Commission (ATSIC), 69.
Aboriginal land rights, 25, 60, 61, 64, 65, 66, 69, 70, 148, 207–245.
Abortion, 7, 116, 122, 123, 181, 191, 193, 194, 195, 198–203, 301, 316.
Abortion Law Reform Act (Vic), 191, 193, 194, 195, 198, 199, 201, 203.
Adoption, 88, 159, 326, 335, 336, 339, 353, 357.
Aggiornamento, 45.
Al Hussein, Zeid Ra'ad, 274, 275.
Alaska Native Claims Settlement Act (US), 215.
Alberigo, Giuseppe, 44.
Allen Consulting Group, the, 151, 152.
Allouache, Sophie, 334.
Amnesty International, 1, 146, 207.
Anton, Ron, 111.
Applegarth, Peter, 170, 171.
Arinze, Francis, Cardinal, 28, 51.
Arrupe, Pedro, 10, 11, 123.
Assisted Dying Bill (UK), 193, 312, 314, 315, 317, 321.
Assisted Dying for the Terminally Ill Bill (UK), 193, 321.
Assisted reproduction technology, 326.
Asylum, 247, 253, 254, 256, 261, 262, 264, 273, 276, 282, 285, 287
Assylum seekers, 13, 151, 247, 249–290. 360,
Australian Capital Territory v JT, 307n.
Australian Catholic Bishops Conference, 25, 51n, 59, 63, 70, 92, 128, 301.
Australian Christian Lobby, 349.
Australian Human Rights Commission, 149, 152, 156, 159, 160, 185, 196, 265.
Australian Medical Association (AMA), 197–202, 304.

B

Barwick, Garfield, 167, 347–350.
Bathurst, Thomas, 174, 175, 177.
Beazley, Kim (Snr), 347.
Belo, Carlos Filipe, 181.
Benedict XVI, Pope, 48, 55, 57n, 118n, 119n, 138, 184, 341, 342.
Benjamin, Raymond, 31, 32.
Bergoglio, Jorge, 5, 9, 341.

Bishop, Bronwyn, 353.
Bjelke-Petersen government, 66.
Bjelke-Petersen, Joh, 25, 65, 66, 165, 236, 237.
Blackburn, Richard, 221, 222.
Blair, Tony, 115, 182, 183n.
Bleijie, Jarrod, 175.
Brennan Committee, 159
Brennan, Gerard, 167, 168, 192, 212n, 361,
Brennan, Patricia, v.
Brennan, William, v, 23, 26,
Broad, Candy, 201.
Brown, Bob, 302, 303.
Brown, Ian, 177n,
Burnside, Julian, 200, 202
Bush, George, 257, 258.

C

Callinan, Ian, 229n.
Campbell, Alistair, 115, 182.
Campion, Edmund, 84.
Canadian Conference of Catholic Bishops, 40, 41n.
Caritas in Veritate, 55.
Carmody, Kevin, 220.
Carmody, Tim, 165, 166, 175–179, ,
Carter v Attorney General of Canada, 314n, 317.
Carter, Bill, 33,
Carter, Kay, 321.
Casey, Michael, 84.
Cassin, Rene, 184, 185.
Catechism of the Catholic Church, 288, 331, 332n.
Catholic Health Association, 396f.
Ceyrac, Pierre, 111.
Chaput, Charles, 24, 26–29, 53–55.
Charter of Human Rights and Responsibilities Act (Vic), 159, 196, 203, 205.
Chernov, Alex, 101.
Child sexual abuse, 27, 55, 74, 81–105.
Clinton, Bill, 123, 257, 258.
Coleridge, Mark, 33, 34n, 338, 339, 340, 343.
Collins, Edward, 64.
Collons, Paul, 43.
Colmar Brunton Social Research, 146, 148, 150.
Commonwealth Conciliation and Arbitration Commission, 230.
Congregation for the Doctrine of the Faith (CDF), 19, 96, 107, 325, 328, 329n, 341, 343n.342.

Conscience, 1, 2, 11, 30, 40, 41, 46, 110, 114, 135, 136, 137, 167, 173, 181–205, 233, 242, 243n, 293, 294, 295, 301, 308, 353, 361.

Conscience vote, 330, 336, 345, 347, 350, 352, 356.

Convention Relating to the Status of Refugees, 254, 265n, 288.

Cosgrove, Peter, 181, 182.

Council for Aboriginal Reconciliation, 68, 69, 78.

CPCF v Minister for Immigration and Border Protection, 265n, 286.

Crennan, Susan, 101.

Crimes Amendment (Protection of Children) Act (Vic), 91.

Crisp, Jeff, 276.

Crumlin, Rosemary, 72.

Cunneen, Margaret, 83, 92, 93.

Curtain, David, 101.

D

Davis, Peter, 176, 177.

Davoren, John, 84.

Dawson, Daryl, 227n, 332.

de Chardin, Teilhard, 47, 184.

de Jersey, Paul, 169, 174, 175, 176, 178, 179.

Deane, Helen, 68,

Deane, William, 68, 227n.

Death with Dignity Act, 305.

Declarations of incompatibility, 158, 159, 160.

Defense of Marriage Act (DOMA), 327, 337.

Dening, Greg, 242, 243.

Director of Public Prosecutions, 308, 309.

Discrimination, 38, 49, 65, 66, 67, 114, 116, 148, 152, 156, 161, 212, 213, 244, 313, 324, 326, 327, 329, 331, 332, 334, 335, 336.

Dodson, Michael, 68,

Dodson, Patrick, 62, 64, 68, 71, 239, 240, 241n.

Dolan, Timothy, 238.

Dorfield, Peter, 24, 25.

Drinan, Robert, 112, 122–126.

E

Ellacuria, Ignacio, 135, 136.

Ellis v Pell, 81, 82.

Ellis, John, 83, 85, 86, 87, 89, 95.

European Convention on Human Rights, 171, 266, 268, 312.

European Court of Human Rights, 157, 256n, 265, 266, 267.

Euthanasia, 116, 291, 292, 293, 295, 296, 299, 300–306, 308, 310, 311, 312, 314, 316, 349.

Euthanasia Laws Act (Cwlth), 302.

Evangelii Gaudium, 30, 31n.

Evangelium Vitae, 294–296.

F

Faircloth, Sean, 8.

Falconer, Charles, 312, 314, 315, 317, 321.

Finnis, John, 117, 118.

Flood, Philip, 145.

Foley, James, 32, 33n.

Forché, Carolyn, 135

Francis, Charles, 101,

Francis, Pope, 2, 5, 6, 7n, 8, 9n, 10, 11–18, 21, 27, 31n, 34, 36, 136, 137, 270, 271, 341, 344, 361.

Fraser government, 167.

Fraser, Malcolm, 221.

Freedom of Conscience, 40, 41, 110, 114, 181–205.

Freedom to Marry Bill (Cwlth), 335.

G

Gageler, Stephen, 352.

Gandhi, Mahatma, 184.

Gardiner, Anne, 71.

Gerace, Maria, 89.

Get Up!, 146,

Gill, Matthew, 72,

Gillard, Julia, 95, 247, 327,

Glendon, Mary Ann

Gobbo, James, 101, 230, 231n.

Goodwin-Gill, Guy, 253, 254, 255, 257, 259–264, 265n

Grahl-Madsen, Atle, 259.

Grayling, AC, 8.

Greens Party, the, 300, 301, 327.

Grossman, Jerome, 123, 125.

Gummow, William, 256.

H

Habermas, Jürgen, 271, 272.

Habersberger, David, 101.

Haddrick, Ryan, 176, 177.

Halik, Tomas, 47, 48.

Hanger, Ian, 97, 98n, 99.

Hawke government, 65.

Hawke, Robert, 59, 68, 69.

Hayes, Michael, 71.

Heaven, Ray, 71.

Hehir, Bryan, 116, 117.

Heiss, Elsie, 70, 73.

Heaney, Seamus, 1, 2.

Henderson, Paul, 302.

Heyes, Tasman, 253.

Higgins, Terrence, 307.

Hirsi v Italy, 265.

Hirst, John, 153.

Hitchens, Christopher, 116.

Hockey, Joe, 333, 334.

Hope, Alistair, 139,

Hope, 8, 14, 17, 20, 21, 31, 40, 48, 56, 57, 60, 74, 75, 79, 94, 110, 116, 122, 127, 136, 205, 207, 216, 298, 304, 309, 325, 326, 346, 347.
Howard government, 67, 69, 302.
Howard, John, 68, 226, 239, 240, 247, 249, 250, 253.
Human rights, 1, 2, 109, 110, 111, 113, 114, 117, 118, 119, 120, 121, 123, 124, 126, 130, 131, 136, 139, 145–163, 167, 184, 189, 192, 197, 236, 240, 252, 258, 261, 270, 275, 285, 290, 324, 326, 327, 328, 329.
Human Rights (Parliamentary Scrutiny) Act (Cwlth), 161.
Human Rights Act, 145, 146, 152, 157, 159, 160, 161, 163, 166, 268.
Human Rights Commission, 152, 156, 159, 160, 186, 187, 203, 265.
Human Rights Consultation, 138, 141, 145, 163, 171, 181.
Humanae Vitae, 19, 20, 23.
Humphrey, John, 185, 186.

I

In re Southern Rhodesia, 210, 211.
International Covenant on Civil and Political Rights, 149, 192, 252, 254, 256, 289, 326.
International Covenant on Economic, Social and Cultural Rights, 149.
Irving, Helen, 159, 160.

J

Jenkins, Harry, 161.
Jennings, Gavin, 201, 202.
Jesuit Refugee Service, 13, 14, 111, 181.
Joffe, Lord, 193, 303, 314.
John Paul II, Pope, 10, 35, 53, 59, 62, 64, 65, 69, 72n, 75n, 79, 123, 294f.
John XXIII, Pope, 44, 45n, 277.
Johnson v *McIntosh,* 207, 243.
Jones, Tony, 333.

K

Keane, Patrick, 172, 178, 250, 288.
Keating government, 167
Keating, Paul, 66, 266, 240, 244.
Keim, Stephen, 166.
Kelly, Edward, 25.
Kelly, Michael, 48.
Kelly, Paul, 220.
Kennedy, Anthony, 203, 337.
Kennedy, Edward, 122, 125.
Kennedy, Ted, 71.
Kennett, Jeff, 101.
Kerr, John, 221.
King, Martin Luther, 172.
Kirby, Michael, 228n.
Knight, Anthony, 72.
Kostakidis, Mary, 145.

Krajewski, Konrad, 16.
Kupka, Karel, 76.
Lambie, Jacqui, 353.
Lampedusa, 13, 14, 265, 270, 272.
Langan, John, 124n, 125.
Lange, David, 217.
Langton, Marcia, 226.
Lash, Nicholas, 52, 53n.
Leary, John, 71.
Levada, William, 51.
Leyonhjelm, David, 354, 355, 356, 357.
Liberty Victoria, 200, 201, 203.
Lingiari, Vincent, 219, 220.
Little, Frank, 102.
Locatelli, Paul, 113, 130, 131n.
Lucas, Brian, 92, 93, 94.
Lumen Gentium, 35, 127.

M

Mabo v *Queensland (No 2), 67, 165,* 212n, 213, 223n, 224, 226, 227, 228n, 249, 360.
Mabo, Eddie Koiki, 66, 222, 223, 237, 242, 243,
Mahoney, Jack, 52.
Malcolm, Arthur, 71.
Malik, Adam, 184.
Mansell, Michael, 241.
Mansfield, Lord, 359, 360.
Marriage Act (Cwlth), 327, 332, 346, 347, 350.
Marriage Equality (Same Sex) Act (ACT), 351.
Marriage Equality Bill (ACT), 345.
Mason, Anthony, 192, 212n.
McAdam, Jane, 257n, 264, 265n.
McClellan, Peter, 82, 89, 90, 97, 98, 99, 110.
McGarvie, Richard, 101.
McGuckin, Robert, 33.
McHugh, Michael, 212n, 227.
McIntyre, Stuart, 242.
McKelson, Michael, 71.
McLachlan, Ian, 224.
McMurdo, Margaret, 173.
Medical Services (Dying with Dignity) Exposure Draft Bill (Cwlth), 312.
Micciche, Francesco, 51.
Milirrpum v *Nabalco,* 221n.
MIMA v *Ibrahim,* 256n.
Monan, Donald, 136.
Morris, William, 23–36, 43, 51–55, 126, 128,
Morrison, Scott, 276, 277, 286.
Muir, Ricky, 353, 354, 357.
Mullins, Pat, 71.
Mundine, Kaye, 69.
Mung Mung, George, 72.
Murray, John Courtney, 112, 116, 117n, 122, 129.
Murray, William, 237n.

N

National Aboriginal and Torres Strait Islander Catholic Council (NATSICC), 59, 70, 75. 78.
National Aboriginal and Torres Strait Islander Ecumenical Commission, 73.
National Indigenous Council, 69.
National Human Rights Consultation, 138, 139, 141, 145, 146n, 147, 152n, 159, 160, 163, 171, 181, 188.
Native title, 66, 211, 222, 225, 226, 227, 228, 240,
Native Title Act, 67,
Native Ttitle Tribunal, 228,
Neate, Graeme, 228.
Neuberger, David, 267, 268n, 315.
Newman's government, 165, 173
Newman, Campbell, 174, 175, 178, 339.
Newman, John Henry, 12.
Nichols, Vincent, 324, 325n, 331.
Nicolas, Adolfo, 113, 114n.
Nitschke, Philip, 302, 303, 306, 314, 315.
Non-refoulement, 257n, 259.
Nungalinya College, 73.
Nussbaum, Martha, 181, 182, 190, 191, 192, 193, 204, 205.

O

O'Farrell, Barry, 92, 93, 94, 352.
O'Loughlin, John, 76.
O'Malley, John, 46.
O'Neill, (Tip) Thomas Phillip, 124.
O'Rourke, Anne, 199.
Orsy, Ladislas, 112, 113, 127.

P

Pacem in Terris, 117.
Pacific solution, 249, 250.
Palliative care, 296, 300, 305, 310.
Palmer, Michael, 145,
Plamer United Party, 278.
Parliamentary Joint Committee on Human Rights, 159, 160, 161.
Parliamentary scrutiny, 152, 163.
Passi, David, 223, 224, 237.
Pastoral Response Office, 102.
Pearson, Noel, 228, 235, 239, 240, 241.
Pell, George, 26, 30, 81, 82, 84, 85, 86, 89, 90, 95, 96, 99, 100–104, 106, 107, 301, 330.
Pellegrino, Edward, 310n.
Pelosi, Nancy, 125.
Peng-chun Chang, 184.
Peter, Alwyn, 234, 235, 237.
Peters, Michael, 71.
Phoktavi, Jub, 48.
Physician assisted suicide, 291, 292, 300, 304, 305, 306, 310n, 311, 312, 317, 319, 320.

Peile, Anthony, 71.
Pike, Betty, 73, 74n.
Pincus, Cecil William, 170.
Plunkett, Mark, 177.
Purdy, Debbie, 308.

Q

Queensland Coastal Islands Declaratory Act (Qld), 223.
Queensland Council for Civil Liberties (QCCL), 165, 170, 179.
Quinn, Kevin, 109, 112, 113.

R

R (on the application of Nicklinson and another) v Ministry of Justice, 315n, 316n.
Racial Discrimination Act, 66, 223.
Rahner, Karl, 10.
Ramsay, James, 169.
Ratzinger, Joseph, 328, 342.
Rawls, John, 38, 118, 205, 271.
Reagan, Ronald, 257, 258.
Rebora, Clemente, 137.
Refugees, 14, 111, 249, 251, 252, 254–259, 265n, 267n, 268, 278–284, 289, 301, 360.
Rhatigan, Patricia, 271.
Rhodes, Cecil, 207, 210.
Rights of the Terminally Ill (Euthanasia Laws Repeal) Bill (Cwlth), 302.
Robb, Andrew, 232.
Robinson, Geoffrey, 30.
Romer v Evans, 203.
Romero, Oscar, 135.
Roosevelt, Eleanor, 184, 186.
Rossiter, Christian, 306, 307.
Royal Commission into Aboriginal Deaths in Custody, 81.
Royal Commission into Institutional Responses to Child Sexual Abuse, 81.
Royal Commission into the Home Insulation Program, 97.
Rubuntja, Wenten, 62, 63, 64, 76.
Rudd government, 145,
Rudd, Kevin, 130, 188, 247, 249, 250, 282, 236, 237n, 345.
Rush, Francis, 25.
Rykmans, Pierre, 129.

S

Sale v Haitian Centers Council, Inc, 258.
Same sex marriage, 312, 321, 323–357.
Sandaloo, Hector, 72.
Santa Cruz, Hernan, 184.
Santamaria, Joseph, 101.
Savulescu, Julian, 203, 204.
Scalia, Antonin, 191.
Scheepers, Ross, 333.

Schroth, Raymond, 122, 123, 124n, 125.
Scott, Leslie, 210.
Scully, Jeff, 26, 27, 30.
Searson, Peter, 102.
Shanahan, Tim, 226.
Slavery Abolition Act (UK), 359.
Smith, Greg, 174.
Somerset's Case, 359.
Sparksman, Brian, 29,
Spe Salvi, 48, 57.
Spence, James, 88, 89n.
Spigelman, James, 174.
Stanley, Fiona, 217.
Stanner, WEH, 220, 234.
Stephens, Ursula, 162.
Sumner, Lord, 210, 211, 212.
Sumption, Jonathan, 316.
Sweeney, Brian, 76.
Synod on the Family, 16–21.
Szoke, Helen, 196.

T

Tan, Vivian, 284.
Tapsell, Kieran, 84.
Taylor, Ben, 139,
Taylor, Charles, 56,
Taylor, Gloria, 317, 318, 319, 321.
The Commonwealth v The Australian Capital Territory, 351.
The Rights of the Terminally Ill Act (NT), 301, 302.
Tiernan, Bryan, 71, 139.
Towards Healing, 86, 100.
Travers, Douglas, 198, 199.
Truth Justice and Healing Council, 84.
Turnbull, Malcolm, 330.

U

UN Declaration of Human Rights, 2, 118, 119, 120, 184, 186n, 187, 252, 256n.
Ungunmerr, Miriam Rose, 73, 76.
United Nations High Commissioner for Refugees (UNHCR), 251, 259, 260, 263, 264, 276, 280, 281, 282, 284.

United States Conference of Catholic Bishops, 338.
US v Windsor, 337, 338.
Usher, John, 84.

V

Vallely, Paul, 8, 9n.
Vatican II, 35n, 39–46, 127.
Vicarious liability, 87, 88, 99, 100, 105.
Victorian Scrutiny of Acts and Regulations Committee, 194, 195n.
Vincent, Frank, 92.

W

Waldron, Jeremy, 271, 272, 273, 285.
Wanstall, Charles, 168.
Ward, Ian, 139, 140, 141,
Ward, Tess, 71.
Washington, George, 190.
Waters, Ian, 33.
West, Morris, 361.
White, TW, 252.
Whitlam government, 221.
Whitlam, Gough, 167, 219, 220, 236n, 348.
Wik Case, 67, 226n.
Wilberforce, Lord, 359.
Williams, George, 346, 347
Williams, Roger, 191, 204
Williams, Rowan, 81, 118, 120, 121, 184,
Williams, Tammy, 145,
Wilson v Anderson, 228n.
Wilson, Philip, 51.
Wilson, Ronald, 68, 226, 228.
Wilson v Ward, 226n.
Windschuttle, Keith, 242,
Wolterstorff, Nicholas, 121, 122n.
Wong, Penny, 133, 334, 343.
Wontulp-Bi-Buya, 73.
Woods, John, 343.
Wootten, Hal, 359, 360.
Wright, William, 93, 94.

Y

Young, Neil, 201.

CPSIA information can be obtained at www.ICGtesting.com
Printed in the USA
BVOW03s1549200415

396565BV00003B/6/P